Before the Storm

Before the Storm

The Story of
Royal Air Force Bomber Command
1939-42

Robert Jackson

Arthur Barker Limited
Winsley Street London W1

Copyright © Robert Jackson 1972

ISBN 0 213 99409 7

Printed in Great Britain by
Bristol Typesetting Co. Ltd
Barton Manor, St Philips, Bristol

Contents

Illustrations

This book is respectfully dedicated to
Flight Lieutenant Bob Jones, DFM, RAFVR,
who flew with Nos. 61, 97 and 207 Squadrons
1940-2 and whose luck held out.

I

The British Bomber Force, 1918-34

13 June 1917 was a brilliant day. The sun beat down on the streets of London from a clear morning sky and by eleven o'clock the heat was almost unbearable. Suddenly, at 11.15, a new sound intervened over the workday hubbub of the capital: the drone of massed aero-engines. Thankful to escape from the sweltering confines of their shops and offices for a few minutes, people streamed out into the open air and peered skywards at the cluster of miniature crosses that slid across the blue backdrop. There were fourteen of them, maintaining a ragged formation which, in 1917, still presented a sight rare enough to arouse considerable excitement. All but a handful of the spectators believed that they were watching a squadron of the Royal Flying Corps either on manoeuvres or returning from the Western Front.

As the people watched, a white flare shot from the leading aircraft and arched downwards, leaving a smoky trail. It was the signal for the squadron to spread out, the flights on its flanks peeling away. A few seconds later, the first bombs came whistling down into the heart of London.

The aircraft were in fact Gotha G.IVs of the German Military Aviation Service's 3rd Bomber Wing, a unit specially formed to carry out air attacks on Britain and based in Belgium. Two earlier attempts to raid London by the German airmen had failed because of bad weather; during the first of these, on 25 May 1917, twenty-one Gothas had penetrated to within twenty miles of the British capital before deteriorating weather conditions had compelled the crews to drop their bombs at random and turn for home. Many of the raiders had bombed Folkestone, causing considerable damage and loss of life. Fighter

aircraft based in southern England and at Dunkirk had intercepted the Gothas, but only one had been shot down. The
bombers had returned on 5 June, but once again their loads of
high explosive had gone down on Essex and Kent and they had
turned back short of the capital. One of the raiders had been
shot down by anti-aircraft fire.

Finally, on 13 June, the Gothas succeeded in reaching their
main objective. Four tons of bombs went down on London,
killing 162 people and injuring a further 432. The damage to
property amounted to £132,000. Ninety-four fighters took off
to intercept the raiders and chased them far out to sea, but few
of them actually engaged the enemy and all the Gothas returned
to base.

The raid came at a time when the future of British air power
was the subject of heated debate in government circles. The
first eighteen months of the war had shown the British flying
services to be generally inferior to those of the enemy in terms
of organization and equipment; a fact that had been brutally
hammered home in 1915, when the Royal Flying Corps on the
Western Front began to suffer appalling losses at the hands of
the new German Fokkers with their synchronized machine-guns.
In February 1916 a Joint War Air Committee was set up under
the chairmanship of Lord Derby with the broad responsibility
of effecting closer collaboration between the Royal Flying Corps
and the Royal Naval Air Service, as well as endeavouring to
streamline the process of supplying equipment to both arms.
The venture was, however, doomed from the start; the Committee had no executive power and any recommendations it
made had to be passed on for further discussion to the Board of
Admiralty and the Army Council. Since these departments had
been at each other's throats over the ownership and application
of military air power since its inception, it was hardly surprising
that the Committee's proceedings quickly became bogged down
in a morass of parochial wrangling.

It was left to Lord Derby, the Lord President of the
Council, to salvage something from the confusion. After a careful study of the factors that had hampered the effectiveness of

the Air Committee, he recommended the formation of an Air Board as a first step towards the creation of a separate Air Ministry. The recommendation met with considerable opposition from the Board of Admiralty and the Army Council, both of which made it clear that such an Air Board should not be permitted to interfere with their respective policies governing the use of naval and military aircraft. On this somewhat forbidding note the Air Board came into existence on 11 May 1916, but it was still not granted executive powers and to all appearances it was just as hamstrung as the earlier Air Committee had been. Relations between the Air Board and the Admiralty became increasingly strained until, in August 1916, there came an open explosion. Without even a hint to the Air Board, the Admiralty had obtained approval from the Treasury to spend three million pounds on the purchase of new aircraft and equipment. The Air Board protested, only to be told bluntly that it had no authority to do so. The Board countered by submitting a report to the Cabinet which amounted to a demand that the Board should have full control of aircraft design, supply and finance. Reaction to this proposal was not long in coming from the Admiralty. In a heated reply, the First Lord – Arthur Balfour – stated that the design and procurement of aircraft for service with the RNAS was the Navy's business, and that the idea of any aspect of naval aviation being under the control of any organization other than the Admiralty was intolerable.

Matters were complicated still further when, spurred on by points of view put forward by a visiting French Military Air Service delegation, the Admiralty became interested in the possibility of mounting a strategic bombing offensive against German targets. In fact it would be more accurate to say that the Navy's interest was reawakened, for as long ago as the autumn of 1914 Captain Murray Sueter, Director of the Admiralty's Air Department, had stressed the vital need for a new bomber aircraft that could hit the enemy hard deep inside his own territory; a ' bloody paralyser of an aeroplane ', as Sueter put it. But although the ' bloody paralyser ' – in the shape of the twin-engined Handley Page O/100 – had flown successfully and had been ordered in quantity, it was still not operational by October 1916, and in the meantime German targets – mainly Zeppelin sheds – had been attacked with varying degrees of success by RNAS airmen flying a collection of aircraft that were totally unsuited to the task. The majority of these raids had been carried out by the Naval Wing at Dunkirk, and the Admiralty now proposed that this station be turned into a major operational centre for future strategic attacks, with large reserves of aircraft and spares to ensure a continual offensive. The spares, particularly engines, could if necessary be diverted from stocks earmarked for the Royal Flying Corps. The immediate effect of the proposal was to arouse the indignation of Sir Douglas Haig, Commander of the BEF, who had made constant requests for more aircraft to support his ground forces in France and Belgium and who now retaliated with a demand for a further twenty fighter squadrons to be sent to the Western Front. The whole situation was getting out of hand, and the Air Board found itself powerless to intervene in what looked like developing into an all-out clash between the two Services.

Meanwhile a serious crisis was looming in the British Government, and the Cabinet's conduct of the war was coming under heavy attack in the press. The immense burden of responsibility, coupled with the personal tragedy of the death of his eldest son at the front that autumn, had imposed an intolerable strain on the Prime Minister, Asquith; the Foreign Office was being widely criticized for its diplomatic entanglement with King Constantine of Greece; and a series of unopposed attacks on British shipping in the Channel by small units of the German Fleet had dealt a severe blow to the prestige of the Admiralty and to Balfour in particular. The first hint of the wind of change came on 29 November 1916, when it was announced that Sir John Jellicoe had been appointed to succeed Sir Henry Jackson as First Sea Lord and that Admiral Sir David Beatty had been promoted to the command of the Grand Fleet. Two days later matters came to a head when Asquith announced his decision to reconstruct the Government. His proposals were totally rejected by David Lloyd George and the Unionist members of the Cabinet. Weary and disillusioned, the Prime Minister tendered his resignation, as did his Liberal colleagues. The King then summoned Bonar Law to form a new government, but he declined and it was left to Lloyd George to assume the reins of power.

The following days saw the Cabinet of representatives of the principal Government departments replaced by a War Cabinet of five members, with Lloyd George at its head and consisting of Bonar Law as Chancellor of the Exchequer, Arthur Henderson representing Labour, and Lords Curzon and Milner. Lord Derby was appointed Minister of War, while Balfour was installed at the Foreign Office and his cousin Lord Robert Cecil was made Minister of Blockade.

One of the first acts of the War Cabinet was to shift the responsibility for the design and supply of aircraft from the Admiralty and the War Office to the Ministry of Munitions, and to increase the power of the Air Board. In February 1917 the Board was substantially reorganized under the direction of Lord Cowdrey and moved to the Hotel Cecil, where it worked alongside the Aeronautical Department of the Ministry of Munitions. The Board was faced with a formidable task, made infinitely more complex by the indecision, bickering and general confusion of the previous year; its members were acutely aware that every week's delay in supplying desperately needed combat aircraft to the front-line squadrons meant the needless sacrifice of more young airmen. Major-General Hugh Trenchard, the able Commander of the Royal Flying Corps, was continually hammering home the urgent need to raise the strength of the RFC on the Western Front to fifty-seven squadrons, but by the beginning of April 1917 the number of squadrons in France, including four RNAS fighter units placed at Trenchard's disposal by the Admiralty, stood at only fifty, and not all of these were fully operational.

The situation showed no sign of improvement at the beginning of June. Then, on the thirteenth, the Gothas raided London and, literally overnight, a general clamour was raised in support of Trenchard's demands. A matter of hours after the raid, the

War Cabinet was holding an emergency session and within a week the War Office was recommending an expansion of the RFC's total strength from 108 to 200 squadrons, eighty-six of which were to be allocated to the Western Front and Italy. The War Office also proposed the formation of forty long-range bomber squadrons, whose task would be to strike at targets deep inside Germany in retaliation for the German raids on British cities. There was an immediate objection from Haig, who feared that any emphasis on building up a strategic bombing force would lead to delays in the formation of the additional fighter and close-support squadrons that would be allocated to his armies in France if the recommendation was accepted; in his view, the only logical role of the long-range bomber was to mount attacks on enemy airfields, immobilizing a portion of the enemy's first-line air strength on the ground and enabling the Allies to establish air superiority over the battlefield. It was an opinion that was not shared by Trenchard, who was firmly convinced that attack was the best form of defence. On two points, however, Trenchard and Haig were in complete agreement; the first was that Belgium should be reoccupied as quickly as possible, depriving the Germans of the bases they used as a springboard for raiding London, and the second was that an air offensive should be mounted against the enemy's airfields in conjunction with the land campaign.

Impetus was given to the execution of these plans when, on 7 July, the Gothas paid another visit to London. Their bombs killed sixty-five people and injured 245, and there was no escaping the fact that of the ninety-five home defence fighters that took off to intercept the raiders, only one was successful. There was a grim undertone to the proceedings when the Air Board held its next meeting on 11 July; it was apparent that the Germans intended to step up their raids on the capital, sowing confusion and terror at the heart of Britain's war effort, and the attacks so far had shown that the bombers were able to achieve their objective almost without interference from the defences. The raids had brought into sharp focus not only the inadequacy of the British air defences, but the shaky foundation of the nation's air policy as a whole – a foundation that was continually being eroded still further by inter-Service antagonism.

While the Air Board could do little more than stress the urgent need for new policies to be thrashed out with no further waste of time, the War Cabinet took a firm step towards this goal when it appointed a two-man committee to review the entire field of air policy and supply. The Prime Minister was one of the two men elected to serve on the committee, but in the event he delegated full responsibility to the other: the redoubtable Lieutenant-General Jan Christiaan Smuts.

Smuts lost little time in drafting his first report, which he compiled after deep consultation with senior Admiralty and War Office representatives and aircraft industry executives, and which was submitted to the War Cabinet on 19 July. This preliminary report dealt mainly with the question of defending London against air attack, and on the recommendation of Smuts all aspects of air defence – anti-aircraft guns, searchlights, balloons and fighters – were brought together in a unified command under Major-General E. B. Ashmore. Three new fighter squadrons (Nos. 44, 61 and 112) were hurriedly formed within the Home Defence Brigade, and while these were being worked up to operational status Nos. 46 and 56 Squadrons were temporarily withdrawn from the Western Front to bolster London's defences. It was not long before the reorganized defensive network began to produce results; two more attempts to raid London in August met with determined opposition and the Gothas suffered some losses at the hands of the British fighters and anti-aircraft guns. The second raid, which took place on 22 August, was the last made in daylight. Although the air offensive against London was by no means over, from then on the bombers came only by night.

Smuts's second report, dated 17 August 1917, had wider implications and was to have a far-reaching effect on the future structure of British air power. In it the General recommended a one hundred per cent increase in the strength of the British air services and the formation of a powerful long-range bomber force. This would make necessary a fundamental change in air strategy; with brilliant foresight, the General envisaged that the conduct of future air warfare might revolve round the concept of strategic bombing. What Smuts proposed was not simply a reorganization of the existing air services; he realized that the experience of their respective staffs would not be sufficient to put into practice the kind of strategy he advocated. Instead he recommended the creation of an independent Air Service, which would be born out of an amalgamation of the Royal Flying Corps and the Royal Naval Air Service; while working in close co-operation with Army and Navy, such an Air Service would be in a position to exercise full control over its own operational strategy. Furthermore Smuts recommended the setting up of an Air Ministry 'to control and administer all matters in connection with air warfare of every kind'.

The Cabinet accepted the report, and the decision was taken to go ahead with the plan to establish a separate Air Service. On 24 August an Air Organization Committee was formed to discuss proposals on the formidable task of amalgamation, the composition of the Air Ministry, and to hammer out the decisions that had to be taken on a whole range of matters such as King's Regulations and discipline – all time-consuming work, but business that had to be completely and satisfactorily tied up before the new Service could be born. The committee's task was made no easier by the fact that it had to work in secrecy; this decision had been taken by the Cabinet at an early stage because it was feared that if the Germans knew that an independent British Air Service was in the making they might revise their own air strategy on the Western Front and take steps to expand their Military Aviation Service. As was to be expected, the committee had to endure several attacks from both Admiralty and War Office, although these were not as severe as had been anticipated; even Sir Douglas Haig's protest semed less acid than usual, although he forcefully repeated his view that any emphasis on the creation of a large bomber force was almost certain to have an adverse effect on the supply of aircraft for the support of his ground forces, and complained that little had yet been done to increase the strength of the RFC on the Western Front.

On 16 October the House of Commons was finally informed

that a Bill to amalgamate the air services and create an Air Ministry was being drawn up. The Air Force Bill, later known as the Air Force (Constitution) Act, was passed in November, and on 3 January 1918 the list of new Air Ministry posts was headed by the appointment of Lord Rothermere as Secretary of State for the Air Force. Trenchard was summoned from France to be the first Chief of Air Staff, but he and Rothermere were unable to agree on some matters of policy and Major-General Frederick Sykes succeeeded Trenchard in the post of CAS on 14 April 1918, exactly two weeks after the Royal Air Force officially came into being. Rothermere, whose health had been giving cause for grave concern, was himself replaced as Secretary of State for the Royal Air Force on 27 April by Sir William Weir.

Both Weir and Sykes were determined to press forward with the plan to form an independent bombing force. It was a scheme that enjoyed overwhelming public support, for London had been subjected to a number of severe bombing attacks at night since September of the previous year. To meet the demand for retaliation, an embryo strategic bombing – the 41st Wing – had been formed at Ochey, near Nancy, under the command of Lieutenant-Colonel C. L. N. Newall. The 41st Wing, which began operations on 17 October 1917, consisted of three squadrons: No 55, which used its D.H.4s for day bombing, No. 100 F.E.2Bs) and No. 16 (Handley Page O/100s), both of which were earmarked for night bombing operations. The wing operated in conjunction with two French bomber units, which shared the same airfield, and the operational headquarters were at Bainville-sur-Madon.

In February 1918 the bomber force was redesignated the VIII Brigade, and in May the three squadrons already in action were joined by two more, Nos. 99 (D.H.9s) and 104 (D.H.9s), fresh out from England. This increase in strength permitted the formation of a second Wing – the 83rd – within the VIII Brigade; this new unit comprised Nos. 100 and 216 Squadrons – the latter being the former No. 16 (Naval) Squadron with a new number – and was used for night bombing, while daylight operations were the function of the 41st Wing's Nos. 55, 99 and 104 Squadrons.

Between 17 October 1917 and 5 June 1918 this small force carried out fifty-seven bombing raids on German targets, the principal objectives across the Rhine being Saarbrücken, Mainz, Koblenz, Stuttgart, Cologne, Mannheim and Karlsruhe. Eighty-five raids were also made on other targets – mainly lines of communication – behind the enemy lines during the same period. It was a sound enough base on which to build the proposed Independent Force, and this came into being on 5 June 1918 under the command of Major-General Trenchard. The French raised strong objections to the plan; although the idea of an independent strategic bombing force had the whole-hearted support of General Duval, the commander of the French Air Services, Marshal Foch – the supreme commander of the Allied forces on the Western Front since the start of the great Ludendorff Offensive of March 1918 – saw the bomber as a tactical weapon and demanded full control over its employment. In the end, the Air Council placed Trenchard under the Marshal's orders and instructed him to give priority to tactical requirements.

This, however, did not prevent the early expansion of the Independent Force – although it went ahead at a slower rate than Trenchard had hoped. Fortunately much of the ground-work had already been done by Colonel Newall, who had initiated the construction of several new airfields in the Nancy area to house additional squadrons. While these were being completed Trenchard took steps to increase the frequency and range of the Force's bombing raids. His first task was to select alternative targets in the event of the bombers being unable to reach their objectives deep inside Germany.

'I decided [he wrote] that railways were first in order of importance, and next in importance the blast furnaces. The reason for my decision was that the Germans were extremely short of rolling stock, and also some of the main railways feeding the German Army in the West passed close to our front, and it was hoped that these communications could be seriously interfered with, and the rolling stock and trains carrying reinforcements or reliefs of munitions destroyed. They were also fairly easy to find at night. I chose blast furnaces for the second alternative targets as they were also easy to find at night, although it was difficult to do any really serious damage to them owing to the smallness of the vital part of the work.'

In its operations during June, July and August the Force was favoured by excellent weather and in general the bomber pilots had little difficulty in locating their targets. During August, reinforcements arrived in the shape of Nos. 97, 110, 115 and 215 Squadrons; No. 110 operated D.H. 9As but the others were equipped with the Handley Page O/400, a more powerful variant of the O/100. No. 100 Squadron also re-equipped with O/400s in August and September, but the process of conversion was slow and it was some weeks before the unit was fully operational once more. Another squadron which joined the Independent Force in September was No. 45, a fighter unit whose Sopwith Camels Trenchard had planned to use on escort duties. The range of the Camels, however, was not sufficient for this purpose and Trenchard decided to await the arrival of longer-range Sopwith Snipes. In the event, these did not materialize before the Armistice and No. 45 was assigned to patrol duties along the front.

During June, July and August the Independent Force carried out 249 raids on German targets, dropping 247 tons of bombs on a stretch of the Rhine Valley 250 miles long, from Cologne in the north to Baden in the south; an area crammed with war industries and intersected by a network of strategic railways. Two of the major railway targets were Thionville and Metz-Sablon, which were raided forty-six times during the three months. Both were badly hit; during one attack on 16 July, for example, twenty-four D.H.4s and D.H.9s of Nos. 55 and 99 Squadrons caused a massive blaze at Thionville and blew up an ammunition train. Air reconnaissance the next day revealed that several trains and the goods station had been completely burned out.

By mid-July, however, the Germans had reinforced their fighter defences across the Rhine with units from the Eastern Front – where the Treaty of Brest-Litovsk had brought an end to hostilities – and the British bombers were soon running into determined opposition. During one particularly disastrous attack, carried out against Mainz by twelve D.H.9s of 99 Squadron on 31 July no fewer than seven of the British aircraft were shot down. Only five of the raiders got through to the target, and of these only two returned to base. Three more turned back early with engine trouble.

One of the biggest industrial targets attacked by the Independent Force was the Badische Anilin factory at Mannheim, which among other war materials produced large quantities of poison gas. The plant was raided eleven times and parts of it were badly hit. During August, in addition to raiding twenty-one German towns, the Independent Force also stepped up its attack to German airfields; the principal targets were Boulay, Morhange, Bühl, Friesdorf and Haguenau, which together were bombed seventy-two times. In September the Force dropped more than 178 tons of bombs on German military targets: almost double the previous month's total. The Metz-Sablon rail complex came in for considerable punishment, being attacked twenty-four times in the four-week period.

As the Allied offensive gathered momentum during the closing weeks of the war, a large part of the Independent Force's operations was devoted to tactical bombing in support of the armies, with heavy attacks concentrated on enemy transport and aerodromes. Strategic bombing operations were hampered during September, October and the first week of November by bad weather; several attempts to raid targets beyond the Rhine had to be called off because of high winds, heavy rain or fog. The weather gave rise to particular frustration at night-time, when thick white mist clung to the ground and made it impossible for the aircraft to take off – yet at about 150 feet the sky would be crystal clear. And if the bombers did manage to get off the ground, the crews would often find their targets completely obliterated by the same white murk.

In October the Independent Force received a new weapon: a small stock of 1650-pound bombs, the biggest used by the Allies during the First World War. The Handley Page O/400 was capable of carrying one of these missiles, and they were used against several German targets in the weeks before the Armistice with considerable success. On 14 October a single 1650-pounder sent a munitions factory sky-high at Kaiserslautern, while another dropped by mistake on Wiesbaden caused a blaze that lasted for three days.

Gradually the Independent Force was paving the way for an aerial assault on a target which had been at the top of Trenchard's list of future priorities for some time: Berlin. In September 1918, while the Independent Force was engaged in tactical operations in conjunction with the American First Army during the bitter attack on the St Mihiel Salient, a new bomber Group – the 27th – had begun to form at Bircham Newton under the command of Lieutenant-Colonel R. H. Mulock. The Group, consisting of the 86th and 87th Wings, was to be equipped with a formidable new bomber aircraft: the Handley Page V/1500. The V/1500 was the first true strategic bomber to be produced by the British aircraft industry and was the largest British aircraft to enter production during the First World War. Powered by four Rolls-Royce Eagle engines, it stemmed from an Air Ministry requirement for an aircraft with a 600-mile radius of action. It was armed with six machine-guns and could carry a variety of bomb loads, ranging from thirty 250-pounders to a pair of specially designed 3300-pounders. The machine had a normal crew of six.

The prototype V/1500 was built by Harland and Wolff of Belfast and flew for the first time in May 1918. However, this aircraft crashed in June and it was not until October that a second machine was flight-tested. An order was placed for 250 production V/1500s; the first unit within the 27th Group earmarked to receive the new type was No. 166 Squadron, which formed part of the 86th Wing. The V/1500's 600-mile combat radius meant that it was not dependent on French bases to mount deep-penetration raids into Germany, and the 86th Wing was intended to make the non-stop flight from Bircham Newton to Berlin and back, each of the V/1500s carrying a 1000-pound bomb load. When the Austro-Hungarian Empire surrendered on 4 November 1918 hurried plans were made to send the 27th Group's other wing – the 87th – to Prague, which would also bring Berlin comfortably within the V/1500's range; in preparation for this Trenchard arranged to send a train to Prague carrying enough spares and supplies to support six of the big Handley Page bombers and their air and ground crews for a month.

On 8 November, the first three V/1500s were delivered to No. 166 Squadron at Bircham Newton. The aircraft were hastily bombed-up and placed on immediate alert, waiting for the signal to take off for Berlin. They were still waiting three days later, when the Armistice was signed. The German capital had had a narrow escape; it was to be nearly a quarter of a century before Berliners were to know and dread the wail of sirens and the drone of enemy aero-engines.

The war was over, and the great air offensive against Germany envisaged by Trenchard had not materialized. As to the actual achievements of the Independent Force in its five months of operations, these were summed up by Trenchard in a despatch which appeared as a supplement to the London Gazette dated 1 January 1919, as follows:

The total weight of bombs dropped between the 6th June and the 10th November was 550 tons, of which 160 tons were dropped by day and 390 tons by night. Of this amount no less than 220¼ tons were dropped on aerodromes. This large percentage was due to the necessity of preventing the enemy's bombing machines attacking aerodromes and in order to destroy large numbers of the enemy's scouts on their aerodromes, as it was impracticable to deal with them on equal terms in the air. I think this large amount of bombing was thoroughly justified when it is taken into consideration that the enemy's attacks on our aerodromes were practically negligible, and not a single machine was destroyed by bombing during the period 5th June to 11th November. It must also be remembered that of the 109 machines which were missing, the majority dropped bombs on targets before landing. The amount of bombs dropped by these machines is not included in the above figures.

The 109 aircraft referred to by Trenchard had all been brought down over enemy territory, either as a direct result of enemy action or through other causes. The total, however, did not include a further 243 machines which had been destroyed in the course of other operations or wrecked accidentally; this brought the Independent Force's total aircraft losses to 352. The D.H.9s had suffered the heaviest casualties of any type in service with the Force, having lost 148 of their number during the five months of operations.

A large amount of photographic reconnaissance was done by individual machines at a great height [Trenchard continued]. This work was nearly always successfully carried out, and only one photographic machine was lost during the whole period of operations. Photographs have proved time and time again the efficiency of the work of the bombing machines. Captured correspondence testified to the great moral effect of the bombing attacks on Germany.

It was apparent by the end of June that the enemy was increasing the number of fighting machines opposed to us. These machines were presumably being provided from squadrons he had withdrawn from the Russian front and re-equipped for home defence work. In September and October our day-bombing squadrons had to fight practically from the front line to their objective, and from there home again. In several cases they had to fight the whole way out and the whole way back. This necessitated the most careful keeping of formation in order to avoid undue casualties, as once the formation was split up the enemy's machines could attack individual machines at their leisure. When our machines were in formation he generally concentrated on the rear machines, occasionally making attacks on the machines in front,

Trenchard's assessment of the Independent Force in action

25

was important, for the views he formed in the light of the experiences of 1918 were to have great influence not only on the development of the British strategic bombing force in the years after the First World War, but also on the policies that governed the development of the Royal Air Force as a whole. History has shown that, at least in part, Trenchard's appraisal was at fault; for example, he overestimated the effectiveness of the Independent Force in terms both of the material damage it caused and its effect on the morale of the German people. Trenchard had realized at an early stage of the bombing offensive that with the limited number of bomber aircraft at his disposal he could not hope to embark on the systematic destruction of German industrial and military targets one after the other; instead, he had chosen the policy of spreading out the bombing attacks over as wide an area as possible with the object of sowing panic and disruption among a large sector of Germany's population. He was convinced that under the circumstances this policy was the right one, and in fact he later stated that the moral effect of bombing had proved to be twenty times greater than the material effect. This notion was later expanded into an extreme and widespread belief that a civilian population could be totally demoralized and brought to its knees by sustained bombing attacks. It was a belief that played no small part in dictating both British and German strategic bombing policies during the Second World War, and it was not until the available evidence was sifted after that conflict that the fundamental error of such a concept was made clear.

On the other hand, there were those who assessed the RAF's limited strategic bombing experience at the end of 1918 and formed other opinions as to where its true effectiveness lay. One of them was Winston Churchill, who rejected the idea that a strategic bombing force could win a future war single-handed by terrorizing an enemy population; instead, he advocated the development of precision bombing as a strategic air force's most valuable form of employment. A very limited amount of precision bombing had been carried out by the Independent Force, and because such operations had been undertaken in good weather conditions, at relatively low level and over short distances, the crews had achieved a fair degree of accuracy even at night. If the Force had been called upon to fly precision bombing missions against German targets from bases in Britain, however, the results would probably have been very different, for at the end of 1918 no special instruments and navigational aids for pinpointing targets over long ranges had yet been developed.

At the beginning of 1919, however, any speculation over what the Independent Force might have achieved had the war continued – or what a strategic bombing force might achieve in a future conflict – seemed to be a purely academic exercise. There would be no more wars; from the blood and savagery of the battle-fields a bright new world would grow, and the long-range bomber would join the other appalling weapons in the arsenal of modern warfare on the scrap-heap. Never again would the people of Britain stand in the front line.

On 11 November 1918, the total strength of the Royal Air Force stood at over 380 squadrons and 22,000 aircraft of all types. It was the most formidable array of air power in the world; a mighty organization built almost from nothing in the space of four years, a force which – honed to a razor-edge in combat – had emerged from the war with an unparalleled reputation for skill and bravery that was to form the basis of a lasting tradition. Yet the speed with which the RAF had been brought to the peak of its strength was to bring it to the brink of disaster at the close of hostilities, for unlike the Army and Navy it did not have the advantage of being able to fall back on permanent peacetime stations and establishments. In other words it lacked a firm base, and as a consequence the RAF suffered more devastating and rapid blows from the post-war axe than did either of the other two Services. Within weeks of the Armistice, the wholesale running-down of the RAF's strength, both front-line and reserve, had begun.

It was therefore a gloomy picture that faced Trenchard when, on 11 January 1919, he was reappointed Chief of Air Staff in place of Major-General Sykes, who had received a new post as

Controller-General of Civil Aviation. The immediate concern of the new CAS was to maintain at least the nucleus of an efficient air force, no matter what the odds might be against it; a self-sufficient organization in which the emphasis was to be placed on a high standard of training and a full programme of aeronautical research, providing a sound basis from which expansion might take place at a later date. Trenchard's detailed proposal was agreed by Winston Churchill, who at that time held the twin post of Secretary of State for Air and War, and was duly submitted to the Cabinet, who also approved it. But the Cabinet flatly refused to spend more than five million pounds a year on the scheme, and this represented the barest fraction of the amount Trenchard considered necessary.

The result was almost complete stagnation of a promising project for a much reduced, but streamlined and highly competent air force; and if this did not present problems enough, Trenchard was once again faced with attacks on the RAF from the Army and Navy. For the second time in two years the young Service was fighting for its existence as an independent force.

Trenchard's main ally in the inter-departmental battle that followed was the fact that however much the Admiralty and War Office opposed the RAF, they showed no inclination to join forces in their attempts to suppress it. Had they done so, their combined broadsides might have carried enough weight to force the Government into taking a decision that would have meant the end of the Royal Air Force as a separate service and the piecemeal division of what was left of its combat strength between Army and Navy. Admittedly there was a great deal of justification for the Admiralty's demand for the resurrection of the Royal Naval Air Service, or something like it; later events were to prove that the RAF's resources were totally inadequate to ensure effective air support for the fleet, but the best part of two decades was to pass before the Admiralty finally won its battle and assumed full control of naval air power.

The forceful argument that Trenchard put forward time and again in favour of an independent air force was that it would enable Britain's air power to be concentrated wherever and whenever it was required with the minimum delay. If the air force were split up between Army and Navy, this vital flexibility would in the main be lost; aviation would become tailored to the requirements of each individual Service and there would be little possibility of effective co-operation. It was to overcome this very obstacle that the RAF had been formed as a separate service in the first place. The Admiralty and War Office, on the other hand, were convinced that the future strategy of an independent air force would be based on independent action, and that the only way of ensuring full air co-operation was for the Army and Navy to possess their own air services. Trenchard's argument on concentration made little impact on them, for during the First World War both of the older Services had followed a policy of dispersing their available air power as widely as possible and this was still regarded as the best solution to the problem of providing effective close support for land and sea operations. Neither Admiralty nor War Office shared Trenchard's faith in the aeroplane as an offensive weapon.

The all-important question, however, was one of economy. In the eyes of the economists, the continued peacetime existence of the RAF could be justified only if air power could in some way take over part of the task of the Army and Navy; this would permit a reduction in the Army and Navy estimates, and the money saved in this way could then be used for the upkeep of a small but effective air force. The Admiralty and Army Council rejected out of hand any idea of the RAF assuming even a minor part of their traditional roles; Trenchard, on the other hand, believed implicitly that in certain areas of responsibility the RAF could perform the task of the other two Services – particularly that of the Army – not only more efficiently, but at a fraction of the cost, and it was not long before the turn of events was to prove his point.

In 1918 the collapse of the Ottoman Empire had resulted in the creation of several new Middle East states, the administration of which had been one of the biggest problems facing the planners of the Versailles Treaty. A solution of sorts had been worked out in the form of the mandates system, under the terms of which one or other of the major powers was made responsible for the development and security of the new states. A considerable share of the burden fell on Britain's shoulders; she was given the mandates for Iraq, Palestine and Transjordan, and a more troublesome combination would have been difficult to imagine. Iraq presented perhaps the toughest problem of all, threatened as it was by outside pressures and torn by internal strife, and when a wave of rebellion broke out in 1920 the British Government was faced with a massive public demand to pull its military forces – already seriously overstretched in their task of policing thousands of miles of turbulent frontier – out of the area. To have taken such a step, however, would have opened the way for a general Arab uprising in the Middle East, and that in turn could have led to the bloody extermination of another of Britain's mandatory responsibilities: the Jewish colony in Palestine.

In an attempt to find a workable solution, a conference of senior military and government officials assembled in Cairo on 12 March 1921 under the chairmanship of Winston Churchill, who was then Secretary of State for the Colonies. At first the dilemma confronting the conference seemed insurmountable, with both withdrawal and substantial reinforcement of the land forces in Iraq equally out of the question – the former for the reasons given above and the latter on grounds of economy.

It was then that Sir Hugh Trenchard played his trump card. With Churchill's support he put forward a scheme whereby a handful of RAF squadrons would take over the Army's task of policing Iraqi territory, releasing the large numbers of troops who were tied down there and effecting a considerable financial saving. Such a scheme was without precedent, but there were a number of arguments in favour; for example, a single aircraft could cover in a day an area that would take weeks for several ground patrols to reconnoitre thoroughly. Another big advantage was that an aircraft had a far better chance of catching rebel forces out in the open and unprepared; the rebels almost always knew the whereabouts of army patrols at any given moment, and consequently the ground forces were seldom able to achieve an element of surprise.

The Cairo Conference reached the conclusion that although Trenchard's scheme had yet to be proven and would be something of a gamble, it was nevertheless by far the best alternative, and it was consequently accepted. The Conference decided to try out the scheme initially in Iraq and Transjordan, and if it was successful to extend it to other troubled areas. At the time of the decision there were already five RAF squadrons in Iraq; these were Nos. 6, 8, 30, 55 and 84, all equipped with D.H.9As except No. 6, which operated Bristol F2Bs. With the exception of No. 8 – which did not arrive in Iraq until January 1921 – they had all been in action against the rebels and in the five-month period from July to December 1920 they had dropped over 97 tons of bombs and fired 180,000 rounds of ammunition.

These five squadrons accounted for over a quarter of the Royal Air Force's first-line strength, for in 1920 – with the Air Estimates fixed at only £11 million – the Service possessed only eighteen operational units scattered throughout the Empire. As an immediate result of the Cairo Conference's decision, the RAF's strength in Iraq was raised to eight squadrons, and these proved to be so effective in their role as a flying police force that by 1922 the RAF had assumed full responsibility for internal security in Iraq and Transjordan, enabling the British Government to withdraw all ground forces except an Anglo-Indian Brigade and four RAF armoured car squadrons, supported by native auxiliaries.

The successful application of air control in Iraq led to its use in other areas, notably the Aden Protectorate and India's North-West Frontier. It was a very important step forward in the development of the RAF, for it meant that the Service now had a definite peacetime role – and one, moreover, which justified its existence as a separate force to the fullest extent. The RAF's operations in Iraq and elsewhere during the early 1920s proved beyond all doubt that its true value lay in its ability to be used independently, while still retaining close ties with the other Services.

The Cairo Conference had enabled Trenchard to win one battle in the struggle for the RAF's continued existence in peacetime, but he was still a long way from winning the war. Police operations abroad were providing the RAF with invaluable experience in tactical bombing, reconnaissance and army co-operation, but the operational strength of the RAF in the United Kingdom was pathetically small and almost totally lacking in any kind of offensive capability. It was not until 1923 that the British Government awoke to the realization that Britain lay almost naked to air attack, with neither the means to defend nor to deter, and the awakening came mainly as a result of rapidly deteriorating relations with France. In the general complacency that had accompanied the first four years of peace, the fact that the French had retained an independent air arm with a strength of some 600 combat aircraft had in the main been overlooked or ignored.

In October 1922, following the resignation of Lloyd George, a new administration had been formed under Andrew Bonar Law, and Sir Samuel Hoare had been given the post of Air Minister. Bonar Law, who was dying from cancer, was compelled to resign in turn the following spring and was replaced by Stanley Baldwin, who on 25 June 1923 stated in Parliament that 'British Air Power must include a Home Defence Air Force of sufficient strength adequately to protect us against air attack by the strongest air force within striking distance of this country'. This statement was made to back up a proposal by Sir Samuel Hoare – approved by the Cabinet – for an increase in the number of RAF squadrons based in Britain to fifty-two, which would have established a degree of parity with the French.

Trenchard, still true to his old theory that the best means of defence was attack, decided that priority must be given to the formation of new bomber squadrons. Fighter defences must be kept at an effective minimum, and his plans had no provision for long-range fighters to act as bomber escorts. The bomber, he asserted, would always be capable of penetrating the enemy defences unaided to find and destroy its target.

The Air Staff were in agreement on this broad outline of

The Vickers Virginia; standard RAF night bomber during the 1920s

Overleaf The Handley Page Harrow: the aircraft with which
Bomber Command nearly went to war at the time of Munich

The Vickers Wellesley long-range bomber. This type saw limited action
in the Middle East during the early stages of the Second World War

Vickers Wellingtons in formation over the Channel during the air exercises of August 1939 (note special 'enemy' markings).

A squadron of Blenheims in formation, January 1939

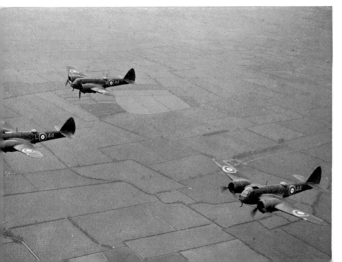

Blenheim Mk Is of No. 44 Sqn, 1938. Note pre-war markings showing squadron number

policy, but on another question – that of whether day and night bombing operations could be carried out by the same type of aircraft – there was a considerable difference of opinion. The problems confronting the CAS and his colleagues were summarized in the following extract from the minutes of an Air Staff conference which took place on 19 July 1923, with Trenchard in the chair:

'CAS . . . thought we might have two types of night bombers, of which one type would be common to day bombing work, one type doing only night work, for close French bombing. He did not mean long distance work where the machine might have to complete its return in the daytime, but in France we should go and come back in the night, and in the summer there would of course be less number of raids than in the winter time. We should have one to carry very big bombs. He would like an opinion on that. Squadron Leader Portal (attached to the Directorate of Operations and Intelligence) said he agreed with the Staff College that night bombers could be used for day bombing work.

'CAS said for the moment he would argue against him. Had he taken into consideration that when it was wanted to get a large number of machines off by day, it was not easy to get these great twin-engined machines off carrying a maximum load of two or three thousand pounds.

'Squadron Leader Portal said he was thinking of making the day bomb smaller.

'CAS asked if he did not think the tendency would be to carry the maximum size bomb possible. It would occasionally be necessary to carry a 4000-lb bomb. For the first 4000-lb bomb dropped here we should carry one and drop it. The pressure would be so great we should have to do it. The question in this hemisphere was whether you could work a large amount at night at certain times, but there were only about four months of the year in which the nights were what he would call short nights.

'Air Vice Marshal Game (Air Officer Commanding the

RAF in India) said it would be an enormous advantage to use night bombers as day bombers, but he thought the night bomber was quite incapable of doing day work.

'DDOI (Deputy Director of Operations and Intelligence – Group Captain C. S. Burnett) said the ideal would be to have one machine to do the two, but it could not be done.

'DCAS (Deputy Chief of Air Staff – Air Vice Marshal J. M. Steel) said that all the arguments used in connection with fighters applied also to bombers in this respect.

'CAS said the arguments were the same, only more so.

'DCAS said he thought there was no question that we must have a separate night bomber.'

The main argument in favour of developing a bomber specifically for operations at night was that such a machine would need less armour plating and defensive firepower than a day bomber; the result would be a substantial reduction in weight, which meant that a bigger bomb-load could be carried. On the other hand, there was a widespread feeling that the development of different types of bomber to carry out the same strategic task would defeat the RAF's all-important policy of concentration and would also probably result in a slower rate of aircraft production. It was a controversy that was never satisfactorily resolved.

The Air Staff's planning was based on the assumption that the RAF's strength in the UK would be raised to the recommended fifty-two squadrons by 1928, but it was not long before all such hopes were abandoned. By the end of 1925 the number of squadrons had risen to twenty-five, but the rate of expansion was slowing down and even the most optimistic forecast could not envisage the target of fifty-two squadrons being reached before 1930. The principal reason for the delay was that the expansion of the French Air Force had also slowed down, and new treaties assuring co-operation between France and Britain effectively removed the threat of open hostilities between the two nations. It was true that other nations – particularly Japan and Italy – were building up their air power at a rapid rate, but in the 1920s these countries were too far away from the British Isles to constitute an air threat of any kind. Moreover, the Cabinet's 'Ten-Year Rule' of 1919 – which affirmed that no major war could be expected to break out for a least a decade – had resulted in a general lack of any sense of urgency.

With these and other factors in mind, the Air Staff now fixed 1936 as the target date for a force of fifty-two squadrons. Urgent consideration was given to the re-equipment of the RAF's squadrons with modern aircraft, but since every British aircraft firm was receiving just sufficient money to keep it going it was impossible to lay any concrete plans for mass production. Nevertheless the years 1926 and 1927 saw many new designs on the drawing-board, many of which reached fruition and provided the RAF with the machines it so desperately needed when the storm-clouds began to gather during the 1930s.

The Air Staff's plans received a further setback in 1928, when Winston Churchill – the Chancellor of the Exchequer – reaffirmed the Ten-Year Rule and extended it for a further five years. The following year, for reasons of economy, the RAF's expansion scheme was delayed yet again and the target date for the fifty-two squadrons put back to 1938. The great depression of 1929 was one of the reasons for this new and stringent economy, but there was a moral factor to be considered too; the efforts then being made by the League of Nations to achieve an agreement on international arms limitation.

When the Disarmament Conference was finally convened in Geneva, it was natural that a major part of the discussion should revolve around the use of air power. The British Government's standpoint on this question had been clear since 1925, when a Preparatory Commission had been first set up to study the possibility of international disarmament; it advocated not only drastic limitations in air armaments, but the abolition of air bombing as an offensive weapon. As an ideal it was commendable enough, as was generally agreed by the Conference when the proposal was tabled as part of the British Delegation's draft convention; but, predictably, it proved impossible to reach any kind of practical agreement. The first obstacle was one of definition; although urging the complete abolition of offensive bombing, the British Draft reserved the right to use the bomber for 'police work in outlying regions'. Precisely what, the other delegations wanted to know, was meant by this reservation? Where was the dividing line between 'police work' and offensive operations? And what was to stop a bomber force stationed in 'outlying regions' being rapidly redeployed and used for strategic attacks in the event of war?

As the discussions went on, this problem – serious enough in itself, and one which was never solved even though the British Government eventually and reluctantly authorized its delegation to give way and agree to the prohibition of bomber aircraft altogether – was gradually eclipsed by a mass of other obstacles that arose. The French delegation, for example, pointed out that if bombers were to be totally prohibited some form of strict international control would have to be exercised over civil aviation, for airliners could be converted to carry bombs without a great deal of difficulty. This proposal was not accepted by most of the other delegations, just as another proposal to prohibit the stationing of bomber aircraft in Europe proved unacceptable on the grounds that France and Italy could deploy a bomber force in their North African colonies.

As far as the Royal Air Force was concerned, the proposals made at Geneva on the limitation and prohibition of bombers were totally contrary to the Air Staff's policy of building up the RAF's strength on the basis of offensive capability. The most serious immediate consequence of the Conference, however, was that the participants agreed to call a halt to military expansion while the disarmament talks were in progress. When this proposal was accepted in 1931 the RAF's home defence force consisted of thirty-seven squadrons, eleven of which were auxiliary units. Five more, then in the process of formation, were added by the spring of 1932, bringing the squadron strength in the UK to forty-two – but thirteen of these were non-regular and much of their equipment was of First World War origin and sadly outdated. There were also four flying-boat and five reconnaissance squadrons. Overseas on 'police' work there were eight squadrons in India, five in Iraq, six in Egypt, three in the Far East and one in Malta. Total aircraft strength was 800, of which 488 were first-line types; a depressing figure compared with the air strengths of France, Italy and the USA, which stood at 1300, 1000 and 900 respectively.

In two aspects – the high standard of its flying training and the total dedication of its personnel – the RAF could justifiably claim superiority over the air force of any other nation. These attributes, however, did not compensate for serious shortcomings in other directions, particularly in the bombing field. At the end of 1932 the RAF had only thirteen operational bomber squadrons at its disposal in the United Kingdom, seven of which were light day-bomber units equipped either with Hawker Harts or Fairey Gordons. Of the remainder, five were heavy night-bomber units; three – Nos. 7, 9 and 58 – used Vickers Virginias, while Nos. 10 and 99 operated Handley Page Hinaidis. There was one medium day-bomber squadron, No. 101, equipped with Boulton Paul Sidestrands.

The Vickers Virginia, which remained in RAF service for fourteen years and equipped nine bomber squadrons during its career, was a development of the earlier Vimy – the aircraft in which Alcock and Brown made their historic Atlantic crossing in 1919. The first production version of the Virginia, the Mk III, became operational with No. 7 Squadron towards the end of 1923, and the total number built – all variants included – was 126. The aircraft's performance was hardly impressive; maximum bomb-load was 3000 pounds, operational ceiling 15,530 feet, range 985 miles – hardly sufficient to allow it to reach targets further afield than the Rhine, even with minimum bomb-load – and maximum speed was a bare 108 mph at 5000 feet, which made the machine's groundspeed painfully slow in even a moderate headwind.

The Virginia's contemporary, the four-seat Handley Page Hinaidi, was also sadly lacking in terms of performance. It stemmed from the Hyderabad, which was developed in turn from the HP 24 commercial airliner and which went into service with No. 99 Squadron at Bircham Newton in December 1925. One other squadron, No. 10, also equipped with Hyderabads in 1928, and a total of forty-five aircraft were built. In 1927 an early production Hyderabad had its twin Napier Lion engines replaced by a pair of 440 hp Bristol Jupiter VIIIs, and in this guise the aircraft became the Hinaidi. Nos. 10 and 99 Squadrons re-equipped with this type early in 1931. The Hinaidi could carry up to 1448 pounds of bombs; maximum speed was 122 mph at sea level, operational ceiling 14,500 feet and range 800 miles.

The RAF in 1932 was, therefore, ill-equipped to undertake the strategic bombing role envisaged by Trenchard and the Air Staff ten years earlier. Quite apart from the general unsuitability of the bomber types in services, there were no facilities to instruct pilots in the handling of multi-engined aircraft at the RAF's flying training establishments; conversion had to be carried out on the operational squadrons. There was no provision for long-range bombers to carry a separate navigator; the pilot did his own navigation, and long-range navigational techniques had not advanced at all since the end of the First World War. Opportunities for live bombing practice were also few and far between, since the geography of the British Isles made it difficult to select areas where live bombing could be carried out without fear of endangering lives and property. Research into bombing techniques went on in a small way – one squadron, No. 15, was employed almost exclusively on experimental work and bomb ballistic trials at the Aeroplane and Armament Experimental Establishment between 1924 and 1934 – but techniques generally were based on the results of the tactical bombing operations carried out by the 'police' squadrons overseas and took little account of such factors as the effect of enemy opposition or the difficulty associated with pinpointing a target after a long-range flight over unfamiliar territory.

Despite all the difficulties, however, the Air Staff never lost sight of the principal reason for the existence of the Royal Air Force. In a lengthy memorandum to the Chiefs of Staff Sub-Committee dated 2 May 1928, Trenchard had defined firmly that 'the aim of the Air Force is to break down the enemy's means of resistance by attacks on objectives selected as most likely to achieve this end.' He went on to justify this aim as one conforming fully with the principles and laws of war, and stated his firm belief that full use would be made of strategic bombing in a future war :

'There may be many [he wrote] who, realizing that this new warfare will extend to the whole community the horrors and suffering hitherto confined to the battlefield would urge that the air offensive should be restricted to the zone of the opposing armed forces. If this restriction were feasible, I should be the last to quarrel with it; but it is not feasible. In a vital struggle all available weapons always have been used and always will be used. All sides made a beginning in the last war, and what has been done will be done . . .

'Whatever we may wish or hope, and whatever course of action we may decide, whatever be the views held as to the legality, or the humanity, or the military wisdom and expediency of such operations, there is not the slightest doubt that in the next war both sides will send their aircraft out without scruple to bomb those objectives which they consider the most suitable.'

They were prophetic words which, five years later in 1933, began to take on a grim significance in the light of a rapidly deteriorating international situation. The general deterioration may be said to have begun in 1932, when Japanese forces invaded China and a startled Britain reluctantly awoke to the realization that Japan was not only a leading military power, but one strong enough to present a potential threat to Britain's interests in the Far East.

Press and newsreel coverage of the events in China was dramatic enough; audiences saw for themselves the horror that the systematic Japanese bombing attacks were bringing to the populations of densely packed Chinese cities. But both China and Japan were a long way off; events nearer home in Germany, where the new Chancellor Hitler appeared to be openly flaunting the terms of the Versailles Treaty, were far more alarming.

The hope of peace, which the League of Nations had sought

for so long, was now receding fast under the dark clouds that covered the horizon. When the Geneva Disarmament Conference finally broke up and the League itself begain to disintegrate following Germany's withdrawal, it was clear to both the government and people of Britain that the time for complacency was over.

In March 1934, during a debate on the Air Estimates in the House of Commons, Stanley Baldwin made a statment of considerable importance. 'This Government,' he said, 'will see to it that in air strength and air power this country shall no longer be in a position of any inferiority to any country within striking distance of our shores.' On 19 July that same year he told Parliament of a new expansion scheme under which the strength of the RAF would be raised by forty-one extra squadrons over a five-year period, bringing the total first-line squadron strength of the Service throught the world to 128.

Known as Expansion Scheme A, the plan envisaged a home-based force consisting of forty-three bomber squadrons, eight of which were to be heavy bomber squadrons, eight medium, twenty-five light and two torpedo-bomber, twenty-eight fighter squadrons with a total strength of 336 aircraft, four general reconnaissance squadrons, four flying-boat squadrons and five army co-operation units. When it was announced in July, the British Government hoped that it would act as a suitable deterrent to Germany's plans for large-scale rearmament, but it was not long before any such illusion was shattered.

Even as the expansion scheme was being debated in the House of Commons, Germany made public her defence estimates for 1934. They called for an air strength of forty-eight squadrons and 1000 aircraft by the end of 1935, with a further 400 machines to be added the following year. Hitler, certain now that neither Britain nor her allies were prepared to use force to curtail his rearmament programme, had contemptuously thrown down the gauntlet.

2

The Years of Crisis, 1935-9

Although Germany's rearmament plans were alarming enough, the Air Staff were confident that the Germans would not be in a position to offer a serious challenge to Britain in terms of first-line air power until at least the end of 1936. This belief, however, was based on the assumption that there would be no dramatic increase in the rate of German aircraft production; if such an increase took place, the Air Staff were well aware that the Germans had the capability to build up a combat force of two thousand aircraft, with reserves, in a relatively short time. Air Chief Marshal Sir Edward Ellington, who had taken over the post of CAS in May 1933, stated this danger in very clear fashion at a Chiefs of Staff Committee meeting on June 1934.

Parliament, however, seemed unable to grasp the sense of urgency. It was absent even in November 1934, when – since it was by then apparent that the Germans had no intention of limiting their arms production – Baldwin told the House that although further increases would be necessary in the strength of the RAF's metropolitan air force, it would not be difficult for Britain to maintain the necessary degree of air superiority.

One of the major reasons for the British Government's dangerously optimistic attitude was that even at this late stage, its diplomatic representatives were still seeking to achieve the limitation of air power in Europe by means of a proposed air pact between the signatories of the Locarno Treaties. Italy, Germany and Belgium were invited to take part in the negotiations, and the immediate German reaction was to ask for representatives of the British Government to visit Berlin. It was when the British emissaries – Sir John Simon and Anthony Eden – arrived in the German capital in March 1935 that the first big

shock came; during an early meeting with Hitler they were informed that Germany already had an air force equal in first-
line strength to Britain's home-based force, and that before long
equality would have been achieved with France's combined
metropolitan and North African air forces. In numerical terms,
that meant up to 2000 aircraft – the number predicted by Sir
Edward Ellington nine months earlier.

The light of history has shown that the German claim to
parity in air power with Britain was false at the time it was
made, even though the prediction of future equality with France
was accurate enough. In March 1935 the Luftwaffe possessed
twenty-two squadrons and about 500 aircraft, 200 of which were
operational first-line types. The British Cabinet, however, was
not aware of this and the report submitted by Sir John Simon
and Anthony Eden on their return from Berlin was taken very
much at face value. The alarm it caused within the Cabinet was
considerable, particularly since it came in conjunction with other
reports – this time fully substantiated – that the Germans were
building up an efficient civil defence system and that Berlin had
already experienced an air-raid warning exercise involving a trial
blackout.

To carry out a full investigation into the growth of German
air power, the Cabinet appointed a special committee under the
initial chairmanship of Sir Philip Cunliffe-Lister. The findings of
this committee showed that the position was more serious than
had previously been supposed. The Secretary of State for Air,
Lord Londonderry, had already been urging a reorganization of
the British aircraft industry so that its production lines would
be geared up to meet the demand of a rapid increase in RAF
aircraft strength. The Air Staff, for their part, now realized that
Expansion Scheme A was inadequate in the light of what was
known of Germany's plans; they were, however, not in favour of
a crash expansion programme, as the equipment available to
implement such a scheme at that time was for the most part
obsolescent. The feeling was that it was better to aim for a
gradual expansion based on the new range of combat aircraft
then on the drawing board or flying in prototype form, with

a strength of about 1500 first-line machines by 1937 as the target.

The new plan – known as Scheme C – was laid before both Houses of Parliament on 22 May 1935. It called for a home-based force of sixty-eight bomber squadrons and thirty-five fighter squadrons, to be ready by March 1937. One-third of the bomber force, about 200 machines, was to consist of aircraft with sufficient range to reach targets in the Ruhr from British bases; the remainder would be able to achieve this only by operating from advanced bases on the Continent.

Seventeen of the new squadrons had been formed by April 1936 and, to accommodate the further increases envisaged, thirty-two new RAF stations were being constructed in the British Isles. Meanwhile, in February 1936, Scheme C had been supplanted by Scheme F, under which a front-line force of 1736 aircraft was planned for 1939. This was to be made up of twenty heavy-bomber squadrons, forty-eight medium bomber, two torpedo-bomber, thirty fighter and twenty-four reconnaissance, with an additional thirty-seven squadrons based overseas. Scheme F was of particular importance because it laid considerable emphasis on the provision of reserves; front-line squadrons were to have a minimum of seventy-five per cent reserves available for immediate use, and there was to be a further reserve of 150 per cent available to maintain the RAF at full combat strength in the event of war.

Until the new light and medium monoplane bombers became available in quantity, the mainstay of the RAF's bomber force was the Hawker Hind biplane. Designed as a replacement for the ageing Hawker Hart, the Hind first flew in September 1934 and entered service with Nos. 18, 21 and 34 Squadrons at Bircham Newton towards the end of 1935. Hinds subsequently equipped twenty-five home-based bomber squadrons up to 1938, and was used by eleven Royal Auxiliary Air Force units for some time after that.

The Hind was in reality an interim aircraft, filling the gap between the Hart and the first of the monoplane bombers: the Fairey Battle. The prototype Battle flew on 10 March 1936, powered by a Rolls-Royce Merlin engine, and production of an initial batch of 155 machines began in May of that year. In May 1937, the first Battles were delivered to No. 63 Squadron at Upwood, and aircrew were enthusiastic about the aircraft's clean lines and its ability to carry a 1000-pound bomb load. Nevertheless, the Battle was underpowered and sadly lacking in defensive armament, two serious drawbacks that were to remain with it throughout its operational career, resulting in a fearful rate of attrition when the type was sent into action during the early stages of the Second World War.

A far more promising aircraft was the twin-engined Bristol Blenheim medium bomber, which had its origin in the Bristol 142 'Britain First', ordered as a transport by Lord Rothermere and later presented to the Air Ministry. An order for 150 Blenheim Is was placed in August 1935 and the prototype flew ten months later, on 25 June 1936. The first production machines were completed at Bristol's Filton factory towards the end of that year and went into service with No. 114 Squadron at Wyton early in 1937.

When it first made its appearance, the Blenheim was a good 40 mph faster than the biplane fighters that equipped Europe's air forces. Its maximum speed of 285 mph, coupled with its ability to carry a 1000-pound war load as far as German targets, represented a sensational advance in the design of bomber aircraft and in 1936 the Air Ministry placed follow-on orders for 1130 more. Production of the Blenheim Mk. 1 went ahead very rapidly and by 1938 the type was available in sufficient numbers to permit the re-equipment of RAF bomber squadrons in India, Iraq and Egypt.

Two more 'interim' bomber aircraft which formed part of the mid-1930s expansion scheme were the Vickers Wellesley and Handley Page Harrow. The Wellesley was a revolutionary aircraft in more ways than one. The brainchild of Rex Pierson and Barnes Wallis, it featured geodetic construction; a method consisting of comparatively light strips of metal forming a web of the aeroplane's wings and fuselage, first pioneered by the Vickers team in the R.100 airship. This type of structure resulted in a weight saving of about forty per cent, giving the aircraft a satisfactory performance on the power of a single Bristol Pegasus engine – an unusual layout for a machine designed as a long-range medium bomber. Two thousand pounds of bombs were carried in two containers under the aircraft's long wings, and defensive armament consisted of one Vickers machine-gun in the port wing and a second mounted in the rear cockpit. Range was 2590 miles, but in November 1938 two Wellesleys of the RAF Long Range Development Unit, stripped of their military equipment and with extra fuel tanks, made a record-breaking non-stop flight of over 7157 miles from Ismailia to Darwin. A third aircraft also set off, but was forced to land on the island of Timor. Before production ended in 1938, 158 Wellesleys were built, equipping six medium-bomber squadrons in the United Kingdom and three abroad.

The Handley Page Harrow was a very different aircraft. Originally developed as a night bomber, it was eventually selected by the Air Ministry to meet a requirement for a bomber-transport and one hundred machines were ordered in August 1935. Delivery of production Harrows began in April 1937 and the type equipped Nos. 37, 75, 115, 214 and 215 Squadrons until it was finally replaced by more modern equipment in 1939. Powered by two Pegasus engines, the Harrow had a top speed of 200 mph, a range of 1250 miles and could carry a bomb load of 3000 pounds.

The mainstay of the RAF's heavy-bomber force during the expansion period was the four-seat Handley Page Heyford bi-plane, designed in 1927 to replace the Hinaidi and the Vickers Virginia. Powered by two Rolls-Royce Kestrel engines, the first Heyford flew in June 1930 and production machines entered service with No. 99 Squadron at Upper Heyford in December 1933. The aircraft could carry up to 3500 pounds of bombs and was armed with three Lewis machine-guns. Heyfords served with eleven RAF bomber squadrons until 1937, when they began to be progressively phased out in favour of new monoplane bomber types.

The other aircraft designed to the same specification as the

Heyford was the Fairey Hendon, which was selected in 1934 to be the main RAF heavy-bomber type. An ugly-looking low-wing monoplane with twin fins, the Hendon prototype made its first flight in November 1931 powered by two Bristol Jupiter VIIIs but a lot of trouble was experienced with these, and later aircraft were fitted with Kestrels. The Hendon entered service with No. 38 Squadron at Mildenhall in November 1936, but by this time the prototypes of more advanced bombers were already flying and only fourteen production Hendons were built, an order for a further sixty being cancelled. In June 1937, No. 38 Squadron detached one of its Hendon flights to Marham; this formed the nucleus of No. 115 Squadron, which re-equipped with Harrows shortly afterwards.

On 14 July 1936 Royal Air Force Bomber Command was formed, with its headquarters at Uxbridge. Initially, the Command consisted of four Bomber Groups, Nos. 1, 2, 3 and 6, the last being an Auxiliary Group. By this time the Air Ministry was giving priority to the design and production of heavy bombers at the expense of light bombers and even medium types. The requirement now was for maximum range and maximum bomb load.

The first of the new heavy bombers was the Armstrong Whitworth Whitley. Designed to specification B.3/34, the Whitley prototype flew on 17 March 1936 and a contract for eighty production aircraft was placed in August 1935. The first squadron to receive Whitley Mk. Is was No. 10 at Dishforth in Yorkshire, deliveries beginning in March 1937, and the aircraft also went into service with No. 78 Squadron at the same station the following July. Thirty-four Mk. Is were built, and these were followed by forty-six Mk. IIs which entered service with Nos. 51, 58 and 97 Squadrons from January 1938.

A second contract, placed in 1936, led to the production of eighty Whitley Mk. IIIs, and delivery of these machines to operational squadrons began in August 1938. All Whitley variants so far had been powered by two Armstrong Siddeley Tiger engines, but after the Mk. III a changeover was made to Rolls-Royce Merlins. The last Whitley version to go into service before the outbreak of war was the Mk. V, which became operational with No. 77 Squadron at Driffield, Yorkshire, in August 1939. The Whitley V had a maximum speed of 230 mph at 16,400 feet, an operational ceiling of 26,000 feet and a range of 2400 miles. It could carry a maximum bomb load of 7000 pounds, and defensive armament consisted of one Vickers gun in the nose turret and four Brownings in the tail turret.

The other two heavy-bomber types which, together with the Whitley, were to form the backbone of the RAF's strategic bombing force on the outbreak of the Second World War – the Handley Page Hampden and the Vickers Wellington – were both designed to Air Ministry Specification B.9/32. Only a matter of days separated the first flights of the respective prototypes of these two machines, the prototype Wellington flying on 15 June 1936 and the Hampden on 21 June.

An order was placed for 180 Wellington Is, powered by two Bristol Pegasus XVIII engines, and the first of these were delivered to No. 99 Squadron at Mildenhall on 10 October 1938. By August the following year eight squadrons of Wellingtons were operational with No. 3 Group in East Anglia. Like the earlier Wellesley, the Wellington was of geodetic construction, which enabled it to withstand fearful punishment when it was put to the test in combat. The aircraft's maximum speed was 255 mph at 12,500 feet, and range was 2200 miles with a 1500-pound bomb load.

The Wellington's contemporary, the Hampden, showed outstanding promise during its early flight trials. Air Ministry experts liked the machine's radical design; the deep, narrow fueselage with its high single-seat pilot's cockpit; the slender tail boom supporting twin fins and rudders; the long, tapering wings with their twin Pegasus radial engines. The view from the pilot's seat was exceptionally good, and the Hampden possessed almost fighter-like manoeuvrability; an important factor and one which, coupled with its maximum speed of 265 mph at 15,500 feet, the experts believed would give it more than a fighting chance of survival during daylight operations in a hostile environment.

The Hampden's main disadvantage, in fact, appeared to be that the crew's positions in the three-foot-wide fuselage were far too cramped to permit any degree of comfort, and this resulted in excessive crew fatigue. The defensive armament of four hand-operated machine guns was also inadequate, as Hampden crews were to learn to their cost during early war flights over enemy territory.

Such, then, was the equipment available to Bomber Command during the latter part of the troubled 1930s; the sharp edge of the sword which, it was still fervently hoped, would act as a deterrent to the growing air might of Nazi Germany. Early in 1937, the Air Ministry realized that if the Luftwaffe continued to expand at its present rate the provisions of Scheme F would not be sufficient to maintain first-line parity in 1939, as had been planned; accordingly, a revised plan – Scheme H – was submitted to the Cabinet. This called for an increase in the RAF's metropolitan first-line force to nearly 2500 aircraft at the earliest possible date after April 1939, and the total figure was to include 1659 bombers. The increase was to be made possible by drastically cutting down the number of machines in reserve and channelling them into first-line units.

Although this would have given the RAF numerical equality with the anticipated first-line strength of the Luftwaffe, it would also have meant that obsolescent aircraft would have been committed to battle in far greater numbers when war came than was actually the case. This, however, was not the principal reason why the Cabinet rejected the new scheme; they did so mainly because of German assurances that the limit of the Luftwaffe's expansion would be much lower than the British feared. And this at a time when, in Spain, German and Italian air force units were already in training for the war!

It was nevertheless clear to the Cabinet during the spring of 1937 that, with the threat to European peace posed by the activities of Germany and Italy, and the potential threat to peace in the Far East created by the expansionist aims of Japan, the whole question of Britain's defence policy was in need of review. Defence thoughts so far had been dictated by the prospect that Britain would have to cope with one enemy – first France, and then Germany – and now it looked as though she might find herself faced with three at the same time.

To reconsider the whole area of defence, a Defence Plans (Policy) sub-committee was set up and Sir Thomas Inskip appointed to the new post of Minister for the Co-ordination of Defence. The sub-committee's first task, in July 1937, was to instruct all three armed services to make an exact assessment of their present and future requirements so that accurate estimates of the cost of their respective re-equipment programmes might be made. The immediate reaction of both Army and Navy was to submit greatly inflated estimates of the cost of their future programmes in the hope that more funds might be allocated to them; to counter this move, in October, the Air Ministry submitted the most detailed expansion plan so far.

Under the proposals outlined in the new plan – Scheme J – Bomber Command's strength was to be increased to ninety squadrons, with 1442 aircraft. These squadrons were to be progressively re-equipped with a second generation of monoplane heavy bombers: large four-engined machines, still in the design stage in 1937, which would be capable of carrying more than twice the bomb load of the Whitley, Hampden and Wellington and over a considerably greater range. The scheme, which was to reach completion by the beginning of 1943, was to cost £650 million – an increase of £183 million over the original estimated cost of Scheme F.

After considering the new scheme, however, Sir Thomas Inskip informed the Secretary of State for Air that he proposed to reject it mainly on the grounds that he believed the Air Staff's emphasis on strategic bombing as a means of winning a war to be misplaced. He believed that if war came with Germany, the decisive factor in the first few weeks would be the fighter aircraft. Priority should be given to strengthening Fighter Command to the point where it would be capable of winning a decisive victory over the Luftwaffe bomber forces that the Germans might be expected to commit to a large-scale air offensive against Britain. This would gain vital time and allow

D

49

a war of attrition to develop, in which the Royal Navy could exploit its command of the sea to the full by imposing a blockade on the enemy.

Inskip's view was that Germany's air strength could be destroyed more effectively in combat with Fighter Command over Britain than by the Air Staff's policy of sustained attacks against the German aircraft industry and operational airfields. What he proposed was a drastic reduction in the proposed strength of Bomber Command, with large cuts in the bomber reserves and a concentration on the development of light and medium bombers rather than on long-range heavy bombers. He considered that the Air Staff should give up any idea of attempting to reach parity with the Luftwaffe in terms of numbers. Apart from the fact that the possibility of achieving parity was fast receding, the operational requirements of the Luftwaffe and the RAF were so different as to make it unnecessary. The Luftwaffe's aim was the creation of a large tactical bombing force to support the Wehrmacht, whereas the RAF's main need was for a strong fighter force to defend Britain herself, and if necessary to establish air superiority over the battle-field.

Although this view provoked a predictably hostile reaction from the Air Staff, it was nevertheless accepted by the Cabinet in December 1937 and the estimated cost of implementing Scheme J was drastically slashed to £100 million. Together, the Air Ministry and Sir Thomas Inskip hastily thrashed out a new plan – Scheme K – in which it was decided that the money would be allocated to the retention of the fighter strength envisaged in Scheme J, while cutting down the number of first-line bomber squadrons and reserves. Progressive re-equipment of Bomber Command with new types of heavy bomber would go ahead, but much more slowly than planned.

The resulting picture was a gloomy one. At an Air Staff meeting held on 18 January 1938 the CAS pointed out that the changes recommended in Scheme K meant that the RAF would have only nine weeks' reserves, and if war came the full potential of the aircraft industry would not have time to develop. He saw the provision of more heavy-bomber reserves as a vital necessity, but to achieve this object with the funds allocated under Scheme K presented an apparently insurmountable problem. The only possible solution appeared to lie in effecting a saving by making cuts in other areas, notably training schools.

That the Air Ministry was prepared to consider such a step was proof enough of the extent to which the situation had deteriorated. Despite the advice of the Air Staff, despite an increasing wave of public criticism, the Government still had its head firmly in the sand as far as the air defence needs of this country were concerned. It was only in March 1938, when German troops marched across the border into Austria, that the Cabinet was galvanized into action. Scheme K was quietly forgotten and replaced by Scheme L, which was drawn up under conditions of near panic that same month. This envisaged the rapid expansion of the RAF's strength to 12,000 aircraft over a period of two years, should war make it necessary, but the emphasis was still on fighter production and there was still no provision to increase the strength and efficiency of Bomber Command to the point where it could launch an effective counter-attack on Germany.

It was in September 1938, at the height of the Munich crisis, that the tragically weak position of Britain's armed forces – and particularly of RAF Bomber Command – was made brutally clear. Six years earlier, Britain's failure to maintain strong offensive forces had helped to weaken her power to negotiate at the Geneva Conference, and now history repeated itself – with infinitely more serious consequences for Europe and the world – as Britain, France and Germany haggled over the Sudetenland. France and Britain threatened war if the Sudetenland was annexed, but in Britain's case at least it was an impotent threat. As far as the RAF was concerned, only one hundred Hurricanes and a mere six Spitfires had as yet reached Fighter Command's first-line squadrons, and although forty-two Bomber Command squadrons were mobilized thirty of them were equipped with light and medium bombers of insufficient range to reach German targets from British bases. Worse still, a critical shortage of spares meant that less than half this force was ready for combat; reserves amounted to only ten per cent, and there was a reserve of only 200 pilots.

It is a matter of history that in 1938, the Luftwaffe was not in a position to launch a large-scale air offensive against the British Isles. Because of the limited range of its bomber aircraft, such a plan could only be put into action with the capture of air bases in France and the Low Countries, and the tanks with which the German Panzer divisions smashed their way westwards in the spring of 1940 were not then available in sufficient numbers to make a 'blitzkrieg' practical in 1938. It is also a matter of history that if France – whose army was still numerically superior and in some respects better equipped than the Wehrmacht – had taken the initiative and invaded Germany in 1938, her chances of success would have been more than favourable.

This fact, however, and the fact that – if war had come in 1938 – the Luftwaffe would have been incapable of taking reprisals for any strategic RAF raids on Germany, were totally eclipsed by the Allies' frantic desire to buy time almost at any cost. As they bartered Czechoslovakia in return for a few months' respite, Chamberlain and his colleagues in the British delegation could think of the relative strengths of the RAF and the Luftwaffe only in terms of numbers, and in the light of these statistics Britain's air striking power seemed distinctly inferior to that of her potential opponent. Greatly exaggerated German claims about the Luftwaffe's strength were accepted at face value and there was little that either the British or French politicians could do to dispute Hitler's bluff, for accurate intelligence on the organization of the Luftwaffe and the performance of its latest combat aircraft was practically non-existent. Although it was known that modern German fighters and bombers were operating on the Nationalist side in Spain, the full extent of their commitment to this conflict was not realized; nor was the fact that regular Luftwaffe air and ground crews were being rotated for Spanish duty under conditions of great secrecy. A golden opportunity to assess the quality of the Luftwaffe's men and machines at first hand, and to observe the air tactics which were to take the Allies completely by surprise in 1940, was consequently wasted.

On the other hand British Intelligence had, at the time of Munich, a reasonably accurate picture of potential targets vital to a German war effort. The means by which this information was acquired had been extensively reviewed in 1936, when an Industrial Intelligence Centre had been set up under the direction of Major D. F. Morton. The Centre's primary task was to assemble every scrap of information which, in the event of war, would enable plans for a crippling economic blockade of Germany to be put into action quickly. The information collated by the Industrial Intelligence Centre, and that from other intelligence sources, was turned over to the Air Ministry; there it was co-ordinated by the Deputy Director of Plans, Group Captain John Slessor, whose staff was responsible for arranging selected targets in order of priority for Bomber Command.

In the autumn of 1937, the broad priorities that would govern Bomber Command's air offensive had been set down in thirteen directives known as Western Air Plans, approved at an Air Ministry conference on 1 October. At the head of the list was plan W.A.1, which envisaged a major air strike on the Luftwaffe's bomber force and its maintenance organization; W.A.2 and W.A.3 involved co-operation between Coastal Command and the Royal Navy, while W.A.4 called for a bombing offensive against German rail, road and canal communications with the object of hindering an advance into France and the Low Countries by German forces. W.A.5 was the blueprint for an attack on Germany's war industry in the Ruhr, Rhineland and Saar, with particular reference to oil installations; W.A.6 was a plan for attacking manufacturing resources in Italy; W.A.7 envisaged bombing attacks on the enemy fleet and its bases in co-operation with the Navy, with the big Kriegsmarine base at Wilhelmshaven as the primary target; W.A.8 was a scheme for attacking various kinds of enemy supply depot; W.A.9 was a tentative plan for putting the Kiel Canal out of action, subject to the availablity of bombs large enough to do the job; W.A.10 was another co-operative plan between Bomber Command and the Royal Navy, with shipping and German merchant ports in the Baltic area as its main objective; W.A.11 was a scheme for the destruction of large tracts of German forest by incendiary bombing; W.A.12 was a plan for attacking units of the enemy fleet at sea; and W.A.13 envisaged precision raids against administrative centres and other headquarters in Berlin and other major German cities.

A searching review of Bomber Command's capability following the Munich crisis revealed that the three Western Air Plans to which priority had been allocated – W.A.1, 4 and 5 – could not be undertaken with any real hope of success at this stage. It was unlikely that Bomber Command could inflict any substantial damage on the Luftwaffe by an offensive against those German aerodromes already targeted by the Air Ministry Plans Division for the simple reason that the Germans were building large numbers of emergency airstrips on which their bombers would be deployed before the outbreak of hostilities, and the locations of most of these were not known. Also the C-in-C Bomber Command, Sir Edgar Ludlow-Hewitt, informed the Air Ministry that a sustained attack on the German aerodromes as envisaged in W.A.1 would in all probability result in the complete annihilation of his medium- and heavy-bomber forces in a matter of weeks. Assuming that Holland and Belgium remained neutral, such an offensive would have to be undertaken mainly by the Blenheim and Battle squadrons operating from French airfields, and of the two aircraft types only the Blenheims would stand anything like a fighting chance of getting through to their German targets. Crippling losses might only be avoided if the bombers were escorted by long-range fighters, and as yet no aircraft of this kind had been developed for RAF use.

It was also realized that Bomber Command would encounter overwhelming obstacles in the execution of W.A.4, the plan to attack German communications to slow up an invasion of France and the Low Countries. The main obstacle here was a difference of opinion between the Air Staff and the General Staff on the type of target to be attacked; the General Staff favoured a concentration on railway bridges and viaducts, while the Air Staff believed that better results could be achieved by attacks on railway stations and junctions. Whichever strategem was adopted, however, both Air Staff and General Staff were agreed on one point: it would involve the commitment of almost the whole of the medium-bomber force based on the Continent and would result in severe losses – and, because of the mass of rail and road systems available to the enemy, its success was bound to be strictly limited.

There remained, therefore, only one Air Plan which Bomber Command might put into action with any hope of success: W.A.5, an attack on Germany's war industry. In a report made to the Air Ministry, the Air Targets Sub-Committee of the Industrial Intelligence Centre had indicated that the German war effort could be crippled by a sustained bombing offensive in the first weeks of the war against forty-five selected power stations and coking plants in the Ruhr. The Air Ministry, however, realized that this report was based on the assumption that Bomber Command could find and hit these targets every time; an assumption which, taking into account existing navigational and bombing techniques, was very far removed from reality. The Air Ministry view was that it would be more profitable to concentrate on the destruction of two major targets on which much of the Ruhr's industry depended: the Möhne and Sorpe dams. Again, this plan could not be activated until Bomber Command had sufficiently large bombs at its disposal. Meanwhile, considerable disruption of the enemy's war effort could be achieved by attacks on the canal system which connected the Ruhr with northern Germany.

There was, however, a major obstacle in the path of the plan to attack German industrial targets. On 21 June 1938, the Prime Minister had announced in the House of Commons that only military targets would be attacked by the RAF, and that every possible care would be taken to avoid civilian casualties. This immediately gave rise to a problem of definition; could, for example, a factory producing military equipment as well as other materials be classed as a military objective? Despite the difficulty in determining what was a military objective and what was not, the principle of a restriction on strategic bombing was generally viewed favourably in Parliament, mainly because it was thought that such a restriction would be to Britain's advantage as it would give the potential enemy no excuse to attack targets in British cities. Accordingly, Sir Edgar Ludlow-Hewitt was ordered to take no action to execute W.A.5 in the event of war; instead, Bomber Command was to confine its initial activities to carrying out W.A.1 and W.A.4 – both of which had already been assessed as unsatisfactory, as we have seen.

The initiative, therefore, was handed to the Germans. Only if the Luftwaffe embarked on a policy of unrestricted strategic bombing could Bomber Command retaliate by attacks on German industrial targets. If strategic attacks by the Luftwaffe did not materialize, the best course for Bomber Command to follow – as Sir Edgar Ludlow-Hewitt was informed in an Air Council letter dated 15 September 1938 – was to conserve its strength in view of the slender reserves available, rather than fritter away its resources in carrying out either W.A.1 or W.A.4 in return for a result that would probably be negligible.

Meanwhile, although all too conscious of the fact that Bomber Command's ability to penetrate into industrial Germany was poor, and would remain so until the new four-engined bombers entered service, the Air Staff continued to work on W.A.5, extending it to include a wider variety of targets. Among the new objectives now being considered were German oil plants and refineries, many of which were situated in western Germany and therefore within range of existing RAF bombers operating out of bases in Britain.

Useful though these considerations were to be in the long run, they did nothing to solve the immediate problem of the manner in which Bomber Command was to be employed if war broke out. Attacks on the German Fleet were, of course, outside the bombing restriction, and it was decided that these would be among Bomber Command's priorities in the first days of war. Another scheme involved the dropping of propaganda leaflets over Germany and this crystallized into Air Plan W.A.14, a co-operative venture on the part of the Air Ministry, the Foreign Office and the Stationary Office.

By March 1939 it was clear to both the British and French Governments that the policy of appeasement towards Hitler's Germany no longer held good. Somewhat belatedly, the British and French General Staffs now met to work out a common defensive policy in view of the increasing aggressiveness of the Axis powers; the German absorption of Czechoslovakia in March had been followed rapidly by the Italian invasion of Albania during the first week of April, and the probability that Britain and France would be drawn into war if Hitler turned his armed might on Poland now loomed large. It was decided that a British Expeditionary Force, together with an Air Component, should be sent to France; the Air Component would be given full facilities on French airfields on the understanding that its aircraft would not be used for unrestricted bombing of German targets from these bases. France, unlike Britain, was vulnerable to heavy attacks by Luftwaffe medium bombers based on German territory, and the French Government's fear of large-scale reprisal raids by the German Air Force was considerable. The French General Staff insisted that the British air component in France must be employed in full to hold up a probable advance by German ground forces, and the British Air Staff – although the shortcomings of Air Plan W.A.4 were well known – had little alternative but to agree.

Even then, the Air Staff and the French General Staff could not reach a firm agreement on how best to use the British bombers in the effort to stem a German drive westwards. The French wanted the RAF to attack German columns, railway communications and airfields; the Air Staff, considering the inadequacy of the equipment at its disposal in the light of the heavy fighter and anti-aircraft opposition that was likely to be encountered, were still sceptical that any favourable result could be obtained. In the end the Air Staff, while promising that the RAF bombers would be used to the fullest advantage in support of the Allied ground forces, warned the French General Staff not to expect too much help from this quarter.

The question had still not been resolved when, on 1 September 1939, the Wehrmacht stormed over the frontier into Poland, a path blasted ahead of it by the Luftwaffe's bombers. A week earlier, on 24 August, No. 1 Group – comprising most of Bomber Command's Fairey Battle squadrons – had been ordered to mobilize in readiness to go to France as an advanced air striking force. The Group had been held at a high state of alert ever since the Munich crisis, and the new order to mobilize came immediately following the news that Germany and the Soviet Union had signed a non-aggression pact; a step that made Germany's intentions all too clear with regard to Poland. In the early afternoon of 2 September ten Battle squadrons – 160 aircraft in all, led by No. 226 Squadron – flew in impeccable formation over the English coast near Shoreham, on course for their new bases in France. They made an impressive sight and the crews were in high spirits.

Less than twenty-four hours later, Great Britain was at war with Germany.

3
The Opening Round:
September-December 1939

During the first weeks of the war, the Air Staff had a clear two-fold objective: to conserve the existing strength of Bomber Command while putting into effect plans for the rapid expansion of the RAF's offensive power. The prime concern was to train, as rapidly as possible, the large numbers of air and ground crews without whom the proposed expansion could not take place, and front-line units found a large part of their task devoted to operational training commitments. In the meantime nothing must be done which might destroy the vital nucleus around which Bomber Command's strategic force was to be constructed. It was for this reason, as much as for any consideration of the restricted bombing policy dictated by the Government, that Bomber Command confined its activities during the initial phase of the war to the dropping of propaganda leaflets and actions against units of the German Navy.

Bomber Command had, in fact, been held in readiness to carry out leaflet raids – Air Plan W.A.14 – since the early morning of 1 September, when nine Whitley IIIs of No. 58 Squadron at Linton-on-Ouse and seven of No. 51 at Leconfield – two of 4 Group's Yorkshire airfields – were each loaded with over half a million propaganda leaflets in bundles of 1500. The total weight of paper carried by each machine was 1800 pounds.

The order to take off on the operation – code-named 'Nickel' – finally came through from Group HQ at five o'clock in the afternoon of 3 September. Three Whitleys of No. 51 Squadron were detailed to drop their loads on Hamburg, while seven of No. 58 were to fly to Bremen and the Ruhr. The aircraft took off shortly after dusk and headed for their respective objectives. To the amazement of the crews, no enemy opposition was encountered during the flight; it was exactly like a peacetime training mission. Three of 58 Squadron's aircraft, however, had engine trouble on their way back from the Ruhr. The pilot of Whitley K.8990, Flight Sergeant Ford, had to make a forced landing near St Quentin, while Flying Officer J. A. O'Neill in K.8969 came down near Amiens. K.8973, which had been the first aircraft to take off, ran out of fuel during the return trip at about 5.45 am and the pilot, Squadron Leader J. J. A. Sutton, made an emergency landing at Fécamp. There were no casualties, but it was a far from auspicious end to Bomber Command's first operational mission over Germany.

The following afternoon, seven Whitleys of No. 51 Squadron flew to Rheims and refuelled there in readiness for a leaflet raid on the Ruhr after dark. This time, their load was reduced to 1200 pounds. Engine trouble once again plagued the operation and in the event only four aircraft took off for their objectives, which were reached without incident. It was the same story on 9 September, when four aircraft of No. 58 Squadron arrived at Rheims to refuel for another Nickel raid. After a delay of twenty-four hours because of bad weather, the four Whitleys took off – but only one reached the target and dropped its leaflets successfully. The other three were forced to return to Rheims with engine trouble.

On 14 September Nickel operations were brought to a temporary halt while the Air Staff and War Cabinet reviewed the results of the missions carried out so far. Despite the fact that these results were not impressive, and that the value of the leaflet raids was being subjected to increasing doubt and criticism from several quarters in both political and Service circles, the operations were resumed on 24 September. This time, however, the War Cabinet affirmed that the actual dropping of leaflets was only a secondary task; the primary aim of the missions was reconnaissance and operational training. Considering the state of Bomber Command's navigational art in the autumn of 1939, there is little doubt that the training value of these early Nickel operations was considerable. They made possible not only a refinement of existing navigational techniques, but revealed serious shortcomings in the range of navigational equipment available to Bomber Command, permitting at least some of these to be rectified before the RAF's strategic offensive began to develop in earnest. One such shortcoming, for example, became apparent when, on the night of 24-5 September, two Whitleys of No. 10 Squadron set out for a leaflet raid on Cuxhaven. On this occasion the target was reached without undue difficulty; the trouble started when the two aircraft picked up direction-finding bearings on the homeward trip which should have brought them on a heading for their home base at Dishforth in Yorkshire. The D/F beam was, however, ninety degrees out of true, with the result that instead of heading in over the coast the bearing given brought the aircraft parallel to it. After flying up and down over the North Sea for some time, the two pilots realized what had happened and, ignoring the D/F reading, turned on to a new course which, fortunately, brought them over the coast at approximately the right place. Both Whitleys landed at Leconfield with their fuel tanks almost dry.

Despite the somewhat hit-or-miss navigational techniques of 1939, it was not the task of finding their way to and from the target that made life difficult for the Whitley crews taking part in Nickel operations. The most serious problems arose from engine trouble, which was a constant affliction of the Whitley's Tiger VIII motors, and from adverse weather. Although everything possible was done in an effort to ensure that weather forecasting was as accurate as available information could make it, the crews all too frequently ran into extremely severe weather en route. A good example of this occurred on the night of 27-8 October, when five Whitleys of No. 51 Squadron took off from their advanced base at Villeneuve to drop leaflets on Stuttgart, Munich and Frankfurt.

All five aircraft were airborne shortly after 6 pm. The crews had been told that they could expect moderately good weather en route, yet within minutes of taking off the Whitleys had begun to encounter heavy showers of hail and sleet and severe icing. One crew gave up and turned back, but the other four continued through weather that showed no sign of improving.

The pilot of the leading Whitley, Flying Officer H. Budden, pressed on towards Munich. Behind him, in the observer's seat, was Wing Commander J. Silvester, No. 51 Squadron's Commanding Officer. It was not long before troubles began to mount up. First of all the front gunner, Sergeant Buckwell, reported that his gun was frozen and incapable of being fired; then the trimming tabs iced up and became completely immovable; and finally the ventral 'dustbin' turret, through which the leaflets were normally jettisoned, stubbornly refused to be lowered from its recessed position under the fuselage. This meant that the crew had to drag the heavy leaflet bundles over to the flare chute on the other side of the fuselage. It was exhausting work, and to make matters worse two hours of flying at altitudes of between 16,500 and 20,000 feet had used up the crew's supply of oxygen. As soon as the leaflets had been dropped Budden brought the aircraft down to a more comfortable level. The Whitley now encountered some anti-aircraft fire, but this was inaccurate and did not present any real hazard. A far worse enemy was the severe turbulence that buffeted the aircraft as it flew along in cloud; most of the crew were airsick and at one stage Budden himself became so ill that he had to hand over complete control to the second pilot, Flying Officer Gould. The Whitley finally returned to base at 00.40 hours, after following D/F bearings which fortunately, on this occasion, were accurate.

The second Whitley bound for Munich dropped its leaflets successfully, but its ventral 'dustbin' jammed in the down position, seriously affecting the aircraft's handling qualities during the return flight. Then, as the Whitley recrossed the French border at 13,000 feet, a cylinder head on the starboard engine blew off and the aircraft lost height rapidly, dropping down into dense cloud. The machine broke through the cloud base at 2000 feet in snow, with the starboard engine out of action and the port engine also beginning to give trouble. There was high ground in the Whitley's path and the pilot, Sergeant T. W. Bowles ordered the crew to bale out. The front gunner was the first to go, but he forgot to disconnect his intercom lead and became trapped in the hatch. The navigator managed to free him, then jumped in turn, followed closely by the wireless operator.

The pilot, believing himself to be alone in the aircraft, trimmed the Whitley to glide and baled out. He was unaware that the rear gunner was still on board; the latter's intercom was unserviceable and he had no idea that the others had all abandoned the aircraft. He was still sitting there, frozen stiff and wondering what was happening, when the Whitley hit the ground. The aircraft bounced along on its belly, slewed to a stop and burst into flames. Shaken but unhurt, the rear gunner clambered out of his turret and ran round to the cockpit, which to his astonishment was empty. The mystery was only solved when he made his way to a nearby estaminet and found the others already there, recovering over a glass of wine.

A third Whitley on this raid, which took off for Frankfurt, ran into trouble almost from the start. A matter of minutes after take-off severe icing began to develop, and then as the aircraft approached the target the vacuum pump on the port engine became unserviceable. In this case, too, the ventral turret stuck two-thirds of the way down, but two crew members – Sergeant Hide and Aircraftman Heller – succeeded in raising it manually. A few moments later Hide, suffering from the combined effect of oxygen lack and exertion, collapsed. He had barely recovered when the pilot, Flight Sergeant Wynton, also fainted. Hide took the controls; by this time, so much ice had accumulated on the Whitley's wings that the aircraft was critically unstable.

Then, without warning, the starboard engine burst into flames. It was hurriedly shut down, but the next instant the aircraft entered a steep dive with a lurch that knocked both front and rear gunners unconscious. By this time Wynton had returned to his senses and, together with Hide, he hauled back on the control column with all his strength. The combined efforts of the two men brought the Whitley out of its dive at 7000 feet, but now both rudders and elevators were jammed and the aircraft, athough on an even keel, continued to lose height at a rate of 2000 feet per minute. As Wynton was on the point of collapse once more, Hide took over the controls and prepared for a crash landing. The Whitley was skimming over a forest and at first the chances of getting down safely seemed remote, but at the last instant Hide spotted a clearing and brought the aircraft in for a belly landing. The machine touched down and skidded broadside on into some trees. The crew, who were dazed but otherwise unhurt, managed to put out the engine fire and spent the rest of the night huddled together for warmth in the fuselage.

The leaflet raids continued until late January, when a spell of exceptionally bad weather brought them to a halt until the third week in February. They were finally abandoned altogether – except by aircraft of the Advanced Air Striking Force – on 6 April 1940. By this time Bomber Command had dropped over sixty-five million leaflets, the Whitleys ranging as far afield – during the later raids – as Vienna, Prague and Warsaw. There had been an almost total lack of enemy opposition, and in fact no aircraft engaged on Nickel operations was brought down by enemy action during the entire period of the raids.

The reason for this lack of enemy opposition at night was not due to any lack of foresight on the part of the Luftwaffe High Command. The latter had, in fact, been working on the assumption that enemy bombers would be forced to operate at night because of German fighter superiority during daylight, and a night-fighter squadron equipped with Messerschmitt 109s – fitted with searchlights to illuminate their targets – had been formed in the summer of 1939. By February 1940 the German night-fighter force comprised several squadrons, forming Gruppe IV/JG 2 at Jever. This unit, however, scored only one success, and that was the result of sheer luck when one of its pilots surprised a Blenheim in brilliant moonlight in April 1940.

The trouble was that the Messerschmitt 109, an admirable day-fighter, was totally unsuitable for night operations. Its pilot had to rely on visual navigation, which depended to a great extent on good moonlight conditions. More than one pilot of

Blenheim
Mk. Is of
No. 90 Sqn,
RAF Bicester,
late 1938

Whitleys in
echelon
formation

Handley Page Hampden of No. 106 Squadron, RAF Finningley, April 1940

Blenheim Mk. IV of No. 139 Squadron at Bétheniville, France, after a sortie over the Siegfried Line, January 1940

Opposite
Fairey Battles. Underarmed and underpowered, the type suffered appalling casualties during the Battle of France

The bomber and the men behind it: Short Stirling, with war load, air and ground crew

Vickers Wellington releases a 1,000-pound bomb over enemy territory

The Handley Page Halifax

Halifax B.II L9619 ZA-E of No. 10 Squadron, RAF Leeming, December 1941. This aircraft was lost during a training sortie over Cumberland on 15/16 February 1942

IV/JG 2 was forced to abandon his aircraft when he became lost and ran out of fuel during a night sortie, and others were killed trying to land in darkness and bad visibility. It was not until the summer of 1940, when the night-fighter units began to convert to twin-engined Messerschmitt 110s, that their operations started to meet with limited success.

Even though the bombers of No. 4 Group were able to range over Germany with relative impunity during those early months of the war, however, Bomber Command was left in no doubt as to the effectiveness of the Luftwaffe's day-fighter defences. At the beginning of the war, the high degree of accuracy called for by the British Government's restricted bombing policy meant that Bomber Command had no choice other than to attack selected targets by daylight, and the same policy made only one objective possible: the German Fleet. This presented the Air Staff with a serious problem, for the major German naval bases in the Elbe Estuary were known to be heavily defended by both fighters and all calibres of anti-aircraft gun. There were only three ways in which bombers might hope to survive, in daylight, in a hostile environment of this kind; they must either be fast enough to elude enemy interceptors, be themselves escorted by long-range fighter aircraft, or fly in tight defensive formations which allowed the maximum firepower to be concentrated on their attackers. Once again, Bomber Command could only adopt the last alternative.

Following armed reconnaissances over the North Sea by Hampdens of No. 5 Group on the afternoon of 3 September 1939, a lone Blenheim of No. 139 Squadron was sent out from Wyton to make a reconnaissance of Wilhelmshaven and the Schillig Roads. The photographs it brought back revealed the battleship *Admiral Scheer* riding at anchor in the roads, surrounded by an armada of light cruisers and destroyers, and the battlecruisers *Scharnhorst* and *Gneisenau* moored in the Elbe. It was too good a target to miss; a golden opportunity for Bomber Command to strike a crippling blow at the German Battle Fleet in the first hours of the war.

At Wattisham, in Suffolk, the ground-crews of Nos. 107 and

110 Squadrons laboured throughout the early hours of 4 September to get their Blenheims ready for the expected attack, loading them with armour-piercing bombs. They had just finished the job when a new order came through from 2 Group Headquarters; in order to escape the worst of the anti-aircraft fire, it had been decided that the attack would have to be made at low level. Since armour-piercing bombs were of little use unless they were dropped from medium or high altitude, the ground crews had to start all over again and replace the armour-piercing bombs with ordinary 500-pounders, fitted with eleven-second fuses. It was the fifth time the bomb-loads had been changed in twenty-four hours.

Ten crews were selected for the operation, five from each Squadron. At the briefing, they were told that German 'pocket' battleships of the *Scheer* class were armed with only two types of anti-aircraft weapon: heavy guns and machine-guns. By going in low the Blenheims should be able to avoid the worst of the fire because – theoretically at least – the barrels of the warships' main armament could not be depressed far enough to engage a low-flying aircraft. The Blenheims were to spread out and attack from three directions. It was hoped that their bombs would embed themselves in the warships' superstructures, where they would explode after a delay of eleven seconds. Precise timing was essential, otherwise each Blenheim ran the risk of being caught in the explosion of the bombs dropped by the preceding aircraft. If for some reason an attack on the warships proved impossible, the crews were to bomb the ammunition depot at Marienhof as their secondary target. Under no circumstances however, were they to endanger civilian lives by bombing the nearby dockyard. The orders were quite definite about that, and they came from very high level.

The first Blenheim, piloted by Flight Lieutenant Ken Doran of 110 Squadron, took off at 16.00 hours, followed by the other nine aircraft. Five Blenhims of 139 Squadron also took off from Wyton at about the same time, and an hour later twelve Hampdens – six from 49 Squadron and six from 83 – left Scampton in Lincolnshire. None of these aircraft, however, was destined to find the target; after cruising round for hours on end over the North Sea, hopelessly lost in thick cloud and fog, they were compelled to return to their bases.

The ten Blenheims from Wattisham flew on under a steadily lowering cloud base. Cloud was 10/10ths at 500 feet, with a north-westerly wind blowing the rainclouds towards the German coast. The cloud tops were at twenty thousand feet, so there was no possibility of climbing above them. At times, the cloud base was so low that the Blenheims were skimming along only fifty feet above the waves. The formation altered course and turned south-east, heading in towards the north coast of Germany. Some trawlers flashed beneath the bombers' wings and were instantly swallowed up behind them in the rain. Ahead of him now, Doran could make out the hazy outline of a coast, broken by a wide bay and with an island to starboard. It was the Jade estuary.

The weather was beginning to clear a little, and the cloud base had risen perceptibly. The Blenheims flew steadily on towards their target. Suddenly a long dark shape rose out of the water dead ahead. It was the *Admiral Scheer*. Led by Doran, the first three Blenheims roared towards the battleship while the other two broke to left and right and shot up into the clouds. The five aircraft from 107 Squadron were still some minutes behind. Doran held his course as the *Scheer* loomed bigger; so far, the flak had not opened up. He could see what looked like a line of washing strung across the after-deck. There was a hazy impression of white upturned faces and some of the sailors waved, no doubt thinking that these were Luftwaffe aircraft. Then they saw the roundels stamped on the Blenheim's wings and scattered in all directions.

Doran hauled back the stick as his navigator pressed the bomb release. The grey superstructure shot past beneath the aircraft, terrifyingly close. The two 500-pounders dropped away and curved down towards the *Scheer*; one burrowed its way into the superstructure, the other bounced off the armoured deck and fell into the sea. Neither of them exploded. As the second Blenheim made its attack, it came under heavy fire from the *Scheer*'s

20-millimetre twin-barrelled cannon – armament which RAF Intelligence sources had apparently known nothing about. One of the second aircraft's bombs exploded close to the battleship's side; the other, like Doran's, failed to go off.

The dull sky was suddenly filled with a brilliant light as more than a hundred guns opened up on the warships and heavy batteries on the shore. The pilot of the third Blenheim pulled up into the clouds halfway through his run-in. He was obeying his instructions; he knew that he could not bomb within the eleven-second time limit. A few moments later, a blazing aircraft dropped out of the clouds and crashed in the sea near Mellum Island. It was one of the diversionary Blenheims, caught in the meshes of the flak.

After a brief respite the five Blenheims of 107 Squadron attacked in turn, making their approach from the north-west and running through the concentrated fire of every gun in and around the anchorage. The leading Blenheim was hit and exploded and the second, both its engines in flames, crashed on the deck of the cruiser *Emden*, killing the first German sailors of the war. The third crashed near the shore; the fourth, bracketed by a cluster of heavy shells, cartwheeled across the water and sank. Only the fifth somehow managed to come through the barrage unscathed, dropping its bombs in a beautiful straddle across the *Scheer* before vanishing into the overcast. Again, the one bomb that hit the battleship failed to explode.

As the surviving Blenheims flew homewards, their crews were bitterly conscious of the fact that the raid had failed: not because of any lack of courage and determination on their part, but because of useless bombs. Old bombs, stored for too long in poor conditions. And the price of failure had been five aircraft and fifteen men.

Later that day, in greatly improved weather conditions, fourteen Wellingtons – six from No. 9 Squadron at Honington and eight from No. 149 at Mildenhall – set out to attack the warships lying off Brunsbüttel in the river Elbe. Of the No. 9 Squadron aircraft, three bombed an unidentified German warship with no apparent result and one jettisoned its bombs over the harbour, hitting a merchantman and setting it on fire. The 149 Squadron Wellingtons had less luck; one claimed to have bombed the target area and the others jettisoned their bombs in the sea. Two of 9 Squadron's aircraft failed to return; one was destroyed by anti-aircraft fire and the other was shot down by a Bf 109 of II/JG 77, operating out of Nordholz. The pilot was Sergeant Alfred Held, and to him went the honour of scoring the Luftwaffe's first victory against the RAF.

It was to be three months before the opportunity again presented itself for an attack in strength on the German Fleet in its home waters. During this period, Bomber Command confined its activities – apart from the leaflet raids – to armed reconnaissance flights over the North Sea, much of the squadrons' time being taken up with operational training. It was an uncertain, frustrating time, with long monotonous hours spent in searching for elusive warships that were seldom seen. Only very occasionally did the crews have a chance to drop their bombs in anger, and when they did the result was more often than not a complete miss – fortunately so in the case of a Whitley of 51 Squadron which bombed a submarine during a security patrol over the North Sea on 13 December, only to discover later that the craft had been British. This type of work was not without its risks; on 29 September, for example, eleven Hampdens of 144 Squadron carrying out an armed reconnaissance of the Heligoland Bight were surprised by German fighters and five of them were shot down.

Reconnaissance sorties over north Germany were also carried out during this period and, although most of these were undertaken by aircraft of the Advanced Air Striking Force, some were flown by the Blenheims of No. 2 Group. On 27 September, for example, three Blenheims of 82 Squadron, operating out of Watton, made a photographic reconnaissance of a number of airfields and the surrounding country in north-west Germany. An attempted reconnaissance of the Ruhr by two Blenheims of 21 Squadron that same day proved abortive because the cameras of one machine went unserviceable and the other was forced to turn back by bad weather.

On 17 November a series of photo-reconnaissance missions by the Blenheims of 21 Squadron revealed a growing concentration of German warships in the Heligoland Bight. No plans were made to attack these immediately as they were positioned inside the strong air defence zone between Heligoland and Wilhelmshaven – the area where the Hampdens of 144 Squadron had been destroyed. Bomber Command was now treading cautiously; it could not afford to sustain heavy losses for no tangible result. The Admiralty, however, and particularly the First Lord, Winston Churchill, began to exert considerable pressure for a bombing offensive against the enemy fleet and its bases while the opportunity still existed, and before the German battleships and cruisers broke out in strength to wreak havoc on Britain's trade routes.

On 3 December, in response to this pressure, Bomber Command detailed twenty-four Wellingtons to attack enemy warships in the Heligoland Bight. The aircraft – a mixed force from Nos. 38, 115 and 149 Squadrons under the leadership of Wing Commander R. Kellet – took off from their bases at Marham and Mildenhall and made rendezvous over Great Yarmouth at 09.40, climbing to 10,000 feet over the sea en route to their objective. The leading flight of three aircraft sighted Heligoland at 11.26 and the crews made out the outlines of some ships, including two cruisers, lying in the vicinity.

The Wellingtons ran through heavy anti-aircraft fire as they made their approach and two of them were hit, although not seriously. A few moments later the bombers were attacked from astern by Messerschmitt 109s and 110s. These attacks were ineffective and at least one of the fighters was damaged. The Wellingtons bombed from 8000 feet, but although some of their bombs fell in the target area no hits were registered on the warships. All the aircraft returned safely to base.

This operation appeared to vindicate the claim that a tight bomber formation was sufficient defence against fighter attacks in daylight. The Messerschmitt pilots had seemed wary of facing the Wellingtons' rear armament at a range closer that 400 yards, and although one straggling bomber had been attacked simultaneously by four fighters it had fought its way clear without having sustained a single hit.

At any rate, Bomber Command was sufficiently encouraged by the result to try again. The opportunity came on 14 December, when it was reported that the cruisers *Nürnberg* and *Leipzig* had been torpedoed by a British submarine and were limping back into the Jade estuary, badly damaged. At 11.45 am, twelve Wellingtons of 99 Squadron, led by Wing Commander J. F. Griffiths, took off from Newmarket to attack the warships. The weather was bad, with 10/10ths cloud at less than 1000 feet, and by the time the Dutch coast was sighted at 13.05 the Wellingtons were forced to fly at 600 feet or less to stay below the overcast. The pilots had been ordered not to attack unless they could bomb from at least 2,000 feet; they nevertheless continued on course in the hope that the cloud would lift.

By this time they were coming under heavy and continuous fire from warships and merchantmen lying in the approaches to the estuary. At this low altitude the bombers presented excellent targets and several were hit. Suddenly, there was a lull in the flak as enemy fighters came speeding up; they were the Messerschmitt 109s of II/JG 77, led by Major Harry von Bülow, and this time the pilots showed no hesitation in pressing home their attacks to point-blank range. The Wellingtons' gunners accounted for one Bf 109, which was seen to crash in flames, but the fighters destroyed five bombers in a matter of minutes. A sixth Wellington crashed on landing at Newmarket.

For some reason, Bomber Command were reluctant to believe that enemy fighters had been responsible for the destruction of half the Wellington formation. In the Bomber Command Report of 28 December 1939 Air Commodore Bottomley, the Command's Senior Air Staff Officer, wrote:

'It is now by no means certain that enemy fighters did in fact succeed in shooting down any of the Wellingtons. Considering that enemy aircraft made most determined and continuous attacks for twenty-six minutes on the formation, the failure of the enemy must be ascribed to good formation flying.

The maintenance of tight, unshaken formations in the face of the most powerful enemy action is the the test of bomber force fighting efficiency and morale. In our Service it is the equivalent of the old "Thin Red Line" or the "Shoulder to Shoulder" of Cromwell's Ironsides.'

A study of the Luftwaffe combat reports on the 'Battle of the Jade Estuary', however, leaves little doubt that the fighter pilots' claims were authentic. The Germans attributed their success to the fact that most of the pilots of II/JG 77 had been recently transferred to the Luftwaffe from the Naval Air Arm and consequently had much more experience of bad weather flying than the average day-fighter pilot.

Air Commodore Bottomley's point of view does not appear to have been shared by his superiors. The Commander of No. 3 Group, Air Vice-Marshal Baldwin, felt that the loss of half of one of his squadrons had been the result of a monumental blunder, while the view of the C-in-C Bomber Command, Sir Edgar Ludlow-Hewitt, was that the bomber leader should have turned back as soon as it became apparent that there was no possibility of bombing from the authorized height.

Notwithstanding the unfortunate outcome of the raid of 14 December, another attack on the German Fleet was planned for the eighteenth. Twenty-four Wellingtons of Nos. 9, 37 and 149 Squadrons under the leadership of Wing Commander Kellet – veteran of the 3 December raid – assembled over King's Lynn about 9.30. The aircraft were loaded with 500-pound semi-armour-piercing bombs and the crews' orders were to patrol the Schillig Roads, Wilhelmshaven and the Jade Estuary and to attack any warships sighted. Any bombing was to be carried out from a minimum level of 10,000 feet.

The bombers climbed to 14,000 feet in four flights of six aircraft. Less than an hour after leaving the English coast they were flying in a cloudless sky, with visibility more than thirty miles. About two-thirds of the way across two aircraft dropped out with engine trouble and returned to base.

At 10.50 the bombers were detected by two experimental radar stations on Heligoland and Wangerooge, both equipped with the new 'Freya' detection apparatus. The officer in charge of the Luftwaffe station on Wangerooge – the other was run by the Navy – immediately telephoned the news through to the fighter operations room at Jever, only to be told by the duty officer that something must be wrong with his radar set; the British would never be foolhardy enough to mount an attack in a cloudless sky and brilliant sunshine, where their aircraft would be sitting targets for the German fighters.

Meanwhile, the twenty-two Wellingtons had made a detour round Heligoland to avoid the anti-aircraft batteries there and were now turning in towards Wilhelmshaven from the south. After a frustrating delay of several minutes the first German fighters – six Messerschmitt 109s of 10/JG 26, led by First Lieutenant Johannes Steinhoff – took off from Jever to intercept. None of the other fighter units at Jever or the adjacent airfield of Wangerooge was on readiness, and there was a further delay before these were 'scrambled'.

Steinhoff's 109s met the Wellingtons on the approach to Wilhelmshaven and scored their first two kills almost immediately. The fighters then sheered off as the bombers flew at 13,000 feet through heavy flak over the naval base. The Wellingtons crossed Wilhelmshaven without dropping any bombs then turned and crossed it again, still without bombing, before heading away towards the north-west. By this time the Bf 109s of 10/JG 26 had been joined by the twin-engined Messerschmitt 110s of ZG 76 and the 109s of JG 77, and the combined force of fighters now fell on the Wellington formation as it passed to the north of Wangerooge. Another bomber went down, the victim of a Bf 110, and crash-landed on the island of Borkum. Only one member of the crew survived. Other Bf 110s accounted for five more Wellingtons in an area some fifteen miles north-west of Borkum, and a sixth bomber was destroyed thirty miles north of the Dutch island of Ameland. Rather belatedly, a pair of Bf 109s from JG 101 at Neumünster arrived and joined the air battle in time to catch the tail-end of the Wellington formation; they shot down one bomber, but one of the 109s was badly hit and the pilot had to crash-land short of his base.

The combat was not entirely one-sided. Although only two German fighters – Bf 109s of JG 77 – were actually shot down, several others received severe punishment from the Wellingtons' defensive rear armament, but all of them managed to limp back to base or make emergency landings. The surviving bomber crews claimed that at least twelve enemy fighters had been destroyed and as many more damaged; such exaggerated claims were to be a feature of daylight bomber operations throughout the war, with several gunners all firing at the same aircraft and claiming it as damaged or destroyed.

Twelve Wellingtons, over fifty per cent of the attacking force, failed to return from the raid. At a time when Bomber Command was following its all-important policy of conservation, such a loss was disastrous – particularly since some of the Wellingtons had been carrying additional crew members to provide them with 'operational experience'. Moreover, the loss had been sustained on the very fringe of enemy territory, which made the outlook for future deep-penetration daylight raids appear black indeed.

The big question-mark was whether the raid of 18 December had experienced unusually bad luck. Sir Edgar Ludlow-Hewitt was of the opinion that the enemy had recently reinforced the Wilhelmshaven defences with some of their best fighter squadrons, and that these had received sufficient warning of the bombers' approach to manoeuvre themselves into a favourable attacking position. In fact, the number of Luftwaffe fighters committed to the action was far fewer than either the C-in-C or the AOC No. 3 Group supposed, and although several later accounts of the raid attributed the fighters' success to the employment of early-warning radar this – as we have seen – had little or no influence on the outcome of the battle.

The AOC 3 Group, Air Vice-Marshal Baldwin, pinned down the real causes of the disaster in his subsequent report to Bomber Command. The fuel tank in the Wellington's port wing, he pointed out, was neither self-sealing nor protected by armour plate, and when hit in this area the bombers had caught fire very rapidly. Those which failed to burn lost vast quantities of fuel through holes punched in these vulnerable tanks, a fact that was observed by the German fighter pilots who reported having chased more than one Wellington out to sea with streams of fuel pouring over its wings. The risk presented by the unprotected tanks had been realized by both Bomber Command and Vickers, and at the time of the 18 December raid modifications involving the fitting of armour plating to the port wings of all Wellingtons were already under way; this latest disaster, however, showed clearly that this step was not enough. If the Wellington squadrons were not to suffer a series of crippling losses at the hands of enemy fighters on future operations, their aircraft had to be fitted with self-sealing fuel tanks with all possible speed.

Secondly, although the German fighters had received some punishment from the Wellingtons' defensive armament during attacks from astern, the bombers had proved particularly vulnerable to beam attacks. The greatly superior speed of the Messerschmitts had been a critical factor, as Captain Reinecke, commanding I/ZG 76, pointed out in his subsequent combat report: 'The Messerschmitt 110 is easily capable of catching and overtaking this English type, even with the latter at full boost. This provides scope for multiple attacks from any quarter, including frontal beam. This attack can be very effective if the enemy aircraft is allowed to fly into the cone of fire. The Wellington is very inflammable and burns readily'.

Air Vice-Marshal Baldwin was also of the opinion that another contributory factor in the heavy losses sustained by the Wellingtons had been their inability to maintain a strong defensive formation. The surviving crews reported that some flights had become split up in the heat of battle, making it easy for the Messerschmitts to pounce on and destroy individual aircraft. Baldwin thought that lack of combat experience on the part of the crews was mainly to blame; on this occasion, he pointed out, the crews had been subjected to severe attacks for the best part of half-an-hour without let-up, and since it had been their first real taste of combat they could hardly be blamed if some of them had deviated from the order to keep formation under the enormous stress of the air battle.

At least one German combat report, however, showed that Baldwin's belief was not entirely correct. Lieutenant-Colonel Carl Schumacher, commanding JG 1, wrote that although much of the damage inflicted on his fighters had been attributable 'to the tight formation and excellent rear-gunners of the Wellington bombers, their maintenance of formation and rigid adherence to course made them easy targets to find'.

Neither Baldwin nor Sir Edgar Ludlow-Hewitt, however, had any way of knowing the German view at the time, and the C-in-C Bomber Command therefore acted in a manner he fully considered to be just when, soon after the raid he ordered Baldwin to assemble his squadron and flight commanders and hammer home the vital necessity for accurate formation flying. Disciplinary action was to be taken against any pilot who wilfully failed to comply with his orders in this respect. The C-in-C further implied that he was not satisfied with the overall standard of efficiency of 3 Group's crews, a view that caused not a little discontent among the personnel of the three squadrons which had been involved in the 18 December raid when they got to hear of it. Their own feeling, and quite rightly, was that they had been sent into action against hopeless odds – albeit unknowingly – in vulnerable aircraft; they had seen their comrades shot down in flames one after the other and they themselves had returned to base in aircraft whose state was in some cases pitiful, with the fabric of their wings torn and flapping in the slipstream and the metal of their engine nacelles punctured by cannon shells. And now, it seemed, the tragedy was to some extent being blamed on the pilots for failing to keep station.

Although – at any rate on the surface – the C-in-C Bomber Command and his Group commanders remained faithful to the theory that bombers could win through in daylight provided they maintained tight formation, the disaster of 18 December was to lead to a complete revision of Bomber Command's policy. The first immediate result was that, a matter of hours after the raid, the Air Ministry ordered a temporary halt to armed reconnaissance of the Heligoland Bight at squadron strength until armour plating had been added to the bombers' fuel tanks. Meanwhile, the Wellingtons of No. 3 Group and the Hampdens of No. 5 were to undertake 'Nickel' operations to give their crews night flying experience.

Armed reconnaissance of the Bight, however, continued on a limited scale, with aircraft usually operating in flights of three. On 2 January 1940, while the C-in-C and the Air Staff were debating the whole future of daylight bombing operations in the light of December's unfortunate record, one such flight of three Wellingtons was attacked off Heligoland by Messerschmitt 110s of ZG 76. Only one of the bombers returned to base.

4
Sparring Across the North Sea, January-April 1940

The British bomber losses over the Heligoland Bight in December 1939 made it clear that if daylight raids were to continue, Bomber Command faced a heavy sacrifice of aircraft and crews. The realization of this fact came at a time when, for the second time that year, the Air Staff was engaged in lengthy controversy with the French General Staff over the employment of Bomber Command if and when the Germans struck westwards.

In September, while the battle for Poland still raged, the British Chiefs of Staff had drawn up a plan of action which was to be executed in the event of a sudden German assault on the west. The main feature of this plan was that Bomber Command, as the best means at Britain's disposal of hitting the Germans hard, would be called upon to launch a maximum effort daylight attack on the Ruhr. It was thought that such an assault on the industrial heart of Germany – which would only be undertaken if an enemy invasion of Belgium and Holland took place, opening up a direct route for the RAF's bombers across these countries to their objectives in the Ruhr – would paralyse a large part of the German war effort and consequently destroy the enemy's hope of a series of rapid advances in the west.

It was an old argument, and once again the French took a firm stand against it. Air power, they insisted, must be used defensively, as a means of army co-operation. Furthermore an attack on the Ruhr by Bomber Command would in all probability result in heavy Luftwaffe attacks on French targets, not on objectives in Britain, and the French Air Force was in no position to retaliate. On 3 October 1939, when the whole question was being debated between French General Staff and British Air Staff representatives in Paris, the state of readiness of France's bomber force was bad enough; two months later it was pitiable. On 14 September two-thirds of the bomber units of the 1st Air Army had been pulled out to the rear for fear that they would be knocked out by a surprise air attack, and on 4 December all bomber groups – with the exception of two equipped with antiquated Farman 222s and Amiot 143s – had been withdrawn to the south of France to be re-equipped with more modern types. By the end of December the entire Air Army bomber force in north-eastern France had been reduced to seventy or so aircraft, all Farmans and Amiots. Throughout the winter months these vintage machines crossed the Rhine on numerous occasions on light reconnaissance or leaflet-dropping missions, their crews braving as many hardships and discomforts as their counterparts in the Whitleys of Bomber Command and, like the latter, penetrating deep into enemy territory.

As a bombing force, however, the Farmans and Amiots were completely ineffective, and their activities were restricted to night operations. By daylight, they were easy targets for both flak and fighters, with their low maximum speeds and weak defensive armament.

It was therefore clear that any major air attack on the Ruhr by daylight would rest entirely on the shoulders of Bomber Command. In October 1939, despite the French attitude, both the Air Staff and the War Cabinet agreed that such an offensive would be necessary should the enemy thrust into the Low Countries; everything had to be done to prevent the Germans from securing a foothold in this area, and consequently from using captured airfields as a convenient springboard for mounting air attacks on the British Isles.

The trouble with the Ruhr Plan, as the Air Staff were the first to admit, was that it left a lot to chance; it was, in short, a gamble. No one at this stage knew the full extent of the opposition likely to be met by a large attacking force in daylight, and consequently there was no way of estimating Bomber Command's probable losses in such a venture. Moreover the bomber force employed could not involve more than 180 aircraft and – as was pointed out in a Bomber Command

appreciation of the Ruhr Plan submitted to the Air Ministry by
Sir Edgar Ludlow-Hewitt on 27 January 1940 – there was considerable doubt that any worthwhile result could be achieved.
This together with the possibility that up to half of the bomber
force might be wiped out – with all the disastrous implications
that the loss of so many trained aircrews would have on the future
development of Bomber Command - prompted the C-in-C to
urge the Air Ministry to reconsider the whole plan, and if
possible to devise some other means of employing Bomber Command to the fullest advantage without such enormous risk. The
severe losses sustained by the Wellington squadrons in daylight
over the German (Heligoland) Bight supported Ludlow-Hewitt's
point of view.

On 22 February 1940 the Ruhr Plan was the subject of a
lengthly discussion at an Air Staff conference under the chairmanship of the CAS, Sir Cyril Newall. At the conference it was
agreed that the Ruhr Plan should only be carried out as a last
desperate resort, and that Bomber Command should instead
concentrate on the development of Air Plan W.A.5(c) – a
proposed attack on the oil resources necessary for Germany's
war effort. This seemed by far the most promising alternative
to the Ruhr Plan, especially since it was felt that even with its
present limited resources Bomber Command would be capable
of finding the oil plants under cover of darkness and, because of
their high vulnerability factor, of inflicting severe damage on them.

During the first two months of 1940, while the Air Staff
attempted to form some kind of firm strategic policy for Bomber
Command, air operations had been curtailed by bad weather and
by the fact that both sides were conserving their strength for
the coming struggle in the west. The Luftwaffe in particular –
which had lost no fewer than 285 aircraft in the Polish Campaign – was reluctant to risk any more heavy losses through
attacks of doubtful value on heavily defended targets. Poland
had shown that the Luftwaffe was strong enough only to undertake a war of limited length and confined to a single front, a
fact that was not appreciated at the time by either the British
or the French.

Since 17 October 1939 – when four Junkers 88s of I/KG 30 had attacked Scapa Flow and sunk the old depot ship *Iron Duke* – the Luftwaffe had confined its activities to reconnaissance along the Franco-German frontier and to mine-laying operations along the British coast, the latter being carried out by Heinkel 115 floatplanes based on Sylt, Borkum and Norderney. The magnetic mines were a serious menace, and at the Admiralty's request Bomber Command initiated a series of nightly patrols over the enemy bases, beginning on 12 December in an effort to prevent the mine-carrying floatplanes from taking off. Forty-two sorties were made on Sylt and forty on Borkum were made before the end of the year, the aircraft occasionally bombing lights seen on the water.

Early in March 1940 there was a sharp increase in air activity on both sides. On the eleventh, Bomber Command's armed reconnaissance missions over the German Bight – which had continued sporadically since December – at last met with a concrete success when a Blenheim of No. 82 Squadron piloted by Squadron Leader M. V. Delap attacked and sank the submarine U.31, which was surprised on the surface in the Schillig Roads.

Five days later a small force of Luftwaffe bombers attacked Scapa Flow; bombs fell on the island of Hoy and killed a civilian. By way of retaliation, Bomber Command was authorized to carry out its first bombing attack of the war against a land target: the seaplane base of Hörnum on the island of Sylt. The raid, which took place on the night of 19-20 March, was carried out by thirty Whitleys of Nos. 10, 51, 77 and 102 Squadrons and twenty Hampdens of Nos. 44, 50, 61 and 144 Squadrons. The weather was bad, with a good deal of fog, but there was moonlight over the target and the bombers attacked at levels varying between 1000 and 10,000 feet, dropping forty 500-pounders, eighty-four 250-pounders and some 1200 incendiaries. Most of the bombs, however, appeared to have fallen in the sea, for a study of photographs brought back by a reconnaissance aircraft some days later revealed no damage whatsoever. One Whitley failed to return.

F

The loss of only one aircraft out of a force of fifty appeared to justify the Air Staff's increasing emphasis on night bombing, but as a rehearsal for future night attacks on other German targets there was no denying that the raid – in so far as actual results were concerned – had been a disappointment. This disappointment was reflected in the Bomber Command report on the raid, which stated :

' The operation does not confirm that, as a general rule the average crews of our heavy bombers can identify targets at night, even under the best conditions, nor does it prove that the average crew can bomb industrial or other enemy targets at night. Our general opinion is that under war conditions the average crew of a night bomber could not be relied upon to identify and attack targets at night except under the very best conditions of visibility, even when the target is on the coast or on a large river like the Rhine. Under the latter conditions about   fifty per cent of the average crews might be expected to find and bomb the right target in good visibility; if the target has no conspicuous aids to its location, very few inexperienced crews would be likely to find it under any conditions.'

This report was influenced not only by the raid itself, but by the months of experience gained by the crews engaged on leaflet operations and by the early results of reconnaissance flights over Germany by the Wellingtons of 3 Group and the Hampdens of 5 Group, which had been undertaking this type of mission since 6 March. The reports of the crews left the Air Staff in no doubt concerning the difficulty of target identification at night, even in conditions of bright moonlight. On moonless nights it was just possible to distinguish land from water at low altitude; otherwise, crews were only able to make out such features as the glow of blast furnaces. They also reported that their night vision was seriously affected by the glare of searchlights under moonless conditions.

In moonlight, areas of water such as lakes and the larger rivers were clearly visible at heights of 12,000 feet and more, while smaller rivers and railways lines – depending on the angle of light – could be seen at 6000 to 8000 feet. Towns and villages could be made out from about 4000 feet, but individual buildings could only be distinguished from a much lower level. According to the crews of 4 Group Whitleys who carried out a series of reconnaissances of the Ruhr in February, marshalling yards presented exceptionally good targets, not least because they were not fully blacked out.

These observations appeared to indicate, however, that even in conditions of bright moonlight bombers would have to fly at an altitude not greater than 12,000 feet if the crews were to have a chance of identifying their targets visually. Earlier, it had been suggested by Air Commodore Coningham, No. 4 Group's commander, that an invisible target might be bombed successfully by timing a bomber's run-in to its position from a known and recognized pinpoint in the vicinity, but at a time when Air Ministry policies on strategic bombing were still dictated by considerations of possible civilian casualties the idea proved unacceptable and was rejected.

Since visual identification was held to be all-important, the only alternative was to find a foolproof method of illuminating the target area artificially; Coningham's suggestion of a timed run-in could theoretically be applied to flare-dropping aircraft, but the latter would have to be followed very closely by a second machine carrying bombs if an attack was to be made before the light of the flares died away. Even then, success depended on the accurate positioning of the flares, and trials so far with the standard 4.5-inch parachute flare had not been encouraging; the flare burned for a very limited period, and large aiming errors had been registered when it was dropped during night exercises.

Over an eighteen-month period between September 1938 and the end of March 1940, Bomber Command repeatedly urged the Air Ministry to initiate the development of new types of flare. The Air Ministry, however, appeared to be completely uninterested in the matter, and Bomber Command was told that the 4.5-inch flares already in use were adequate. Neither was priority given at this time to the development of radio and radar aids to precision bombing, although research was going on in a small way and the subject was discussed from time to time at Air Staff and Bomber Command conferences. The Germans were quicker off the mark; in the spring of 1940 development was well advanced of the blind bombing system known as 'X-Apparatus', a basically simple idea devised as long ago as 1934 by a scientist named Dr Plendl. The principle behind 'X-Apparatus' was a high-frequency radio beam, sent out by a ground transmitter to form an invisible road in the sky that could be followed by a bomber aircraft. A steady signal in the pilot's earphones told him that he was on course, while a series of dots or dashes meant that he was straying off to left or right.

The beam followed by the bomber was intersected by a second 'split' beam, emitted by another ground station. When the bomber reached the intersection, its special radio equipment picked up a signal which told the radio operator that the aircraft was ten miles from the target. He then pressed a switch, starting up a clock on his instrument panel. Five miles further on, in response to another signal, he threw a second switch, stopping the first creeping needle on his clock and starting another. When the two needles were superimposed, the bomber was over its target.

The system, which was used operationally by the Luftwaffe in its raids on British cities during the winter of 1940-1, had its drawbacks; it was, for example, subject to jamming, and it was not long before the British developed effective counter-measures. Nevertheless, the measure of effectiveness may be judged by the fact that when it was used operationally by KG 100 – the Luftwaffe's 'Pathfinder Force' – on the night of 14 November 1940, it enabled them to pinpoint the target with amazing accuracy in pitch darkness and light the way for the 450 bombers that followed. The target was Coventry.

5

The Germans Strike: Norway, April 1940

On the afternoon of 4 April 1940, the crew of a reconnaissance Blenheim returning from a sortie over the Elbe estuary reported a large concentration of warships and merchant vessels – some seventy craft in all – moving northwards in the Schillig Roads. Six Blenheims of No. 2 Group were immediately sent out to attack the naval vessels, but no favourable result was achieved. A second sortie the following morning was abortive because of bad weather, but the leading aircraft flew over the Roads at 200 feet, just below the cloud base, and reported that the ships had gone.

On Saturday 6 April a further reconnaissance showed that units of the German fleet – including the *Scharnhorst* and *Gneisenau* – were in Wilhelmshaven, while that night the crews of British bombers engaged in 'Nickel' operations over north-west Germany reported that they had sighted long lines of motor transport heading along the autobahn from Hamburg to Lübeck with headlights full on. There was also considerable activity at Eckernförde, near Kiel, where a major loading operation appeared to be in progress in the harbour – again with no regard for any blackout.

The indications that the Germans were planning a major operation with Scandinavia as the target had been numerous. As early as 28 March, the Norwegian legation in Berlin had warned its government that a massive build-up of German land and sea forces was taking place in Baltic and North Sea ports, and by 5 April the Norwegian Government was in possession of concrete intelligence that a large-scale German landing on the south coast of Norway was imminent. The first hint that something big and ominous was under way reached London on

1 April, and two days later the British War Cabinet met to discuss the latest reports. The British Government, however, did not view the situation with anything like the gravity it merited; in fact, the War Cabinet clung to the belief that the German concentrations on the Baltic and North Sea coasts were in the nature of a deterrent, designed to prevent the British from following up a plan to lay mines in Norwegian territorial waters with a possible occupation of key Norwegian ports. Such a plan was, in fact, in the process of being actioned. Winston Churchill, as First Lord of the Admiralty, had been campaigning since the beginning of the war for permission to mine the Norwegian Leads by air and sea in an attempt to cut off vital iron-ore shipments to Germany. The plan was finally approved on 3 April, and since it was considered likely that there would be a strong German reaction it was decided that a small Anglo-French force would land at Narvik and advance to the Swedish frontier. This force embarked on transports and warships in the Clyde and Forth at about the same time that Wehrmacht troops were boarding their transports in German harbours, bound for the same destination.

On 5 April, the Prime Minister, Neville Chamberlain, made what was, to say the least, an unfortunate speech to the Central Council of the National Union of Conservative and Unionist Associations. In it, he stated that the German had 'missed the bus' by not taking advantage of their initial superiority to launch an assault on the west before the Allies had time to build up their strength. When Chamberlain delivered his speech, the first wave of German transports was already at sea, bound for its objectives in Norway.

On 8 April, in the early hours of the morning, a small force of British destroyers laid a minefield across the approaches to Narvik. The Norwegian Government delivered strong protests but by this time the British were no longer in any doubt about the Germans' intentions. The previous day, a squadron of Blenheims on armed reconnaissance over the North Sea had sighted an enemy cruiser and four destroyers. The warships were shadowed and a few minutes later the main body of the German

Fleet was located about seventy-six miles NNW of Horns Reef. The Blenheims attacked a cruiser, believed to be either the *Scharnhost* or *Gneisenau,* but with no result.

The Bomber Leader then flashed a message to his base, giving the position and course of the German naval force, but this was not received and the fact that the enemy was at sea in strength was not revealed until the bombers returned. A squadron of Wellingtons sent out that afternoon failed to locate the warships, and a second attempt the following day was frustrated by bad weather. All the British Government could do was inform the Norwegian legation in London that the warships had been sighted off the Norwegian coast, heading northwards.

Then, on the morning of 9 April, with a speed and precision that took the Norwegian and British Governments completely by surprise, the German invasion of Scandinavia began. At 8.30 am the British War Cabinet met in emergency session to discuss what steps to take in the light of the facts that were then known, and it was decided that the C-in-C of the Home Fleet, Admiral Sir Charles Forbes, should be authorized to make the attempt to drive the Germans out of Bergen and Trondheim in preparation for the recapture of both places by a military expedition. Units of the Home Fleet – which had sailed from Rosyth two days earlier after hastily disembarking the troops earmarked for the projected Narvik landing – were in position some eighty miles off Bergen by mid-morning on the ninth, and Forbes planned to attack with seven destroyers while four cruisers stood-off to provide heavy supporting fire. Soon afterwards, however, air reconnaissance reported the presence of two German cruisers in Bergen; the Admiralty considered the odds against a destroyer attack to be too great, and it was cancelled. A few hours later, the Home Fleet was forced on to the defensive when it was attacked by relays of Heinkel 111s and Junkers 88s. The onslaught went on all afternoon, the bombers sinking the destroyer *Gurkha* and damaging the cruisers *Devonshire, Southampton* and *Glasgow.*

With the Home Fleet's offensive capability crippled by continual air attack, it was left to Bomber Command to strike at the warships in Bergen. At dusk, the German naval forces were attacked by a squadron of Wellingtons and one of Hampdens. The bomber crews reported two hits on a cruiser; this turned out to be the *Königsberg*, and she was finally sunk the following day by Fleet Air Arm Skua dive-bombers, operating out of Hatston in the Orkneys.

The Luftwaffe, meanwhile, had begun to concentrate its forces on the newly-captured Norwegian airfields of Stavanger, Vaernes and Fornebu. Stavanger-Sola was the most important of the three, being strategically well placed to command the southern approaches to the Norwegian Sea and therefore to the vital ports of Bergen, Trondheim and Narvik. It rapidly became the main base from which the Luftwaffe mounted its ceaseless attacks on the Home Fleet, and Bomber Command was consequently authorized to try and put it out of action.

It was now that the range limitations of Bomber Command's aircraft became apparent. In order to reach Norwegian targets with anything like an appreciable bomb load, it was necessary to use bases in northern Scotland. The C-in-C Bomber Command had, however, not been slow to realize this, and on 2 April he had given orders for two of his squadrons – Nos. 9 and 115 – to be deployed to Lossiemouth and Kinloss, where they came under the operational control of No. 18 Group Coastal Command.

On 11 April, six Wellington crews of 115 Squadron were briefed to attack Stavanger-Sola. Two Blenheims of 254 Squadron Coastal Command, detailed to act as fighter cover, went ahead and made several strafing runs over the airfield as dusk was falling. Three of the Wellingtons attacked the target and the crews reported that a large fire had been started; the other three failed to attack and one of them was shot down. It was the first time that the RAF bombed a mainland target during the Second World War.

Meanwhile, a force of Hampdens of 5 Group had been held in readiness all day on 11 April to attack a concentration of shipping in Kristiansand. The weather was brilliantly clear, however, and Bomber Command – with bitter memories of the tragedy of 18 December 1939 – was not prepared to authorize the mission. Forty Hampdens and Wellingtons took off that night to attack enemy shipping en route from Kiel to Oslo; a direct hit was claimed on an ammunition ship, which blew up, but the operation was generally hampered by fog and most of the aircraft failed to find a target.

On the morning of 12 April units of the German Fleet – including the *Scharnhorst*, *Gneisenau* and the cruiser *Leipzig* – were reported to be heading south across the entrance to the Skagerrak. No. 3 Group Wellingtons and 5 Group Hampdens flew a total of ninety-two sorties in search of them, but the clear skies of the previous day had given way to fog and nothing was seen. The Hampdens suffered badly during the day's operations; one formation of twelve was attacked by Messerschmitt 109s and 110s, which chased them 200 miles out to sea and shot eight of them down. Two Wellingtons also failed to return.

The tactics the German fighters employed against the Hampdens were brilliant in their simplicity. The Messerschmitt 110s would formate with the Hampdens, flying slightly in front – where the bombers' guns could not be brought to bear – and between fifty and a hundred yards off to one side. The fighter's rear-gunner would then pick off the pilot with an easy no-deflection shot. In this way they systematically picked off almost the entire formation, starting with the wing-men and working inwards. Other fighters stayed above and behind the formation, well out of range of the Hampdens' rear guns, ready to dive down and destroy any bomber that tried to escape.

This catastrophe underlined the total unsuitability of the Hampden for daylight operations in the face of even moderate fighter opposition, and from then on the type was – except on one or two notable occasions – restricted to night missions. The task undertaken increasingly by the Hampdens of 5 Group after the opening of the Norwegian campaign was mine-laying; the first operation of this kind was carried out on the night of 13-14 April, when fifteen Hampdens drawn from Nos. 44, 49, 50, 61 and 144 Squadrons were detailed to lay mines off the Danish coast. Twelve aircraft completed their mission, two more aborted and one failed to return.

The following day, Bomber Command once again struck at Stavanger airfield. This time it was the turn of six Blenheims of 107 Squadron, which had been hurriedly flown up to Lossiemouth from Wattisham. Twelve aircraft actually set off, but six of them either failed to find the target or had to return to base in appalling weather.

' Soon after leaving the Scottish coast, [one pilot told in his report] we ran into rain that was literally tropical in its fury. After some time we climbed and then the rain turned into snow. At 13,000 feet the engines of two of the Blenheims became iced up and stopped. One of the aircraft dropped more or less out of control until only 600 feet above the sea, when the engines started again. The other Blenheim was even luckier. It actually struck the waves at the very moment its engines came to life. It lost its rear wheel, but both aircraft got safely back to base.'

On the night of 15-16 April Whitleys of 4 Group bombed Norway for the first time – and the target was again Stavanger. The Whitleys involved were twelve aircraft of Nos. 10 and 102 Squadrons, temporarily operating from Kinloss under the orders of Coastal Command. Seven aircraft claimed to have found the target and bombed it.

The following night, a lone Whitley of 58 Squadron took off from Linton-on-Ouse, Yorkshire, to attack Oslo-Fornebu airfield, an objective that was beyond the range of any Bomber Command aircraft except the Armstrong-Whitworth type. It turned out to be a harrowing flight. Clouds were low at the start, but the pilot climbed to 11,000 feet into a moderately clear layer between upper and lower cloud masses. Setting a course for the southern promontory of Norway to establish a landfall, and flying by dead reckoning, the bomber made the sea crossing at 10,000 feet. Because of dense cloud the crew failed to locate the coastline and the first sight they had of land was when, shortly after 23.00 hours, a snow-covered hill appeared in bright moonlight through a gap in the clouds.

Recognizing the rolling nature of the country, the pilot fixed his position and set a course to cut the south-east coast of Norway in order to make a landfall, but once again the coast was missed. Thirty minutes later a flat black surface was sighted through a break in the cloud, but it was impossible to tell whether it was land or water. The pilot therefore switched on his landing light and flew down its beam until the reflection showed that the black surface was, in fact, the sea. The pilot then turned to port, flying at 2000 feet, and some minutes later he was able to identify the coastline by the foam of breakers.

For the next half-hour the pilot, his face pressed into the open aperture of the cockpit window, picked his way in and out of cloud along the coast until he reached the entrance to Oslo Fjord. Keeping the rugged cliffs in sight with extreme difficulty, the pilot navigated his way to Drammen Fjord, flying over the docks on the southern side at 1500 feet and observing a great deal of activity around ten cargo vessels anchored there. The docks were floodlit and would have made an excellent target, but the pilot's orders were to bomb Fornebu and he accordingly set course for Oslo at 3000 feet.

At the head of Oslo Fjord the Whitley ran into a severe snow-storm that completely blanketed Fornebu and most of the sur-rounding countryside. The pilot made several attempts to pene-trate the murk, coming down as low as 500 feet, but at this height very heavy icing was encountered and he was forced to climb again. He flew back over Drammen in the hope that the snowstorm would abate, but although Oslo itself showed up clearly in bright moonlight the aerodrome itself remained com-pletely obscured. It might have been possible to judge the position of the target in relation to Oslo, but positive visual identification was still the order of the day and the pilot had no alternative but to set course for England with his bombs still on board.

The Whitley landed at Linton at 04.30, after being airborne for nine and a half hours. It was no mean feat of navigation on the pilot's part; his navigator, a new and inexperienced member of the squadron who was making his first war flight, had become hopelessly lost early in the mission and had been unable to render much assistance.

The following night three more Whitleys of 58 Squadron set off for Fornebu. One aircraft aborted with engine trouble, but the other two found the target and bombed it sucessfully. Fornebu was bombed four more times before the end of the month.

Stavanger, however, continued to receive the biggest weight of bombs, being attacked sixteen times by Bomber Command – as well as by aircraft of Coastal Command and the Fleet Air Arm – between 11 and 24 April. One of the best-executed raids was carried out on 17 April by twelve Blenheims of 107 Squadron; the bombers made their attack in two formations of six, the first bombing from high level and the second from low level ten seconds later. The Blenheims were attacked by enemy fighters and two were shot down, but the remainder maintained their defensive formation and fought their way through.

One of the main assembly points for the German transport squadrons engaged in ferrying troops and supplies into southern Norway was the airfield at Aalborg, in Denmark, and this was attacked for the first time on the night of 20-21 April by Hampdens of 83 Squadron, flying from Lossiemouth. Three aircraft took off; one crew got lost and abandoned the mission when they found themselves near Copenhagen with the sun coming up, but the other two claimed to have made successful attacks on the target. The next night the crews of 83 Squadron were back to their more usual occupation, laying mines in Oslo Fjord. Of the forty-five sorties flown by No. 83 during April, more than half were accounted for by mine-laying operations.

By this time, Allied plans for launching a counter-attack in Norway had belatedly got under way with the landing of a British brigade and three battalions of French Chasseurs at Namsos and a second British brigade at Åndalsnes. The idea, approved by both the British War Cabinet and the French War Council, was that these forces would advance from the north-east and south-west on Trondheim. Possession of this objective, with its large, well-equipped harbour and its neighbouring airfield, would give the Allies the opportunity to land a force of more than 50,000 men with which to block the German's progress northwards. This area of central Norway was eminently suitable for defence; apart from the nature of the terrain, the only access to Trondheim for enemy forces approaching from Oslo was by way of a single road and railway line, and it was felt that the Wehrmacht's progress could be seriously hampered by air attack.

The date for the assault on Trondheim was set for 22 April. While the two 'pincers' advanced on their objective from north and south, a massive frontal attack would be made with the full support of the Home Fleet, including about 200 carrier-based aircraft.

It was a boldly-conceived plan, but the risk involved was enormous. On 18 April both the Admiralty and the War Office expressed serious doubts that the operation could be undertaken with any real hope of success. Their opinions were influenced by reports of the continuing build-up of Luftwaffe bomber forces on the airfields of southern Norway, and by the fact that news of the proposed frontal assault on Trondheim had been somehow leaked to the Press. There were also indications that the Germans were strengthening their defences at Trondheim, but this could not be confirmed as there was a total lack of air reconnaissance information. It seemed certain, however, that the Germans knew of the planned attack and were taking all possible steps to meet it, which made the concentration of the Home Fleet's warships in a small area an extremely hazardous venture. The plan was therefore changed and the frontal assault abandoned. Instead, the Chiefs of Staff recommended an increase in strength of the forces at Namsos and Åndalsnes, making these wholly responsible for the capture of Trondheim.

Because of the overwhelming air superiority enjoyed by the Germans, this revised plan was doomed to failure from the start. The Åndalsnes force pushed sixty miles inland to the railway junction at Dombås, where it joined up with Norwegian units, but the idea of an advance northward to Trondheim was abandoned and instead the force headed south-east down the

Gudbrandsdal with the object of assisting the Norwegian troops engaged in harassing the German forces advancing from Oslo. The first clash between British and German troops took place on 21 April, but the British brigade's rifles and machine-guns were no match for the enemy's artillery, tanks and aircraft. After a day of stiff fighting, the combined British and Norwegian force began the 140-mile withdrawal to Åndalsnes, where they fought a valiant rearguard action until they were evacuated on the night of 30 April-1 May. The Namsos force was also evacuated the following night. Both operations were carried out under heavy and continual air attack.

The RAF was powerless to intervene. Eighteen Gladiator fighters were flown to a frozen lake at Lesjaskog, forty miles from Åndalsnes, but within four days they were wiped out either in the air or on the ground. Bomber Command was asked to mount as many raids as possible on the enemy airfields, but these amounted to mere pinpricks. Both Bomber Command and the Hudson and Blenheim squadrons of Coastal Command could do little more than make repeated attacks on Stavanger in the hope of hampering the Luftwaffe's operations. Direct support of the Allied land operations in Norway was out of the question, for each mission involved a round trip of 600 to 800 miles over open sea and, even with maximum fuel and the smallest worth-while bomb-load, the time that the RAF crews could afford to spend over their targets was measured in minutes.

What effect the capture of Trondheim, with its neighbouring airfield of Vaernes, would have had on the Allied campaign in central Norway is a matter for conjecture. In all probability the outcome would not have been different, for the Luftwaffe was mistress of the Norwegian sky and would certainly have inflicted devastating losses on any RAF units using Vaernes as a base for any operations.

The month of intensive operations over Norway between 9 April and 10 May 1940 cost RAF Bomber Command thirty-three aircraft, not counting those destroyed accidentally. Taking into account the fact that the Bomber Command units operating alongside Coastal Command flew an average of four sorties a week at squadron or half-squadron strength, many of them in daylight and in an area where the enemy enjoyed total air superiority, the loss was not as high as it might have been. It was, however, in no way justified by the negligible results obtained – and for Bomber Command, the sternest test was still to come.

6

Blitzkrieg

If the opening months of the war seemed unreal to the crews of Bomber Command based in Britain, this was doubly true for the personnel of the Advanced Air Striking Force in France. They had been transported, literally overnight, from the familiar routine and surroundings of their well-equipped RAF stations to a series of airfields that seemed incredibly primitive by comparison; they were conscious that they might have to go into action at a moment's notice; they knew that the enemy's equipment was superior to their own in almost every respect, that supplies of fuel and ammunition were extremely limited, that some spare parts were almost non-existent and that if the enemy launched an all-out attack they would probably last no more than a week.

Any doubts that the AASF's equipment was totally outclassed were removed during the very first month of the war, when the Battle squadrons began making armed reconnaissance flights over the Siegfried Line. The rear gunner of one Battle – Sergeant F. Letchford of 88 Squadron – had the distinction of shooting down the first enemy aircraft claimed by the RAF in the Second World War when he destroyed a Messerschmitt 109 during an operation on 20 September, but the jubilation at this achievement was short-lived. Ten days later, five Battles of 150 Squadron flying an armed reconnaissance mission over Saarbrücken were attacked by a formation of Bf 109s and only one aircraft came back.

After this disaster the Battle squadrons went over to night operations, carrying out occasional attacks in support of French ground forces skirmishing with the enemy patrols in the Saar area. Operational flying was severely handicapped by bad weather during the autumn and winter and the squadrons embarked on a period of intensive training, carrying out mock attacks on British and French ground forces, night cross-country flights, practice bombing and air gunnery exercises. Night operations were not resumed until late in February, when the Battles started a series of leaflet raids on the Rhineland.

In December 1939 two of the Battle squadrons – Nos. 15 and 40 – were withdrawn to the United Kingdom to re-equip with Blenheims. This left the AASF with eight Battle squadrons, later reinforced by the Blenheims of Nos. 114 and 139 Squadrons. The latter two squadrons originally formed part of the Second Echelon of the AASF, which was to have followed the Battles to France in the autumn of 1939 and which also comprised Nos. 21, 82, 90, 91, 107 and 110 Squadrons. In the event, the Air Ministry decided to postpone the despatch of the main body of the Second Echelon, and only 114 and 139 Squadrons had arrived in France by 10 May 1940. It was a wise decision, as the tragic events of May and June were to show.

As dawn broke on 10 May 1940 German airborne forces struck at Eben Emael, the vital Belgian fortress commanding the west bank of the Albert Canal. Simultaneously, assault troops captured the bridges over the Meuse at Vroenhoven and Veldwezelt. While the battle for Eben Emael went on and the first armoured spearheads of von Bock's Army Group B smashed their way across the bridges into Belgium in the spreading light, twenty-eight Heinkel 111s of II/KG 4 were thundering inland over the Hook of Holland. They had taken off from their bases in north-west Germany at 05.00 and had made a wide detour around northern Holland. By approaching the target from the west – the direction of England – the bomber leader hoped to achieve the maximum element of surprise.

The target was the airport of Waalhaven, on the outskirts of Rotterdam. At the same time, other Luftwaffe bomber formations were bearing down on the key airfields of Schiphol, Ypenburg and Bergen op Zoom with the object of paralysing Holland's air defences in one blow. The Netherlands Army Air Force's handful of fighter aircraft put up a spirited resistance, but it was useless. Within minutes the Dutch airfields had been put out of action, their runways cratered and their installations in flames.

After the bombers came the Junkers 52s, disgorging their loads of paratroops. Waalhaven was captured within twenty minutes. An hour later three Fokker T. V bombers lumbered over and dropped a few bombs among a group of Ju 52s on the airfield, but the German fighters pounced and two of the Dutch aircraft crashed in flames. In the afternoon, eight Blenheims of No. 15 Squadron – operating from Alconbury in Huntingdon-shire – also attacked Waalhaven, destroying a number of enemy transports. All the Blenheims returned to base, some with extensive battle damage. Twelve Blenheims of 40 Squadron also took off from Wyton to attack Ypenburg; nine aircraft bombed the primary target, another bombed a small landing ground five mile west of Leyden and an eleventh machine strafed some Junkers 52s parked along the beach between The Hague and Noordwijk. Three Blenheims failed to return, two being shot down by anti-aircraft fire and the third by Messerschmitts soon after bombing Waalhaven.

When the storm broke, the total RAF strength in France was 416 aircraft, of which 256 were light bombers, 200 of the latter – 110 of them Battles – were serviceable. The whole force was under the command of Air Marshal Arthur Barratt and was composed as follows :

The BEF Air Component (Air Vice-Marshal Blount): four fighter squadrons, Nos. 85 and 87 with Hurricanes and Nos. 607 and 615 with Gladiators (in the process of converting to Hurricanes); two strategic reconnaissance squadrons, Nos. 18 and 57 with Blenheim IVs; two medium-bomber squadrons, Nos. 53 and 59, also with Blenheim IVs; five army co-operation squadrons, Nos. 2, 4, 13, 16 and 26, with Lysanders; and one liaison squadron, No. 81, with Dragon Rapides.

The Advanced Air Striking Force (Air Vice-Marshal Play-fair): two fighter squadrons, Nos. 1 and 73, with Hurricanes; eight light-bomber squadrons, Nos. 12, 88, 103, 105, 142, 150, 218 and 226 with Battles; two medium-bomber squadrons, Nos. 114 and 139, with Blenheim IVs; and one photo-reconnaissance flight consisting of four unarmed Spitfires of No. 212 Squadron, on temporary attachment.

In all, the Luftwaffe's bombers – flying in formations that varied in size from three to more than thirty aircraft – struck at seventy-two allied air bases in Holland, Belgium and France on that morning of 10 May. Throughout the day, 400 Heinkel 111s, Dornier 17s and Junkers 88s flew over a thousand sorties against airfields and communications. Despite the weight of the attack and the element of surprise, the losses sustained by the RAF and the French Air Force were surprisingly light; this was due in no small measure to the efforts of the British and French fighter squadrons, which got off the ground in time to break up many of the enemy formations. In Belgium and Holland, however, it was a different story; the Belgians lost fifty-three aircraft and the Dutch sixty-two, one-third and one-half of their respective effective strengths.

The Allied reply was slow in coming, and when it did come it was ridiculously feeble in comparison with the Luftwaffe's effort. The carefully-laid plans for mounting a concerted Anglo-French offensive against the enemy's lines of communication proved to be worth less than the paper they were written on. Air Marshal Barratt, besieged by frantic calls for help from the British and French army commanders in the field, spent most of the morning trying to get the French Air Force C-in-C, General Vuillemin, to embark on a joint course of action. It was not until 11.00, however, that Vuillemin gave orders authorizing his small bomber force to undertake offensive operations against the advancing enemy columns, and the French GHQ flatly refused to permit the bombing of road and rail complexes on German territory. The result was complete confusion, with the commanders of the French bomber squadrons deluged with a series of senseless orders and counter-orders – none of which had the slightest bearing on the task they had expected to undertake once the invasion started. Some units were even ordered to carry out unarmed flights over the front line at low level as a 'morale-booster' for the French troops; one or two actually did so and were decimated by the Messerschmitts.

In the end Air Marshal Barratt, on his own initiative, decided to send the AASF into action in support of the hard-pressed Allied forces without the help of the French. He immediately telephoned the French General Georges, commanding the North Eastern Zone of Operations, and informed him of his decision. Quietly, Georges murmured, 'Thank God'. His men had been pounded incessantly by the Stukas since dawn and the Panzer divisions were breaking through everywhere. Now, at last, there was a prospect of some respite.

Nevertheless it was not until noon that the AASF was able to mount its first operation. Most of the squadrons had been on readiness since 06.00, with half their available aircraft ready for take-off at 30 minutes' notice and half at two hours' notice, but a lack of information on the enemy's positions had caused lengthy delays. At last thirty-two Battles – one flight each from Nos. 12, 103, 105, 142, 150, 218 and 226 Squadrons – were ordered to attack enemy troops advancing through Luxembourg. They approached the target in four waves of eight aircraft, escorted by a handful of Hurricanes. No enemy fighters were encountered, but the Battles ran into a storm of anti-aircraft fire from mobile 20-mm cannon and machine-guns and thirteen of them were shot down. Almost all the surviving aircraft were damaged to some extent.

A second low-level attack – again directed against the enemy columns choking the roads of Luxembourg – was carried out towards the middle of the afternoon, again with thirty-two aircraft flying at 250 feet. This time a squadron of Bf 109s put in an appearance, and between them the fighters and the flak accounted for ten more Battles. Throughout the remainder of the day the AASF's ground crews worked like slaves to repair battle-damaged aircraft, making as many as possible airworthy for operations the following morning.

So far neither the AASF's two Blenheim squadrons nor the UK-based 'heavies' of Bomber Command had been committed to the battle. French opposition to the British plan to mount strategic bombing attacks on German marshalling yards and oil refineries in the Ruhr was no longer an obstacle, for this step had finally been agreed at a meeting between the British War Cabinet and the French War Council in Paris in April. The main reason for the delay in taking a decision on the employment of Bomber Command was that, at the time of the German attack, the new British Coalition Government under Winston Churchill was in the process of formation, and although the changeover took place as smoothly as possible under the circumstances there was a certain amount of inevitable confusion and delay. The filling of certain key ministerial posts presented difficulties right from the start; Churchill had, for example to overcome a considerable amount of opposition to install Sir Archibald Sinclair as Air Minister, for his followers in the Liberal Party felt that he deserved nothing less than a seat in the War Cabinet. Churchill was forced to compromise by proposing that Sir Archibald should join the War Cabinet when matters of major political importance were being discussed. Moreover the new Air Minister at this stage had little grasp of the technical considerations that governed the whole concept of strategic bombing; he needed time in order to become familiar with his new task before committing himself to recommendations and decisions of far-reaching importance.

The new War Minister, Anthony Eden, found himself in a similar position. He did not, in fact, assume his post until the afternoon of 12 May, and it was the following day before he was able to put forward the official War Office view on how Bomber Command should be used. Like the French, Eden believed that the RAF bomber force should be committed to attacks on communications rather than industry; a view that was not shared by the Air Staff.

All these arguments consumed vital time, and meanwhile the slaughter in France and the Low Countries went on. On the night of 10-11 May a force of thirty-six Wellingtons attacked Waalhaven and the crews reported having started several fires among the buildings, and that same night eight Whitleys of Nos. 77 and 102 Squadrons bombed lines of communication on the enemy's route to southern Holland at Geldern, Goch, Aldekerk, Rees and Wesel at the request of Air Marshal Barratt –

but no attacks east of the Rhine were as yet authorized and it was to be another twenty-four hours before the UK-based squadrons of Bomber Command again flew in support of the Allied armies.

At dawn on 11 May the crews of No. 114 Squadron were briefed to attack enemy armour pushing through the Ardennes. Their Blenheims stood in a long line on Vraux airfield, not far from Soissons on the north bank of the Aisne, fuelled, armed and ready to go. The crews had collected their parachutes and were lounging on the grass beside their aircraft, waiting for the order to take off, when nine elongated shapes skimmed over a line of trees and fanned out across the aerodrome. They were Dornier 17s, and showers of 100-pound bombs cascaded from their bellies to explode among the British aircraft. Within half a minute a pall of smoke obscured the sky over Vraux, spreading from the blazing wreckage of the Blenheims. No. 114 Squadron had virtually ceased to exist.

The annihiliation of one of the AASF's Blenheim squadrons – fortunately without great loss of life – meant that the burden of the day's operations once again fell on the Battles. Once again, heavy casualties were suffered. In the early afternoon, eight Battles of Nos. 88 and 218 Squadrons went out again to attack enemy concentrations in Luxembourg; they never even reached the target. The fighters pounced, and only one Battle returned.

On the night of 11-12 May, again at the request of Air Marshall Barratt, Bomber Command made its first large attack against the German mainland. The target was road and rail communications around München-Gladbach, and the attack was made by Whitleys of Nos. 51, 58, 77 and 102 Squadrons and Hampdens of 44, 49, 50, 61 and 144 Squadrons. Thirty-six aircraft took off, five Hampdens came back early and about half the remaining aircraft bombed the target. One Whitley and two Hampdens were shot down; both Hampden crews less one pilot, made their way to the Allied lines.

Meanwhile, the Belgians had made a desperate appeal to the British and French to try and destroy the bridges over the Albert Canal at Maastricht, over which a continual stream of tanks, armoured cars and troop carriers was pouring into the Low Countries. The Germans had lost no time in organizing their defences around this objective; there were long-barrelled 37-mm and quadruple 20-mm anti-aircraft cannon every few yards along the banks. An attempt to bomb the bridges by nine Battles of the Belgian Air Force's 5/III/3 Squadron, flying from their base at Aeltre, had met with disaster at noon on 11 May; six of them were destroyed before they reached the target and the 100-pound bombs of the remaining three failed to do any damage. The bridges were then attacked by twelve Blenheims – six from 21 Squadron and six from 110 – operating from their British bases. The attack was made from 3000 feet in the face of very heavy anti-aircraft fire. On approaching the target the Blenheims broke formation in order to make their attacks from different directions, but as they were making their run-in the bomber leader spotted enemy fighters overhead and instructed the pilots to form up once more so that the maximum defensive fire-power could be brought to bear. Four Blenheims were shot down and the others were all damaged; none of the bombs hit the target.

Next it was the turn of ten Lioré-et-Olivier 451s of the French Air Force's Groupes de Bombardement 1/12 and 11/12; escorted by Morane 406 fighters they were making the first French bombing attack of the war. Their bombs started several fires among a group of enemy motor transport, but the bridges themselves remained intact. The Moranes, hopelessly outnumbered, fought a valiant battle against a horde of Messerschmitts, claiming the destruction of five enemy aircraft for the loss of four of their own number. One LeO 451 was shot down; all the remainder except one were so badly damaged that it was several days before they could be made airworthy once more.

Destruction of the bridges still remained a priority task the following morning, despite the fact that air reconnaissance had revealed a threat in the south in the shape of four Panzer divisions advancing towards Marche and Dinant and in the Bastogne-Neufchâteau sector. The first attack of 12 May on the Maastricht-Tongeren axis was carried out by nine Blenheims of

No. 139 Squadron, which took off from their base at Plivot to bomb a German column advancing in the direction of Tongeren. The Blenheims were caught by fifty Bf 109s and massacred; only two aircraft returned. Two of the missing crews later arrived back at Plivot, having crash-landed near the enemy lines.

The attack by 139 Squadron took place at 07.00. An hour later on that Whit Sunday morning, the crews of No. 12 Squadron were also briefed for an attack on the bridges. No. 12 was based on the little grass airfield of Amifontaine, 120 miles from Maastricht. The assembled crews listened in silence as the deputy CO, Squadron Leader Lowe, told them exactly what they might expect. The mission, he said, was so dangerous that he had been instructed to call for six volunteer crews.

The entire squadron volunteered, and in the end Lowe settled for the six crews already on standby. Three Battles would attack the bridge at Veldwezelt and three the bridge at Vroenhoven. The former was to be the objective of B Flight, led by twenty-two-year-old Flying Officer Donald 'Judy' Garland. Garland's opposite number in A Flight was Flying Officer Norman Thomas, who would lead the attack on the Vroenhoven bridge.

Thomas was the first to take off, followed by Pilot Officer Davy. The third member of A Flight, Pilot Officer Brereton, had mechanical trouble with his aircraft and had to be left behind. Five minutes later, Garland's Battle bumped across the grass and roared into the air. Behind Garland came Flying Officer McIntosh and Sergeant Fred Marland.

Thomas and Davy climbed steadily at 160 mph, levelling at 7000 feet. Scattered cloud was creeping across the sky from the east. It was 09.00, and Tongeren was dead ahead. With fifteen miles still to go to Maastricht, the Battle crews got a sudden surprise when light flak started to come up. It was only now that they realized the speed and extent of the German advance.

Five minutes ahead of the Battles, the eight Hurricanes of No. 1 Fighter Squadron, based at Vassincourt, were also heading for Maastricht. Ahead of them, several thousand feet higher, the fighter pilots saw the sky apparently filled with enemy fighters; they were looking at the Messerschmitts of three Fighter Wings, 120 aircraft in all. Disregarding the fearful odds the Hurricane pilots went in to the attack. In a hopeless, unequal fight lasting five minutes they destroyed three Bf 109s, but six Hurricanes went down in flames on the banks of the Albert Canal.

The Battles, meanwhile, were heading for their targets under cover of the diversion. In a long, slanting dive Thomas swept over the Maastricht-Tongeren road, pointing the Battle's nose at the Vroenhoven bridge. A Bf 109 appeared, but the pilot – no doubt wary of following the Battle into the thick of the anti-aircraft fire – sheered off and attacked Pilot Officer Davy's aircraft instead. The latter escaped by diving into a cloud.

Thomas dropped his four 250-pound bombs singly as he passed over the bridge at less than 100 feet. His aircraft was hit again and again; a shell found the engine, which spluttered and died. Thomas crash-landed in a field; the crew, dazed but unhurt, climbed out of the wreck and raised their hands as German soldiers came running up.

Diving behind his leader, Davy saw Thomas's bombs erupt on the far end of the bridge. He dropped his own bombs from 2000 feet and saw them explode in the water and on the canal bank. He turned and ran for home through a web of tracer and anti-aircraft bursts. At that moment he was attacked by a 109; the fighter was driven off by his rear-gunner, but not before its cannon-shells had set fire to the Battle's port fuel tank. Davy ordered his crew to bail out and was about to follow them over the side when he noticed that the fire had gone out of its own accord. He nursed the crippled Battle towards base, and was only a few miles away from home when he ran out of fuel and had to come down in a field. A few hours later Mansell, Davy's observer, turned up safely at Amifontaine. Patterson, the rear-gunner, had not been so lucky; he came down behind the German lines and spent the rest of the war in a PoW camp.

The bridge at Vroenhoven still stood. Five minutes after Thomas's attack, Garland's flight was approaching its metal twin at Veldwezelt. Garland favoured a low-level attack, and the three Battles swept across the Belgian countryside at fifty feet in line astern. Flying Officer McIntosh's aircraft burst into flames on the run-in to the target; despite terrible burns he jettisoned his bombs and made a perfect belly-landing on the left bank of the canal. All three crew members scrambled out of the aircraft and were taken prisoner.

Fred Marland's aircraft was hit and went into a steep climb, burning from wingtip to wingtip. Then it flicked over and dived vertically into the ground. There were no survivors. The third Battle – Garland's – appeared over the bridge, turning steeply. Then its nose went down and it dived into the bridge, disintegrating in the explosion of its own bombs. When the smoke cleared the western end of the bridge was a tangled ruin, sagging into the water.

For their action, Garland and his observer – Sergeant Tom Gray – were awarded posthumous Victoria Crosses. Few people today remember the name of Garland's gunner, LAC Reynolds; for some inexplicable reason he received no award at all.

German sappers were already erecting pontoons alongside the shattered bridge at Veldwezelt when twenty-four Blenheims of No. 2 Group attempted to attack the bridges over the Meuse within the perimeter of Maastricht. Ten of the bombers were shot down. At 13.00 it was once again the turn of the French Air Force when eighteen Breguet 693s of Groupement d'Assault 18, escorted by Moranes, attacked German armoured columns in the Hasselt—St Trond—Liège—Maastricht sector. Eight of the Breguets failed to return. Twelve LeO 451s which bombed enemy columns near Tongeren, St Trond and Waremme at 18.30 were more fortunate; most of them were damaged, but they all returned to base.

The AASF's Battles, meanwhile, had been in action again during the late afternoon, when fifteen sorties were flown against concentrations of enemy troops near Bouillon. Six Battles were shot down. During the day's operations, sixty-two per cent of the Battles sent into combat had failed to return.

Attacks on the German columns in the Maastricht area were maintained after dark by forty Blenheims of 2 Group, drawn from the squadrons that were to have formed the Second Echelon of the AASF. The aircraft operated in relays and, in contrast to the daylight operations, their losses were negligible. The last mission against the bridges at Maastricht was flown in the early hours of 13 May by twelve elderly Amiot 143s of Groupement 9, all of which returned to base.

Reconnaissance carried out during the night of 12-13 May by the Amiots of Groupements 9 and 10 confirmed that the enemy's main thrust was directed along the axes Clairvaux-Bastogne and Neufchâteau—Bouillon—Sedan. Now, more than ever, aircraft were needed to support the field armies which were desperately trying to stem the flood – but the terrible losses of the previous day had left the AASF with only 72 airworthy machines, and Air Marshal Barratt's immediate concern was to conserve the remnants of his striking force until a worthwhile target could be found for them. Accordingly only one mission – by a handful of Battles from 226 Squadron – was carried out on the thirteenth. The Battles bombed a factory in an attempt to block the road near Breda at the request of the 7th French Army, which was pulling back towards Antwerp under heavy pressure from the 9th Panzer Division.

Two missions were flown by the French Air Force's bomber arm during the thirteenth, both of them ineffective. The first was carried out by a single Potez 631, which bombed an armoured column in the Givonne sector during the morning, and the second by seven LeO 451s at 17.00. All the French machines returned to base, but half of them were so badly damaged by flak that they had to be written off. During the night of 13-14 May twenty-four Amiot 143s attacked the enemy's rear at Trèves, Marche, Ciney, Dinant and Rochefort, and Blenheims of 2 Group once again bombed the bridges at Maastricht and the road and rail exits of Aachen and Eindhoven.

'Victory or defeat hinges on the destruction of those bridges.' There were the words used by General Billotte, commanding the French Army Group 1, when he telephoned Air Marshal Barratt in the early hours of 14 May with a request for further air strikes by the AASF. At 04.30 and 06.30, two flights of five

Battles from 103 and 150 Squadrons attacked the pontoons which the German Pioneers had thrown across the Meuse at Gaulier, north of Sedan. All the Battles returned to base. Some of the pontoons appeared to have been damaged, but Guderian's panzers continued to rumble across into the bridgehead established on the west bank in the evening of the thirteenth. Further north, the 6th Panzer Division pushed through a second breach in the Monthermé area, while in the Dinant sector Rommel's 7th Panzers poured into a third bridgehead.

The German thrust in the critical Sedan sector caught the French 2nd Army completely unawares; it would be at least twenty-four hours before a counter-attack could be launched. In the meantime, the French GHQ requested the commitment of the entire available forces of the AASF and the French Air Force in a desperate effort to delay the enemy advance and buy time.

The first attack was carried out at 09.00 by eight Breguet 693s, escorted by fifteen Hurricanes and fifteen Bloch 152s. The Breguets bombed and strafed enemy armour in the Bazeilles region and the pontoon bridges between Douzy and Vrigne-sur-Meuse. Only scattered light flak and a handful of fighters were encountered, and the bombers all returned. At 12.45 thirteen Amiot 143s of Groupements 9 and 10 were also sent in to the attack on the direct orders of General Vuillemin; it was the first time that these old night bombers had been committed to daylight operations. Flying at 2500 feet and escorted by thirty Bloch 152s, Morane 406s and Dewoitine 520s, they bombed enemy concentrations in the Sedan, Bazeilles and Givonne sectors. Two were shot down by flak and two more by fighters. At the same time, eight unescorted LeO 451s attacked targets south of Sedan and armoured columns on the Bazeilles-Sedan axis. One of the LeO 451s was hit by flak in its bomb-bay and exploded in mid-air.

The twenty-nine bombers sent into action by the French that morning represented their entire serviceable bomber force. There were no more reserves immediately available; from now on, it was up to the Advanced Air Striking Force. The French losses since the invasion began totalled 135 fighters, 21 bombers and 76 reconnaissance and observation aircraft.

Air Vice-Marshal Playfair had been holding the AASF in reserve for as long as possible, allowing his squadrons a few more hours in which to scrape together their available resources. Those resources were pitifully small, amounting to only sixty-two Battles and eight Blenheims, but with the French bomber force out of action Barratt and Playfair were left with no alternative other than to send these battered remnants into combat. However hopeless the situation might be, however suicidal a large-scale daylight attack might turn out, the pleas for help from the Allied armies could not be ignored.

Between 15.00 and 16.00 that afternoon, the AASF flung every aircraft that could still fly into the cauldron. It was a massacre. No. 12 Squadron lost four aircraft out of five; No 142 four out of eight; No. 226 three out of six; No. 105 six out of eleven; No. 150 lost all four; No. 88 one out of ten; No. 103 three out of eight and No. 218 ten out of eleven. Of the eight Blenheims sent out by 114 and 139 Squadrons – all flown by 114 Squadron crews – only three returned to base. It was the highest loss in an operation of similar size ever experienced by the RAF; fearful payment for the destruction of two pontoon bridges and the damaging of two more, which was all that was achieved. During the days that followed six Battle crews, all shot down behind the enemy lines, managed to struggle back to their bases. They included a pilot who, although wounded in two places, had nevertheless managed to swim the Meuse; and an observer and gunner who had stayed with their badly injured pilot in enemy territory for more than twenty-four hours, leaving him only when he died. All the other crews – 102 young men – were either dead or prisoners.

At dusk, the bridges were again attacked by twenty-eight Blenheims of 2 Group. Seven aircraft failed to return, including two which crash-landed in French territory.

News of the disasters of 14 May, both on land and in the air, was received with horror by the British War Cabinet. Out of the confusion two facts emerged clearly: first, that the AASF had virtually ceased to exist as an effective fighting force, and second, that it was impossible to comply with repeated requests by the French General Staff for the transfer of ten more British fighter squadrons to France. A decision to this effect was forced by Air Marshal Dowding, the C-in-C Metropolitan Fighter Command. Appalled by the losses suffered by the Hurricane squadrons in France – over 200 machines in the first four days of fighting – he obtained permission to appear before Churchill and his ministers on 14 May, a day after he had been ordered to send a further thirty-two Hurricanes across the Channel. Dowding was adamant that to send a further 120 fighters to France, as requested by the French, would be little short of suicidal for Britain's own air defences. His case was based largely on a draft report being prepared for submission to the War Cabinet by the combined Chiefs of Staff, entitled 'British Strategy in a Certain Eventuality', and on one extract in particular :

> 'While our Air Force is in being, our Navy and Air Force together should be able to prevent Germany carrying out a serious seaborne invasion. Supposing Germany gained complete air superiority, the Navy could hold up an invasion for a time, but not for an indefinite period. In these circumstances our land forces will be insufficient to deal with a serious invasion. The crux of the matter is air superiority. Once Germany has attained this she might attempt to subjugate this country by air alone. We should be able to inflict such casualties on the enemy by day as to prevent serious damage, but we cannot be sure of protecting our large industrial centres from serious damage by night attack. If the enemy presses home night attacks on our aircraft industry, he is likely to achieve such material and moral damage as to bring all work to a standstill.'

Dowding told the War Cabinet that if a German air attack on Britain did come, he would need more than twenty-five squadrons of fighters to repel it. Placing a graph on Churchill's blotter, he said that if the present rate of wastage continued for another fortnight, there would not be a single Hurricane left either in France or in Britain. The possible transfer of Spitfires to France did not enter into the argument, for these were Dowding's first line of defence and were so valuable that such a step was not even contemplated.

Dowding's remarks to the War Cabinet have since been the subject of much controversy, and there have been allegations that he did not lay all his cards on the table – in other words, that he deliberately misled the Cabinet by quoting inaccurate figures both of losses and available aircraft. Whether this was true or not is academic; the real point is that at this stage, not even the provision of an additional 120 Hurricanes would have had an appreciable effect on the enemy's overwhelming air superiority. When he walked into the Cabinet Room on that day in May, Dowding realized that the Battle of France was already lost, his one concern was that the thirty-nine squadrons and 1300 pilots earmarked for the defence of Great Britain should not be frittered away uselessly, and whatever means he used to achieve this end have been amply justified in the light of history.

Such arguments, however, were not likely to appeal to the French, who already appeared to be totally demoralized and on the verge of collapse. The War Cabinet had to make some kind of gesture of help, but with the situation totally confused and concrete intelligence on the military position almost non-existent, it was not easy to decide what to do. In so far as action by the Royal Air Force was concerned – with the AASF shattered and little probability of more fighters being sent to the continent (although the decision not to do so was not actually taken until 19 May) – there remained only the UK-based squadrons of Bomber Command with the means of striking at the enemy.

There were two ways in which Bomber Command might be usefully employed in support of the Allied forces in France. First, they could be used to attack targets such as marshalling yards, railway junctions and trains between the Rhine and the eastern frontiers of Holland and Belgium, the crossing-points over the Meuse and congested areas in the enemy's rear; this was already being done by the Blenheims of 2 Group, operating under cover of darkness, and one large raid (on the night of 11-12 May) had also been made by Whitleys and Hampdens of 4 and 5 Groups with limited success. Second – and this was regarded as a much more drastic step – Bomber Command could be authorized to bomb industrial targets east of the Rhine.

Despite the desperate nature of the situation in France and the Low Countries, it needed a severe jolt before the War Cabinet would agree to put the latter course of action into effect. The jolt in question was the German bombing of Rotterdam on 14 May – one of the most misunderstood, misinterpreted and – from the propaganda point of view – widely exploited actions in the history of air warfare. Because the Rotterdam attack was to play no small part in influencing – at least indirectly – the War Cabinet's policy with regard to strategic bombing, it is worthwhile analysing what took place.

On the morning of 10 May, German paratroops had captured key bridges over the Nieuwe Maas at Dordrecht and Rotterdam. They held these positions for nearly four days, suffering heavy losses, until the first panzers clattered into the outskirts of Rotterdam on 13 May. Command of the German forces in Rotterdam now rested on the shoulders of General Rudolf Schmidt, commanding the 39th Panzer Corps, who had been ordered at all costs to avoid unnecessary casualties among the Dutch civilians. On the evening of 13 May Schmidt called upon the Dutch commander, Colonel Scharroo, to surrender, stating that further resistance would lead to widespread damage in the city and would only delay the inevitable German victory by a few more hours.

Every one of those hours, however, meant a serious loss of time to the Germans. General von Küchler, C-in-C of the 18th Army, feared that British intervention in Holland was imminent. The Dutch had to be broken quickly; the German forces already committed against them were desperately needed for the push through Belgium into northern France. At 19.00 on 13 May, von Küchler ordered that the Dutch resistance in Rotterdam was to be smashed by every available means. The battle-plan

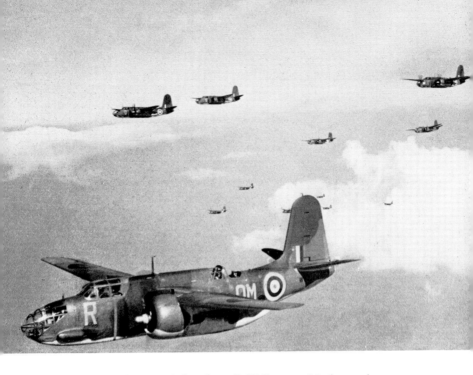

Douglas Bostons of No. 226 Squadron, RAF Swanton Morley, early 1942
Halifax B.II Series IAs of No. 158 Squadron, RAF East Moor, late 1942.
Second aircraft from left, HR719 NP-M, was shot down over Düsseldorf
on 11/12 June 1943

Right Halifaxes of No. 35 Squadron pictured during a daylight attack on the *Scharnhorst, Gneisenau* and *Prinz Eugen* in Brest Harbour of 18.12.1941

Right Halifax B.V of No. 76 Squadron, RAF Linton-on-Ouse, early 1943. This particular aircraft was destroyed in a crash on 31 August 1943

Lancaster B.I of No. 207 Squadron, RAF Bottesford, mid-1942

Bostons taking part in a daylight raid on the docks at Le Havre. Bombs bursting at A and B in the photograph

Lockheed Ventura of No. 21 Squadron over Holland, late 1942

envisaged a tank attack across the Willems Bridge at 15.30 the following day, preceded by a large-scale air-raid on the surrounding area to 'soften up' the defences.

By the morning of the fourteenth the Dutch commander still had not replied to General Schmidt's call for surrender. Two German envoys had been flown into the city to discuss capitulation terms; finally, at noon, they managed to get in touch with Colonel Scharroo and deliver their ultimatum – surrender or suffer the destruction of the city centre by the Luftwaffe. Scharroo found himself unable to make the decision alone and told the envoys that he would have to contact the Hague for further instructions. Half-on-hour later, the Dutch Government replied that it was sending a delegation to Rotterdam to talk terms with the Germans; it was due to arrive at two o'clock.

At 13.30 General Schmidt sent a signal to Luftflotte 2 calling off the impending air attack, which was scheduled to take place at 15.00. He was too late. At 13.25 one hundred Heinkel 111s of KG 54 had taken off from their airfields near Bremen; by the time Schmidt's signal reached Luftflotte 2 HQ, the bombers were already approaching the Dutch border. There was a further delay before the order cancelling the mission reached the headquarters of KG 54; by this time the radio operator in each Heinkel had closed down his position to take up combat station behind the machine-gun in the blister beneath the fuselage.

The Heinkels headed towards Rotterdam in two waves, one approaching from the east and the other from the south-west. Red flares were fired by the troops on the ground as a signal to abort the attack, but the Heinkels of the first group were flying into the sun and their crews failed to see the warning. They dropped their bombs in the centre of the Old City, where the Dutch artillery was in position. So did the first wave of the second group, but then the remainder saw the flares and broke off the attack.

Altogether, fifty-seven out of the hundred Heinkels of KG 54 bombed the target, dropping 100 tons of high explosives and killing 900 civilians. The disjointed reports of the raid that reached the War Cabinet in London the following morning, however, indicated that thousands lay dead beneath the rubble of the city centre; in fact, a figure of 30,000 killed was accepted in many quarters even well after the war.

The raid on Rotterdam had, in the event, turned out to be a tragic blunder – but this did not alter the fact that the Germans had conceived and executed it as a deliberate terror attack against a civilian target, despite the presence of Dutch Army units in the area. The grim conclusion drawn by the War Cabinet was that the enemy had taken off the gloves; the 'gentleman's agreement' of the early months of the war, restricting bombing on humanitarian grounds to targets where there was little chance of civilian lives being lost, was at an end.

Nevertheless it was only after much discussion – and considerable reluctance – that the War Cabinet finally authorized Bomber Command to attack targets east of the Rhine on 15 May. Bomber Command lost no time in launching its first attack against industrial Germany; that same night, ninety-nine Wellingtons, Whitleys and Hampdens of Nos. 3, 4 and 5 Groups were sent out to attack oil plants, steelworks and railway targets in the Ruhr and the area immediately west of the Rhine. Only a small portion of the total force despatched located the industrial targets, but considerable damage was done to the railway junctions and marshalling yards at Aachen, Roermond, Bocholt, Wesel, München-Gladbach and Cologne, the autobahn south of Duisburg and the aerodromes at Duisburg and Eindhoven.

Up to 15 June the heavy bombers carried out twenty-seven night attacks on German lines of communication, ammunition and supply dumps, oil storage tanks and other targets of importance to the enemy's war effort on the Western Front. These early raids into Germany were haphazard; there was little attempt at co-ordination between squadrons. It was left to individual crews to fix their own take-off times, select their own route to the target and the bombing altitude.

Meanwhile, the Luftwaffe continued its systematic destruction of the Allied air forces in France. On 15 May the Germans broke through at Sedan, and there was little the Allies could do to oppose the onslaught from the air. At 11.00, twelve Blenheims of 2 Group attacked enemy forces in the Dinant area, while 150 French fighter aircraft flew patrols in relays over the battlefield. Sixteen more Blenheims, escorted by twenty-seven French fighters, again attacked at 15.00, striking at bridges over the Meuse in the Samoy region and at enemy concentrations at Monthermé and Mézières. Four Blenheims failed to return. The attacks were renewed at 18.30 by nine Breguet 693s and six LeO 451s.

By nightfall on 15 May, the Luftwaffe's losses had reached 539 aircraft – not counting transports and reconnaissance machines – since the start of the invasion. The RAF in France had lost 86 Battles, 39 Blenheims, 9 Lysanders and 71 Hurricanes and Gladiators over the same period. The decimated Battle squadrons had not carried out any operations during the fifteenth, most of their aircraft being too badly damaged to fly, but a small-scale raid was carried out without loss on enemy positions in the Sedan area on the night of 15-16 May.

On the sixteenth two of the Battle squadrons, Nos. 105 and 218 – with only four aircraft left between them – were disbanded. The remainder of the AASF was now pulled back to the Troyes area to be reorganized and for the next five days only very limited operations were carried out, mainly at night. It was left to the French Air Force and the Blenheims of 2 Group to provide direct support for the Allied armies, and both suffered heavily. On 17 May, following an urgent request for air support from General Giraud – who had just assumed command of the 9th Army – eighteen Potez 631s made a low-level attack on enemy columns on the Trélon-Mâcon and Anor-Chimay roads. These aircraft were night-fighters which had been hastily called up from their base in the Paris air defence zone. Six of them were shot down. Twelve LeO 451s, attacking the same objective soon afterwards, lost four of their number, one of them destroyed by French anti-aircraft fire.

The heaviest loss of the day, however, was sustained by the Blenheims of No. 82 Squadron. In the afternoon, twelve aircraft were detailed to attack tanks and troops near Gembloux. A few miles from the target, flying in two formations of six at 8000 feet, they ran into intense and highly accurate anti-aircraft fire which caused them to open out. They were immediately attacked by a large number of Messerschmitt 109s, which shot ten of them down. An eleventh aircraft was shot down by ground fire; the sole survivor, badly damaged, managed to get back to base.

The German advance continued. By 19 May the enemy had reached the Oise-Aisne Canal and the Chemin des Dames in the south and the line of the Scheldt, held by the British Army, in the north. The bases of the BEF's Air Component were now directly threatened, and on the nineteenth three of the seven fighter squadrons – Nos. 3, 54 and 79 – were evacuated to England. They were followed the next day by Nos. 85, 87, 607 and 615, and by the majority of the army co-operation Lysanders. Of the 261 Hurricanes committed to the battle (replacement aircraft included) only sixty-six were evacuated safely. Seventy-four had been lost on operations, the remainder having been either destroyed on the ground or abandoned because there were not enough pilots to fly them home. From 20 May, RAF fighter operations over the battlefield were carried out by the Hurricanes of 11 Group, flying from their bases in southern England.

By this time daylight operations by both the AASF and No. 2 Group had virtually ceased, and there was a consequent dramatic drop in casualties. On the night of 21-2 May, AVM Playfair once again committed almost the whole of the AASF's remaining forces to the fight, twelve attacks being carried out on enemy troops in the Arras area. At dusk on the twenty-second more attacks were carried out on enemy columns heading for Boulogne, these being made in conjunction with 2 Group's Blenheims. One dusk attack by twelve Blenheims, on the HQ of an enemy mechanised division at Ribecourt, was particularly successful; the aircraft hit the target with twelve 250-pound and seventy-two 40-pound bombs, totally destroying it, and made their escape without a shot being fired at them.

The depleted Battle squadrons went on fighting to the end. On the night of 27-8 May they flew thirty-six sorties against airfields, dumps and lines of communication, bringing the total number of missions flown since 21 May to two hundred. Only one Battle was lost during this period. As the enemy advanced further into France and the situation became more confused, however, the AASF's attacks became more sporadic. An almost total lack of information made it difficult for the crews to be given precise targets; during the last days of May they could do little more than fly in the direction of the Germans' last known position in the hope that a worthwhile target would present itself. Often, enemy columns on the move had to be ignored because of the streams of refugees that mingled with them.

By 29 May the incredible swiftness of the German advance had confined the British Expeditionary Force to the area around Dixmude and Armentières. 'Operation Dynamo', the evacuation from Dunkirk, was under way. On 3 June the Battles of the AASF again withdrew to bases near Le Mans, from which they made several attacks on railways at Givet and Charleville, fuel and ammunition dumps at Florenville and Libramont, enemy troops at St Gobain and Gault and the advanced German airstrips at St Hubert and Guise – the latter one of the bases from which the Luftwaffe's Stukas were pounding the Dunkirk beaches.

On 13 June forty-eight Battles attacked troop concentrations along the Seine and Marne. Six aircraft were shot down. Forty-eight hours later, with the French Government suing for an armistice, it became apparent that there was nothing more the AASF could do and the squadrons were ordered to fly their remaining aircraft to England.

In five weeks of fighting the RAF had lost a total of 1029 aircraft, 299 belonging to the AASF, 279 to the Air Component, 219 to Fighter Command, 166 to Bomber Command and 66 to Coastal – most of the latter having been destroyed during the nine days of Dunkirk. Losses in personnel amounted to 1526 killed, wounded or missing.

The Battle of France was over, and it was lost.

7
At Bay

At the beginning of June 1940 the Air Staff were still confident of Bomber Command's ability to wage effective long-range warfare against industrial targets in Germany. Bombing strategy, however, was totally dictated by the course of events in France, and this was reflected in an Air Staff directive issued to Air Marshal C. F. A. Portal, the AOC-in-C Bomber Command since April, on 4 June.

The directive made it clear that priority was to be given to the support of the French land forces, as long as such support was economical and effective. However, the Air Staff would use every possible means to persuade the French that Bomber Command's operations should not be confined exclusively to direct support in the area of the land battle, and that an effective contribution could be made by striking at targets in Germany itself.

Portal was therefore directed that – until it became necessary to divert a large part of the bombing effort in support of the next phase of the land battle – the primary aim should be to continue attacks against Germany's oil resources. The Air Staff believed that if 300,000 tons or more of the Germans' oil stocks could be destroyed, their war effort would be in a serious position by August.

Because of the difficulty of locating and attacking oil targets on moonless nights, German aircraft factories were selected as alternative objectives. Bomber Command was also authorized to attack other targets of opportunity, providing these could be positively identified. 'In no circumstances, the directive continued, 'should night bombing be allowed to degenerate into mere indiscriminate action, which is contrary to the policy of His Majesty's Government.'

Meanwhile there was another factor to be considered in the future employment of Bomber Command. By the end of May, both the British and French Governments were expecting the Italians to declare war on them at any moment. On 31 May, the Supreme War Council in Paris agreed that, immediately on the declaration of war by Mussolini, the Allies would carry out offensive operations against objectives in Italy; this would be a joint venture planned by the French and British naval and air staffs. On 2 June, Churchill wrote to the Secretary of State for Air and the Chief of Air Staff:

'It is of the utmost importance, in view of the possible raids on Lyons and Marseilles, that we should be able to strike back with our heavy bombers at Italy the moment she enters the war. I consider therefore that these squadrons should be flown to their aerodromes in southern France at the earliest moment when French permission can be obtained and when the servicing units are ready for their reception.'

The following day, orders were issued for the creation of a bombing force — code-named Haddock Force — for strategic operations against Italy. With the agreement of the French Air Staff the force was to be based at Salon and Le Vallon air-fields, near Marseilles. An advance ground party arrived at these bases on 7 June, and preparations to receive the bombers were well under way by the tenth, when Italy declared war on the Allies.

The two squadrons earmarked to form Haddock Force were Nos. 99 and 149, which during their detachment in France were to come under the orders of Air Marshal Barratt. The first aircraft to arrive, on the morning of 11 June, were six Wellingtons of 99 Squadron. They were immediately refuelled and bombed-up for a raid on industrial targets in Italy that same night. In the afternoon, however, an unexpected complication arose when local authorities sent a deputation to Salon and expressed their strong objections against the planned raid taking place. The deputation had the backing of the commander of the Zone des Operations Aériennes des Alpes, whose six fighter groups were a long way short of full strength and in no condition to meet a large-scale air onslaught. Italian bombers had already attacked targets in the Nice and Cannes area virtually unmolested, and the authorities feared massive reprisals if the RAF raid was allowed to take place.

The Force Commander protested that the venture had the full support of the French Government, but it was no use. The French insisted that his orders must be wrong; it was well known that the French Government was not in favour of bombing attacks mounted from bases on French territory. In desperation the Force Commander telephoned Air Marshal Barratt, who contacted Lord Ismay, the head of the Military Wing of the War Cabinet Secretariat. Together with Winston Churchill and other members of the Government, Ismay was attending a conference of the Supreme War Council near Orléans when the call came. After some discussion between Churchill, the French Premier Reynaud, Anthony Eden, General Weygand and General Dill (Chief of the Imperial General Staff) it was agreed yet again that the raid was to take place with the approval of the French Government.

This decision was passed on to Air Marshal Barratt, who in turn confirmed his orders with the Force Commander. It made no difference; the French authorities at Salon refused to budge. The argument went on well into the evening until at last the Force Commander, his patience utterly exhausted, ordered his aircraft to prepare for take-off at half an hour past midnight. The Wellingtons were already trundling out when, amid a sudden commotion, a number of French Army lorries and other vehicles raced across the grass and stopped in the middle of the runway.

A French officer informed the Force Commander apologetically that he had been instructed to prevent the British bombers from taking off at all costs. His men were to use force if necessary. He was very sorry, but he was only carrying out his orders. He hoped there would be no trouble and that the whole business could be settled amicably. In order to avoid an open clash, the Force Commander had no choice but to call off the raid. Because of the danger of possible sabotage to the Wellingtons, Air Marshal Barratt ordered them to return to England the following day.

Meanwhile, as an insurance against continued French opposition to the RAF using the bases in southern France, the AOC-in-C Bomber Command had ordered the Whitleys of 4 Group to stand by for a mission to Italy. On the afternoon of the 11 June, thirty-six Whitleys of Nos. 10, 51, 58, 77 and 102 Squadrons flew to the Channel Islands, where they refuelled before taking off on the long flight across the Alps. The Whitleys were the only aircraft with sufficient range to reach Italy from the United Kingdom; even so, they were only able to carry a minimum bomb load.

The primary target was the Fiat aero-engine and motor works in Turin, with the Ansaldo factories in Genoa as the alternative. Ten aircraft claimed to have bombed the primary and two more – both of 51 Squadron – the alternate. One Whitley failed to return; the other twenty-three encountered storms and low cloud over the Alps and returned early. The crews who attacked Genoa reported that the Italians had made no attempt at a blackout; the town remained brightly lit, even while the bombing was in progress. The following report on the raid on Turin was made by the bomber leader:

'We were warned that over Italy fighter opposition would probably be encountered. The Italian fighters – CR.42s – it was pointed out were biplanes, with considerable powers of manoeuvre and probably better suited to the task of night interception than the Me.109 or 110. We must be on the lookout for them. Nothing much happened till we were over France after refuelling in the Channel Islands. Then we ran into electrical storms of great severity. There was a good deal of lightning. When we emerged from these into a clear patch somewhere near Bourges the lightning continued. This time it was produced by French flak through which we flew till we ran into heavy weather again and began to climb in order to get over the Alps. I got my heavily laden Whitley to 17,500 feet flying blind on my instruments, but before the climb started in earnest I got a perfect 'fix' on my position from Lac Léman. The town of Geneva at its western end showed bright with many lights. It was ten-tenths cloud over the Alps, but we knew we were crossing them because of the bumps which the aircraft felt every time it crossed a peak. Down we went through the murk till I altered course fifteen degrees to starboard so as to find the River Po. I reached it in darkness, but I could make it out by the patches of cultivation along its banks which showed a deeper shade against the prevailing black. I could not see the waters of the river. On we went till I judged we were over Turin. Then I let go a flare which lit up the middle of the city. I turned back at once and climbed to 5000 feet. When I got to that height I loosed another flare into a cloud which began to glow and shed a soft light over the whole town including the target. I ran in, dropped two bombs, one of which burst on the Fiat building, the other in the railway sidings beside it.

'The bursting of the bombs seemed to be the signal for the enemy to switch on his searchlights. These could not find us, but innumerable flashes of light, constantly renewed, appeared beneath us. It seemed as though the whole of Turin was firing at us. I have never seen anything like it before or since. But no shells could be seen bursting anywhere. We were still at 5000 feet, but the air about us remained unlit by anything except our flare, though the flashes below winked at us with unabated zeal. I did my second run and hit the north end of the works. There was a large green flash which meant that the bombs had certainly fallen on the annealing plant. I knew that, if I hit that, the flash would be a green one. Having no more bombs I dropped more flares to guide other attacking aircraft and drew off a little to watch the show. I climbed to 10,000 feet, keeping a smart lookout for the CR.42s. I did not see any, and no one else did; but we ran into a heavy A.A. barrage. The shell-bursts made a squeaky, gritty noise. It was only then that we realized what had happened. The Italian gunners, who had been producing all those flashes I had seen below, had evidently decided that we were flying at 10,000 feet when we bombed. As we were only at 5000, naturally we saw nothing of the bursts which were about a mile above our heads.'

On 14 June Air Marshal Barratt was informed that the French Government had at last convinced the authorities in the Marseilles area that they had given their approval to the RAF's use of the bases at Salon and Le Vallon. The Wellingtons of 99 Squadron once again flew out to Salon, this time accompanied by six aircraft of 149 Squadron, to find the airfield guarded by French troops in case of possible outside interference. There was no trouble, however, and that night eight Wellingtons took off to bomb the Ansaldo works in Genoa. Only one aircraft attacked the target; the rest were unable to locate it because of bad weather and returned with their bombs still on board. Eight more aircraft went out the following night to attack Milan, and although the weather was still bad six of them claimed to have bombed the target. It was the last bombing operation carried out from French soil by the RAF; on 18 June Haddock Force was evacuated.

On 19 June it was decided at an Air Staff conference that Bomber Command's main effort should now be directed against targets whose destruction would have the greatest effect on the inevitable German air offensive against the British Isles. Priority, therefore, was given to attacks on the German aircraft industry and its associated equipment depots. At the same time, attacks were to be maintained on canal and railway systems in Germany, principally on the marshalling yards in the Ruhr and Cologne areas, the aqueducts carrying the Dortmund-Ems Canal over the River Ems near Münster and the aqueduct at Minden. One squadron of 5 Group Hampdens was to continue mine-laying operations in enemy waters; 5 Group had by this time become acknowledged experts in 'gardening', as this type of operation was known.

Considerable importance was still attached to the destruction of oil plants and stocks in Germany and the occupied territories, and these were to be attacked whenever the opportunity arose;

this, however, was now a secondary task. As an additional role for the bomber force the Air Staff also envisaged carrying out, during the coming weeks, a series of incendiary attacks on German crops and forests. Such attacks could be carried out on moonless nights, when precision bombing of other targets would be restricted. It was expected that a new pellet-type incendiary, designed to be scattered in showers from a bomber, would be ready for use in July.

The main function of the medium-bomber force would be reconnaissance and attacks on enemy aerodromes in north-west France and the Low Countries. In the event of the enemy launching an invasion of the British Isles, the whole medium-bomber force was to be ready to switch its effort to attacks against the German-occupied ports, the invasion fleet at sea and – should the first phase of an invasion succeed – enemy bridgeheads on the British coast.

This directive was completely revised on 4 July, when Air Marshal Portal was told that Bomber Command should now concentrate its main effort against enemy shipping – particularly the pocket battleships and heavy cruisers thought to be lying at Kiel and Hamburg – and against the German ports themselves. In addition, the force committed to 'gardening' operations was to be increased to three squadrons of Hampdens. Attacks on the aircraft and oil industries were to continue as ordered in the previous directive, but raids on railway and canal communications and forests in Germany were to cease, at least for the time being.

Portal had scarcely begun to implement the new instructions when, on 13 July, he received yet another directive. The Air Staff, discussing the best method of employing Bomber Command during the approaching moon phase, had reached the conclusion that the effort against industrial targets in Germany so far had been too dispersed, with the result that few targets had sustained sufficient damage to put them out of action for any length of time. Portal was therefore asked in this new directive to concentrate the heavy-bomber effort against only fifteen selected targets, consisting of five aircraft depots, five airframe assembly factories and five oil plants. Attacks on communications were to continue, but only on a very small scale.

Portal was openly critical of this directive, and informed the Air Staff of his views on 16 July. For a start, he could not understand why Bomber Command was being restricted to attacks on five aircraft assembly plants when it had already been established that the destruction of twice as many would not deal a serious blow to the Luftwaffe's ability to wage all-out air warfare. Also, he doubted the ability of his bomber crews to locate a large percentage of the allotted targets, even in moonlight. The Air Staff estimated that about 140 500-pound bombs would be sufficient to destroy each target, but Portal knew from previous results that only a small fraction of this number of bombs could be expected to hit the objective. Nevertheless the general outline of the directive was confirmed by the Air Staff on 24 July.

The Air Staff tended to regard Portal's point of view as being unduly pessimistic, and – on the surface at least – the results of the bombing attacks carried out during July and August 1940 provided little evidence in support of it. The new phase of attacks on the German industry had in fact begun on the night of 22 June, with the bombing of the Focke-Wulf aircraft factories at Bremen; the same target was again attacked on 26 June and on six nights in July, and the bomber crews reported little difficulty in identifying it. The Junkers factory at Deichshausen was also bombed twice in June and three times in July, while seven attacks were made during these two months on aircraft assembly factories in Gotha and Kassel. A number of raids were also made on aluminium works, principally those at Cologne, Rheinfelden and Bitterfeld.

Raids on aluminium factories assumed additional importance after the collapse of France, when the supply of raw materials necessary for the production of aluminium was greatly increased by the seizure of large quantities of bauxite from French stocks. The most successful attack on an aluminium plant took place on 19 August, when several hits were obtained on a new plant at Rheinfelden, setting back production by some four months.

Meanwhile, fulfilling its secondary task, Bomber Command continued to attack oil plants. These were usually much more difficult to find than aircraft factories, being well concealed, and some of them lay too far away to be attacked during the short summer nights. The principal oil targets raided during July, August and September 1940 were at Gelsenkirchen, Leuna, Misburg, Emmerich and Pölitz. The refineries at Emmerich were bombed on 5 July, 1 August and 3 August, and those at Misburg on 20 May, 19 and 27 June and 1 August, a considerable amount of damage being inflicted on both objectives. The synthetic oil plant at Gelsenkirchen was attacked twenty-eight times between 27 May and 2 December 1940, one of the most successful raids being carried out by nineteen Hampdens of 5 Group on the night of 22-3 July. The crews reported large fires and a series of heavy explosions.

On 15 July, Bomber Command switched a large part of its effort to the German invasion preparations in the ports, anchorages and harbours stretching from Delfzijl in the north of Holland to Bordeaux in south-west France. These ports were to be attacked frequently during the four years that were to pass before the Allied invasion of Europe, but the most intensive phase of the air offensive against them – the 'battle of the barges', directed against the armada of craft assembled by the Germans for the thrust across the Channel – lasted until the end of October 1940.

Aircraft of every Bomber Command Group took part in this nightly offensive, the importance of which has to a great extent been eclipsed by the massive air battle that dragged its vapour trails over the skies of southern England during that summer of 1940. But the Battle of Britain was, in the broad sense, Bomber Command's victory too; for although the Spitfires and Hurricanes of Fighter Command denied the Germans the air superiority necessary for a successful invasion, the attacks mounted by the RAF bombers on the invasion ports were so effective that, even if the Luftwaffe had succeeeded in obtaining temporary mastery of the air over Britain, Hitler's invasion fleet would not have been in a position to sail on the planned date.

This was clearly substantiated by the Germans themselves on several occasions. On 12 September, for example, only three days before Operation Sealion – the invasion of England – was scheduled to take place, HQ Navy Group West sent the following signal to Berlin:

'Interruptions caused by the enemy's air forces, long-range artillery and light naval forces have, for the first time, assumed major significance. The harbours at Ostend, Dunkirk, Calais and Boulogne cannot be used as night anchorages for shipping because of the danger of English bombings and shelling. Units of the British Fleet are now able to operate almost unmolested in the Channel. Owing to these difficulties further delays are expected in the assembly of the invasion fleet.'

With the invasion thought to be imminent, Bomber Command had now launched a maximum effort offensive against the enemy-held ports. On the night of 13-14 September the bombers sank eighty barges in Ostend harbour, and the following night severe damage was inflicted on concentrations of enemy craft at Boulogne. This raid was carried out by the Fairey Battles of the newly-formed Nos. 301 and 305 (Polish) Squadrons, flying their first operational mission. The Battles of Nos. 12, 103, 142 and 150 Squadrons – at full strength again after the catastrophe in France – also carried out many attacks on the enemy ports during this period. It was the Battle's swan-song as a first-line aircraft; in October it was withdrawn from operations and replaced by Wellingtons and Blenheims.

On 14 September, Hitler issued a Supreme Command directive postponing the start of Operation Sealion until 17 September. On the morning of the sixteenth, however, the German Naval War Staff once again reported that the invasion ports had been subjected to heavy bombing: 'In Antwerp considerable casualties have been inflicted on transports. Five transport steamers in the port have been heavily damaged; one barge has been sunk, two cranes destroyed, an ammunition train blown up and several sheds are burning.'

There was worse to come. On the night of 16-17 September,

only hours before the crucial German Supreme Command conference that would decide whether the invasion would take place
or not, a strong force of Blenheims and Battles surprised a strong
concentration of enemy landing-craft in the open sea off Boulogne. Several barges and two transports were sunk, with heavy
loss of life. The vessels had been engaged in an invasion training
exercise. That same night the RAF also struck at the whole
coastal area between Antwerp and Le Havre, and this prompted
the German Naval Staff to report the following day that:
'The RAF are still by no means defeated; on the contrary,
they are showing increasing activity in their attacks on the
Channel ports and in their mounting interference with the
assembly movements.' This statement was underlined by Bomber
Command on the following night when, in full moonlight conditions, every available aircraft pounded the Channel ports and
caused the biggest damage so far to the invasion fleet. Eighty-
four barges were sunk or damaged at Dunkirk alone, while elsewhere a large ammunition dump was blown up, a supply depot
burned out and several steamers and MTBs sunk. The next day
the Navy Staff report made gloomy reading:

'The very severe bombing together with bombardment by
naval guns across the Channel, makes it necessary to disperse
the naval and transport vessels already concentrated on the
Channel and to stop further movement of shipping to the
invasion ports. Otherwise, with energetic enemy action such
casualties will occur in the course of time that the execution
of the operation on the scale previously envisaged will in any
case be problematic.'

On 19 September, four days after the great air battle over
London and southern England that marked the turning-point
of the Battle of Britain, Hitler ordered the armada assembled
in the Channel ports to be dispersed 'so that the loss of shipping
space caused by enemy air attacks may be reduced to a minimum'. Operation Sealion had been postponed indefinitely;
already, while the Luftwaffe's bombers were still being crucified

over England, Hitler was becoming increasingly occupied with the projected attack on the Soviet Union.

Between 15 July and 21 September RAF Bomber Command – according to German naval sources – sank or damaged 21 transports and 214 barges in the Channel ports, some 12 per cent of the total invasion fleet. These figures should be treated with some reservation, as even at this stage of the war the Germans were in the habit of playing down their actual losses in confidential reports to the Supreme Command. The true loss, both in men and material, was in all probability much higher – but even the figure of 12 per cent is sufficient testimony that Bomber Command's effort during those crucial weeks was far from wasted.

Nevertheless the effectiveness of Bomber Command's operations against the Channel ports was grossly underestimated by the War Cabinet. Churchill in particular expressed disappointment at the results of the attacks, as revealed by reconnaissance photographs in a minute to Sir Archibald Sinclair on 23 September. 'What struck me about these photographs was the apparent inability of the bombers to hit very large masses of barges. I should have thought that sticks of explosive bombs thrown along these oblongs would have wrought havoc, and it is very disappointing to see that they all remained intact and in order, with just a few apparently damaged at the entrance.' Churchill did not take into account the fact that many of the barges, although apparently intact, had been made unseaworthy by damage that the photographs did not show. The bomber crews who were over the ports night after night knew that they were sinking the barges faster than anyone had thought possible; the only question in their minds was – were they sinking them fast enough to thwart the invasion if Fighter Command was annihilated?

The ports were easy to find, but they were not an easy target. Light flak was plentiful and losses were heavy. The anti-aircraft defences were particularly strong around Antwerp, and it was while attacking this target on the night of 15-16 September that Sergeant John Hannah, one of the crew of a Hampden of 83

Squadron, carried out an act of great courage that won him a Victoria Cross. The citation tells the story:

'On the night of 15 September 1940, Sergeant Hannah was the wireless operator/air gunner in an aircraft engaged in a successful attack on an enemy barge concentration at Antwerp. It was then subjected to intense anti-aircraft fire and received a direct hit from a projectile of an explosive and incendiary nature, which apparently burst inside the bomb compartment. A fire started which quickly enveloped the wireless operator's and rear gunner's cockpits, and as both the port and starboard petrol tanks had been pierced there was a grave risk of the fire spreading. Sergeant Hannah forced his way through to obtain two extinguishers and discovered that the rear gunner had had to leave the aircraft. He could have acted likewise, through the bottom escape hatch or forward through the navigator's hatch, but remained and fought the fire for ten minutes with the extinguishers, beating the flames with his log book when these were empty.

'During this time thousands of rounds of ammunition exploded in all directions and he was almost blinded by the intense heat and fumes, but had the presence of mind to obtain relief by turning on his oxygen supply. Air admitted through the large holes caused by the projectile made the bomb compartment an inferno and all the aluminium sheet metal on the floor of this airman's cockpit was melted away, leaving only the cross bearers. Working under these conditions which caused burns to his face and eyes, Sergeant Hannah succeeeded in extinguishing the fire. He then crawled forward, ascertained that the navigator had left the aircraft, and passed the latter's log and maps to the pilot.

'This airman displayed courage, coolness and devotion to duty of the highest order and by his action in remaining and successfully extinguishing the fire under conditions of the greatest danger and difficulty, enabled the pilot to bring the aircraft to its base.'

A few weeks earlier, the bombing offensive against Germany's communications system had brought the award of the Victoria Cross to another member of Bomber Command, Flight Lieutenant R. A. B. Learoyd, who was the pilot of one of five Hampdens of 49 and 83 Squadrons detailed to attack the Dortmund-Ems canal north of Münster. This was the point where two aqueducts carried the canal across the river Ems. The newest of the two aqueducts was attacked several times in June and July, and on 29 July reconnaissance photographs revealed that a section of the canal was closed and under repair. As a result an attack was planned on the older aqueduct in an attempt to stop the flow of canal traffic altogether.

The five Hampdens of 49 and 83 Squadrons which set out on the night of 12-13 August carried 1000-pound bombs, the first time that this weapon was used operationally by the RAF. There was a half moon, and the crews had little difficulty in finding the target. The aircraft were to make their attack singly at two-minute intervals, flying at low level down a heavily-defended corridor on the approach to the canal.

The Hampdens made their run-in from the north, with the moon in the pilots' faces and throwing the target into sharp relief. The first aircraft was hit and the wireless operator badly wounded; the second exploded in mid-air; the third caught fire and the crew baled out; the fourth was crippled and forced to break off the attack and return to base. The aqueduct was still undamaged, and only one aircraft – Learoyd's – remained. Learoyd went in at 150 feet, his aircraft being hit repeatedly. 'After a moment,' he reported later, 'three big holes appeared in the starboard wing. They were firing at point-blank range. The navigator continued to direct me on to the target. I could not see it because I was blinded by the glare of the searchlights and had to keep my head below the level of the cockpit top. At last I heard the navigator say "Bombs gone". I immediately did a steep turn to the right and got away, being fired at heavily for five minutes. The carrier pigeon we carried laid an egg during the attack.'

Apart from the holes in the wing, the hydraulic system was shot to pieces and neither the flaps nor the undercarriage indicators would work. Arriving back at Scampton, Learoyd circled the airfield until it was light enough to see the ground and make a landing, as in the dark he had no way of knowing whether his undercarriage was down and locked or not. It was, and the pilot touched down without injury to the crew or further damage to the aircraft. Learoyd's award of the VC was gazetted a week later.

Learoyd's bomb had done the trick; subsequent reconnaissance showed that the old branch of the canal was out of action. Camouflage netting could not conceal the fact that a large chunk of the aqueduct was missing, nor that the Germans had built a new dam to stop the flow of water. Water was still seeping from the canal five weeks later.

After this successful – albeit costly – attack, Germany's inland waterways gradually faded from Bomber Command's list of priority targets. Although the canals carried as much as thirty per cent of German freight, the Railway Research Department of the Ministry of Economic Warfare insisted that railway systems presented a far more profitable target, and this view was supported by the disruption that resulted from Luftwaffe attacks on British rail complexes during the Battle of Britain. The largest of the railway targets selected for the attentions of Bomber Command was Hamm, standing in the north-east corner of the Ruhr. Together with Osnabrück, Soest and Schwerte, Hamm – the biggest marshalling yard in Germany – regulated almost all the rail traffic flowing to and from the Ruhr and the central and east parts of the country; it had the capacity to handle 10,000 wagons a day.

Between 1 June 1940 and 12 June 1941 Hamm was raided eighty-five times, although many of these attacks were made by single aircraft and the damage caused was not sufficient to create widespread dislocation. In September 1940, aircraft taking part in attacks on Hamm and other enemy communication centres also dropped large numbers of a new type of incendiary on forest areas in Germany. The idea was that the conflagrations they caused would not only deprive the Germans of timber, but might also destroy hidden supply depots and ammunition dumps. The incendiary device, named a 'razzle', consisted of two square sheets of celluloid about six inches across, with a piece of phosphorus surrounded by damp cotton wool sandwiched between them. When the cotton wool dried out the phosphorus began to smoulder and eventually ignited the celluloid, which would then burn fiercely for about ten seconds and set light to the surrounding vegetation. 'Razzling' was not a favourite pastime for the bomber crews, as it often meant that they had to arrange their routes so that they passed over forest areas on their way to and from the main target, which in turn meant more time spent over enemy territory. Moreover, the results achieved were negligible and this type of operation was abandoned after a few weeks, the stocks of 'razzles' eventually being used up during later incendiary raids on German cities.

In August 1940, Bomber Command attacked Berlin for the first time. The raid was mounted as a reprisal for a Luftwaffe attack on London which occurred on the night of 24-5 August, when a number of enemy bombers released their loads over the London area instead of on their target – the Short aircraft factory at Rochester and oil storage tanks on the Thames. Reaction from the German Supreme Command to the blunder was not long in coming; the following morning, a signal from Goering arrived at the headquarters of KG 1, which had been responsible for the attack, stating that the crews who had made the error were to be disciplined forthwith and transferred to the infantry on the orders of Hitler himself.

The British War Cabinet, however, had no way of knowing that the raid had been a mistake; they agreed unanimously that the RAF should make a retaliatory raid against the German capital. Bomber Command protested that such a raid would have little or no strategic advantage and would probably result in heavy losses, but it was no use; Churchill was adamant. Accordingly the next night – 25-6 August – eighty-one Wellingtons, Whitleys and Hampdens of Nos. 3, 4 and 5 Groups set off for Berlin. The mission was hampered by thick cloud – 9/10ths down to 2000 feet – and only twenty-nine crews claimed to have bombed the target. Twenty-seven more claimed that they had located Berlin but had been unable to find their allocated industrial targets within the city's perimeter; twenty-one returned to base with their bombs on board and the other six jettisoned their loads in the sea. Eighteen claimed to have bombed alternative targets, seven more aborted and five failed to return. Three of the latter ditched in the sea on the way home, and their crews were rescued.

On this occasion the heavy cloud undoubtedly saved the bombers from suffering more casualties. Although they were over the German capital for three hours, the searchlights were unable to pick them up. An intense flak barrage was put up by Berlin's two rings of anti-aircraft defences, but the gunners were firing blind and no British aircraft was brought down over the capital. On the other hand the damage caused by the bombs was negligible, most of them falling wide of their targets in unpopulated areas beyond the outskirts of the city; more damage, in fact, was probably caused by the fragments of anti-aircraft shells that showered down on Berlin's streets while the raid was in progress. No civilians were killed, but neutral correspondents in Berlin reported that the raid's effect on morale was tremendous. It was the first time that Germany's capital had been subjected to air bombardment; the surprise and shock was apparent on the faces of the city's inhabitants the following morning. Goering had given his promise that no enemy aircraft would drop bombs on Berlin – and now it had happened. The RAF had dropped leaflets on the capital on several occasions, but the sound of bomb bursts had an immeasurably greater effect. Later, when the initial surprise wore off and the Berliners became hardened to almost continual air attack, their morale actually increased; but this could not be foreseen by the War Cabinet at the time of the first raid, and its results – minimal though they were in terms of material damage – appeared to support the old view that the will of a population could be broken by air attack.

On 21 September, after Berlin had been attacked several more times by Bomber Command and had suffered its first civilian casualties, the Air Staff – influenced by the information that filtered through from the German capital – included the following paragraph in the latest directive issued to the AOC-in-C Bomber Command:

'Although there are no objectives in the Berlin area of importance to our major plans, it is the intention that attacks on the city and its environs should be continued from time to time when favourable weather conditions permit. The primary aim of these attacks will be to cause the greatest possible disturbance and dislocation both to the industrial activities and to the civil population generally in the area. After a close analysis of the objectives available and of the results achieved by the German attacks on London it is considered that not only the quickest but most lasting and effective means of dislocating the life of the community would be by the attack of sources of power serving the city. Electricity and gas plants are accordingly selected as the primary targets for attack . . .'

The Air Staff believed that the bomber crews would have little difficulty in locating precision targets in Berlin and the surrounding area, and the first major raid launched against the enemy capital in accordance with the new directive – on the night of 7-8 October – appeared to bear this out. Forty-two aircraft, thirty Wellingtons of 3 Group and twelve Whitleys of 4 Group, set out on the raid and thirty-three claimed to have attacked their primaries, seven more bombing other objectives. Six Wellingtons attacked the big power station in Berlin's Moabit district, and the crews reported several explosions and a big fire that could be seen seventy miles away. Four more Wellingtons attacked the West Power Station and the crews claimed that their bombs started fires around the target, followed by a series of big explosions. More fires were started by another four Wellingtons which attacked the Wilmersdorf power station, their bombs falling along the railway that passed through the target and on the marshalling yard at Charlottenburg. Meanwhile, eight Whitleys bombed the Reich Chancery building; a fire was seen nearby, but no other results were observed. Another

Whitley attacked the War Office, but again no result was seen.

Two Wellingtons bombed the city's coal-gas works, starting many small fires and two big ones that could be seen for a hundred miles. Two Whitleys and a Wellington bombed the Rummelsburg marshalling yard, the BMW Aero-Engine Factory and the Siemens Cable Factory with no visible result, but seven Wellingtons which attacked Bahrenfeld aerodrome, the Viktoria chemical works and the marshalling yards at Schonenburg reported hits on all these targets, with explosions and a large fire at the chemical works. Two Wellingtons failed to return from this raid.

Such reports made very optimistic reading, and the Air Ministry's Publicity Department received severe criticism from some quarters – mainly from Air Vice-Marshal Harris – for not obtaining more Press coverage of the events described in them. The optimistic note was, however, apparent in the official Air Ministry account of Bomber Command's activities which appeared in July 1941. The publication's account of the damage inflicted on Berlin, based entirely on Bomber Command reports, ran as follows :

' In one of the earliest raids hits were scored on the Neukölln and the Alexanderplatz in the centre of Berlin, and these were followed by hits on the Lehrter and Anhalter stations and the Pariserplatz at the end of the Unter den Linden. A number of factories were also damaged, and one near the Lehrter station burnt out. The Brandenburger Tor, the monument to the success of past aggressions, was also hit. By the end of October 1940, the General Post Office had been gutted and the railway services between Berlin and Cologne severely disorganized. Throughout the month of November damage continued to be caused to railway stations, notably the Lehrter and the approaches to the Stettiner, and considerable damage had been done to the Unter den Linden and a number of other famous streets. Road and tram traffic had been temporarily disorganized. By the middle of the month the Berlin underground railway system had been damaged near the Savigny Platz, and a munitions factory had been closed down and evacuated to Posen. The Siemens works were hit in several raids . . . Before Christmas heavy damage was caused in the Weissensee district and also to power stations. In the last week of the year the arsenal in the Friedrichsplatz was blown up, and the old Royal Palace was hit.'

By the time this account was published, the Air Staff were no longer in any doubt that the results of these early raids on Berlin were greatly exaggerated. During 1940, the assessment of any raid had been based entirely on visual evidence of the crews involved and on reconnaissance photos brought back by Blenheims of 2 Group, but these aircraft often failed to reach the objective and when they did the pictures taken by their cameras were of indifferent quality. It was not until the work of photographic reconnaissance was handed over to specially-modified high-flying Spitfires towards the end of 1940 that any really good results were obtained – and their evidence was damning. It showed that in many cases, targets reported as having been destroyed by the bomber crews the night before were totally undamaged. The inference was that many of the crews were dropping their bombs in the wrong place. The first germ of doubt that this was happening frequently was shown during the Berlin raid of 7-8 October, when one of the Wellingtons involved – the only one fitted with a camera – returned with a photograph of what the crew described as the industrial target they had successfully bombed on the outskirts of Berlin. The photograph revealed that the 'industrial target' was in fact a wood.

On 25 October 1940, Air Chief Marshal Sir Charles Portal replaced Air Chief Marshal Sir Cyril Newall as Chief of Air Staff, and Portal's place as AOC-in-C Bomber Command was taken by Air Marshal Sir Richard Peirse. Five days later, the latter received the newest Air Staff directive, which followed yet another review of the RAF's bombing policy. The basis of the review was the assumption that during the winter months, major operations in the European Theatre would be confined to an air offensive by both sides, and the Air Staff were anxious to do everything possible to make Bomber Command's effort more decisive.

The directive requested the AOC-in-C to regard oil targets as the primary objectives for Bomber Command whenever the weather conditions and moonlight were favourable enough to permit precision bombing. Aluminium plants and component factories were to be the alternatives. The directive also suggested that regular concentrated attacks be made on objectives in large towns and centres of industry 'with the primary aim of causing very heavy material destruction which will demonstrate to the enemy the power and severity of air bombardment and the hardship and dislocation which will result from it'.

Bomber Command's first aim in this respect was to continue its attacks on Berlin, or on towns in western and central Germany should the bombers be unable to reach the capital for some reason. Such towns were to be raided by as many heavy bombers as possible, the first few aircraft in each attack carrying incendiaries on which the remainder were to unload their bombs. Attacks on marshalling yards were to continue on a limited scale, as was the offensive against selected occupied ports and enemy night-bomber airfields in northern France.

In addition to the primary targets, Bomber Command was also requested to continue its attacks on targets in northern Italy. Since the night of 13-14 August, when thirty Whitleys bombed the Fiat aircraft factory in Turin and the Caproni works in Milan, only two ineffective raids had been made on Italian territory up to 21 October, when Whitleys attacked industrial targets in Turin, Milan, Bergamo, Savona and Aosta. Then, on the night of 30-1 October, a small force of 3 Group Wellingtons crossed the Alps to attack oil refineries and a rail complex in Naples. Three more raids were carried out during November, one against Naples and the others against the Fiat works, and three during December, when the main target was the oil stocks and refineries at Porto Marghera. Very little material damage was done, but the raids had a far more adverse effect on the morale of the Italian population than they had on that of the Germans.

8

Day and Night Operations, November 1940-October 1941

The German attack on Coventry on the night of 14-15 November 1940 provoked an immediate outcry, both from the British public and in Government circles, for retaliatory raids to be launched without delay against German cities. Churchill and the War Cabinet, however, were concerned about the loss sustained by Bomber Command during August, September and October; this amounted to 228 aircraft, including those accidentally destroyed, and there were grave fears that a continued loss of this magnitude would completely outstrip bomber production. This was reflected in a minute from the Prime Minister to the Chief of Air Staff, dated 17 November 1940:

' I watch these figures [of RAF losses] every day with much concern. My diagrams show that we are now not even keeping level, and there is a marked downward turn this week, especially in the Bomber Command. Painful as it is not to be able to strike heavy blows after an event like Coventry, yet I feel we should for the present nurse Bomber Command a little more. This can be done (1) by not sending so many to each of the necessary objectives, (2) by not coming down too low in the face of heavy prepared batteries and being content with somewhat less accuracy, and (3) by picking out soft spots where there is not too much organized protection, so as to keep up our deliveries of bomb content. There must be unexpecting towns in Germany where very little has been done in Air Raid Precautions and yet where there are military objectives of a minor order. Some of these could be struck at in the meanwhile.

' I should feel differently about this if our bomber force

were above five hundred, and if it were expanding. But having regard to the uncertainties of war, we must be very careful not to let routine bombing and our own high standards proceed without constant attention to our resources. These remarks do not apply, of course, to Italy, against which the full-scale risk should be run. The wounded " Littorio " is a fine target.'

Even bearing in mind that this minute was prompted by ' much concern' over Bomber Command's losses its content is quite remarkable, for it appears to show that Churchill either failed to understand or chose to ignore the lessons learned by Bomber Command in its attacks on German targets over the preceding months. In the interests of conserving the bomber force, the Prime Minister was advocating precisely what the Air Staff had sought to avoid since the war began; the wastage of effort against targets of limited importance. His ideas ran contrary to the Air Staff's faith in precision bombing, and he failed to appreciate that against certain types of heavily-defended target the low-level attack – which he was suggesting should be abandoned – held the greatest chance of success for minimum losses. The second paragraph of the minute is particularly revealing, for it shows that Churchill's thoughts were dictated by naval considerations. The Italian Navy was a serious threat to British sea power in the Mediterranean, and consequently it was quite in order for the RAF to mount an offensive against Italian warships and naval bases – even though the experience of the first months of the war had shown that it was extremely difficult to hit warship targets and that attacks on naval forces were often attended by heavy losses.

The Air Staff did not agree with Churchill's suggestion that the number of aircraft sent out on each raid should be reduced. They believed, with some justification, that the more aircraft despatched, the better the chances of finding and hitting the objective. Their main concern was that the target should be hit by a high proportion of the bombs carried by the raiders – something that happened only very infrequently in 1940.

At the time of the German attack on Coventry, the Air Staff already realized that, because of the known inaccuracy of the RAF attacks on selected precision targets, a considerable weight of bombs must have fallen on populated areas. This, however, fell into the category of error or accident, and was in no way classed as indiscriminate bombing. With the Coventry raid, the situation changed appreciably; although there was still no tendency towards the indiscriminate bombing of civilian populations, Bomber Command was now given clear instructions to make every effort to find and bomb targets in large industrial areas, where – even if a stick of bombs missed the primary target – they might nevertheless still inflict damage on other worthwhile objectives in the immediate vicinity.

Mannheim was selected as the target for the first of these raids, which were to be known as 'area' attacks. The object of the raid, which was code-named Operation 'Abigail', was to cause as much damage as possible to the centre of the town. War Cabinet approval of the scheme was given on 13 December, and the attack was scheduled for the night of 16-17 December. 134 bombers were despatched on the raid, the largest number of aircraft so far detailed by Bomber Command to attack a single target – although there had been a sort of preliminary on the night of 16-17 November, when 127 bombers attacked a number of targets in Hamburg.

Conditions were good for the Mannheim attack, which was made in bright moonlight. Wellingtons of 3 Group, flown by crews specially selected for their experience, marked the target with incendiaries, the fires started by which were claimed to have been bombed by the crews of forty-seven Wellingtons, thirty-three Whitleys, eighteen Hampdens and four Blenheims. They reported that the whole central area of the town was burning; on their return, Sir Richard Peirse sent a signal congratulating everybody on a highly successful operation.

It was somewhat premature. On 21 December a Spitfire of the Photographic Reconnaissance Unit photographed Mannheim in broad daylight, and a subsequent examination of the prints revealed that although considerable damage had been inflicted on the town, it was by no means all in the central target area. Many of the incendiary markers had been dropped outside the area, and a high proportion of the bomb loads had apparently been aimed at these. Sir Richard Peirse thought that much of the blame lay in the wording of the orders issued to the crews; these had specifically said that bombs were to be aimed at the fires and had given no instructions about identifying the target by any other means. In a memorandum to his Group Commanders, the AOC-in-C made it clear that in future, he expected the majority of the bombs to be placed within half a mile of the aiming point.

None of the Group Commanders, however, seriously believed that the orders had been wholly responsible for the general lack of success that attended the Mannheim raid. Air Vice-Marshal Coningham, the AOC No. 4 Group, thought that the idea of marking targets with incendiaries as a guide for the main bomber stream was a good one; the Germans, in their attacks on British cities, had shown what could be achieved in this respect with the use of picked crews. Coningham was in no doubt that the real trouble lay in the inadequacy of navigational techniques; he cited the cases of crews who flew to their objectives above cloud, relying on the wind forecast given to them before their departure, and claimed to have made a successful attack – only to prove incapable of finding their own base at the end of the return flight. The inference was that many crews, who sighted and bombed what they thought was the target through a gap in the cloud, were in fact many miles off course – and that this sort of thing was happening much more frequently than anyone suspected.

Another unpleasant surprise came a few days later, on 24 December, when Spitfires brought back photographs of the oil plants at Gelsenkirchen. These targets, so it was claimed, had been successfully attacked over the preceding months by 196 aircraft – but the photographs showed only a handful of bomb craters in the area and no evidence at all of any significant damage or repairs.

The photographs brought back by the PR Unit supported

Coningham's view that until improved navigational aids became available, Bomber Command's crews would not be in a position to achieve anything but mediocre results. An urgent request was made to Lord Beaverbrook, the Minister of Aircraft Production, to speed up the development of navigational radio aids and other vital equipment such as reliable aircraft cameras for use at night. But valuable time had been lost, and it would be more than a year before the aircraft of Bomber Command were fitted with apparatus that would enable them to find their way to the targets with a high degree of precision.

The lack of suitable aids to precision bombing was not the only problem. Production of bombers for the RAF, particularly the newer types, was still lagging behind, and so was the training of crews. On 30 December 1940, in one of his famous 'Action this Day' memoranda addressed to the Secretary of State for Air, the CAS and the Minister of Aircraft Production, Winston Churchill wrote:

'I am deeply concerned at the stagnant condition of our bomber force. The fighters are going ahead well, but the bomber force, particularly crews, is not making the progress hoped for. I consider the rapid expansion of the bomber force one of the greatest military objectives now before us. We are of course drawing upon the bomber force for the Coastal Command and for the Middle East. If the bottleneck is, as I am told, crews, we must either have the pilots and personnel we are sending out to the Middle East returned to us after they have delivered their machines, or, what would be less injurious to formed squadrons, have other pilots and personnel sent back from the Middle East in their place . . . In order to increase the number of crews available the training must be speeded up and a certain measure of dilution accepted.

'The figures placed before me each day are deplorable. Moreover, I have been told on high authority that a substantial increase in numbers available for operations against Germany must not be expected for many months. I cannot agree to this without far greater assurance than I have now that everything in human wit and power has been done to avert such a complete failure in our air expansion programme.

'So far as aircraft are concerned, the question arises, from constant study of the returns, whether sufficient emphasis is put upon bomber production. The fighters are streaking ahead, and it is a great comfort that we have so good a position in them. We must however increase our bomb deliveries on Germany, and it appears that some of the types and patterns most adapted to this are not coming forward as we had hoped. I am well aware of the damage done by enemy action, but I ask whether it cannot be remedied, and what further steps are possible.'

Churchill had in mind three principal types of new heavy bomber on which the RAF had pinned high hopes: the Short Stirling, the Avro Manchester and the Handley Page Halifax. In order to understand fully the background to Churchill's comments, it is necessary at this stage to examine the development histories of each of these machines in some detail.

The Short Stirling – the first British aircraft designed from the beginning as a monoplane bomber – originated in an Air Staff requirement of July 1936, which was embodied in Air Ministry specification B.12/36. This specification placed a definite limit on the new bomber's wing span so that it could be accommodated in existing types of RAF hangar. As the Stirling's all-up weight was thirty-one tons, Shorts designed the aircraft with a very low aspect ratio wing in order to keep the wing loading within acceptable limits. This solved the hangarage problem, but it seriously limited the aircraft's service ceiling. Another unfortunate aspect of the bomber's design was that its bomb-bay was divided into compartments which were large enough only to hold bombs not exceeding 2000 pounds. When specification B.12/36 was issued it was not anticipated that the aircraft would be called upon to carry larger bombs than this, a lack of foresight that proved a serious drawback when the Stirling was used on operations.

In 1937 the Air Ministry, concerned about the rapid increases in German air strength, ordered 100 Stirlings off the drawing board. This was followed by another order for a second batch of 100 in April 1938, soon after the Germans marched into Austria. The first batch was to be constructed at Rochester in Kent, and the second at Short & Harland's factories in Belfast, where the firm was already engaged in building Bristol Bombays and Handley Page Herefords (the latter an unsuccessful variant of the Hampden with in-line engines).

The prototype Stirling's maiden flight, on 14 May 1939, ended in disaster when a landing-brake seized and the aircraft swung off the runway. The undercarriage collapsed and the machine was classed as irreparable. It was a severe setback, as the second prototype was not ready for its taxiing trials until 21 November. Fitted with a strengthened undercarriage, it made a successful first flight of thirty minutes on 3 December.

Eight Stirlings had been built and flown by July 1940, and production machines were beginning to roll off the assembly lines at Rochester and Belfast. Then came another setback; on 9 August, German bombers hit Rochester Airport and destroyed six newly-completed Stirlings, and on the fifteenth a heavy attack on Belfast destroyed five more. As a result of this raid, twenty sets of components were hastily moved from the Belfast factory to Aldergrove for final assembly.

These raids and resulting hurried moves added to the confusion and frustration that Shorts were already feeling over their Stirling production, for just as this had been getting nicely under way in May 1940 Lord Beaverbrook, immediately on his appointment as Minister of Aircraft Production, had ordered a complete change of priority to fighter output. The Air Ministry's Scheme L, introduced after the Munich crisis, had placed the emphasis on heavy bomber production, and Short's share in this was to have been 1500 Stirlings. Production had already been delayed because of difficulties in obtaining machine tools and other necessary equipment, and this had just been overcome when Beaverbrook's revised policy resulted in no new contracts or priorities being allocated to heavy bombers for several months. Beaverbrook's action was of course fully justified, but as a result it was not until the end of September that Stirling production really got under way, and the end of the year before it had reached anything like the level envisaged.

It was to Beaverbrook's credit that, as soon as the Battle of Britain had been won and the invasion threat had receded, he did everything in his power to boost heavy bomber production. His adviser, Patrick Hennessy of Ford's, drew up a new programme aiming at a monthly production of 2500 aircraft by June 1941, rising to 2800 by the end of that year. This, however, was far too optimistic and was crippled from the start by the critical shortage of machine tools – many consignments of which were lost on their way over the Atlantic in the growing U-Boat offensive against British convoys – and by the Luftwaffe's night attacks, which made continuous shift work impossible. The few Stirlings completed in July were delivered the following month to No. 7 Squadron at Leeming in Yorkshire, and the remainder of the year was spent in converting crews to the new type and training. It was not until January 1941 that the squadron moved to Oakington in readiness for its first operational mission.

No. 7 Squadron's sister unit at Leeming, No. 35 Squadron, was the first to receive the second of the RAF's new four-engined heavy bombers, the Handley Page Halifax. Together with the Lancaster, this aircraft was to share the main burden of Bomber Command's air offensive against Germany during the years to come.

The Halifax had its beginnings in an Air Staff requirement of September 1936, calling for an all-metal mid-wing medium-heavy bomber to be powered by a pair of the new Rolls-Royce Vulture engines. Handley Page's answer was a twin-engined aircraft known as the HP 56, but it was then learned that there would be a shortage of Vulture engines and so Handley Page altered the design to take four Rolls-Royce Merlins instead. The Air Ministry placed an order for 100 of the new aircraft in September 1937; this was later increased in accordance with

Scheme L, which envisaged 500 Halifaxes in service by April 1942.

The prototype Halifax made its first flight at Bicester on 25 October 1939 and the second protoype on 17 August 1940. As was the case with the Stirling the production programme was subjected to many delays because of Lord Beaverbrook's pre-occupation with fighters, but this was quickly remedied and No. 35 Squadron began to receive its Halifaxes on 23 November 1940, only five weeks after the first production aircraft had flown. The Squadron was at full strength by 5 December, when it moved to its operational base at Linton-on-Ouse.

The third new aircraft to enter service, the Avro Manchester, was a bitter disappointment to Bomber Command. It was designed to the same specification as the original Halifax, but whereas Handley Page abandoned the twin Vulture configuration in favour of four Rolls-Royce Merlins, Avro persevered with it in the Manchester – with unfortunate results. Serious trouble with the Vulture engines dogged the bomber throughout its operational career. They were unreliable in their behaviour; often they would carry the aircraft on long-distance raids without the slightest hint of trouble, only to burst into flames for no apparent reason when the Manchester arrived back over its base.

The first Manchester flew on 25 July 1939. 200 were ordered, and production aircraft first went into service with No. 207 Squadron at Waddington in November 1940. Meanwhile Avro were experimenting with a converted Manchester, known as the Mk. III, fitted with four Merlins in place of the twin Vultures. This aircraft made its first flight on 9 January 1941. A few weeks later it received a new name: the Lancaster.

Churchill was right, at the close of 1940, in describing the heavy bomber situation as deplorable. He tended, however, to pin the blame on individuals rather than circumstances, and in fact Beaverbrook and his staff had already been working miracles for several weeks in an effort to set matters right.

In February 1941, both the Stirling and the Manchester were used operationally for the first time, the former in an

attack on oil storage tanks at Rotterdam on the night of 10-11
February and the latter on 24-5 February, when six Manchesters
of 207 Squadron attacked a Hipper-class cruiser in Brest harbour. The Halifaxes of 35 Squadron flew their first operational
mission on the night of 11-12 March, when six aircraft were
sent out to bomb Le Havre. Four of them attacked the primary;
the crew of another, unable to see either the primary or the
alternate – Boulogne – dropped their bombs on Dieppe. The
sixth aircraft also failed to locate the primary after repeated
attempts and, running short of fuel, jettisoned its bombs in the
Channel. The raid ended in tragedy when one of the Halifaxes
which had bombed Le Havre was mistaken for an enemy by a
night-fighter over Surrey and shot down in flames. Only two
members of the crew escaped.

Meanwhile Bomber Command continued with its new policy
of bombing the industrial centres of selected German cities, and
raids on the lines of the Mannheim attack were carried out on
Berlin, Düsseldorf, Hanover, Bremen, Cologne and Hamburg in
January, February and March 1941. Oil targets, however, were
still the main consideration, and there was still a stubborn
tendency on the part of the Air Staff to ignore the photographic
evidence that attacks of this kind so far had met with little
success. In fact, in January 1941 Sir Richard Peirse asked his
Group Commanders to consider the possibility of attacking oil
plants on nights when there was no moon – even though the
experience of the previous year had shown that many bomber
crews were incapable of finding these targets even under conditions of bright moonlight.

Bearing this in mind, the replies of the Group Commander
were astonishing. All of them – particularly Air Vice-Marshal
Coningham – expressed their confidence that a large proportion
of the bomber crews would be able to find the oil targets in no-
moon conditions. Their sudden optimism, in the face of overwhelming evidence to the contrary, remains unexplained; inter-
Group rivalry may have had more than a little to do with it.
In any event, their illusions were soon shattered. On the night
of 14-15 February, twenty-two Hampdens of 5 Group set out

to bomb the oil plant at Hamburg; despite very favourable moonlight conditions, only six of them located and bombed the target. That same night forty-four Wellingtons of 3 Group took off to raid the plant at Gelsenkirchen, but only seven claimed to have completed their mission. The result was somewhat better the following night, when fourteen out of thirty-three Hampdens claimed to have bombed Hamburg, but none of these claims could be substantiated later because heavy cloud over the objectives during the days that followed prevented PR Spitfires from taking photographs. Even if the claims were accurate, however, there was nothing in them to justify the Group Commanders' confidence in the effectiveness of projected raids on moonless nights.

In any case, the whole question was fast becoming immaterial, for after this brief return to attempted precision attacks on oil targets Bomber Command's policy turned increasingly in favour of area bombing. In March 1941, however, policy was influenced by another urgent consideration: the fearful losses being suffered by British Atlantic convoys at the hands of enemy U-Boats. On 9 March 1941 Sir Richard Peirse received the following directive from Air Chief Marshal Sir Wilfrid Freeman, the Vice-Chief of the Air Staff :

'I am directed to inform you that the Prime Minister has ruled that for the next four months we should devote our energies to defeating the attempt of the enemy to strangle our food supplies and our connection with the United States. In the words of his directive, "We must take the offensive against the U-Boat and the Focke-Wulf wherever we can and whenever we can. The U-Boat at sea must be hunted, the U-Boat in the building yard or in dock must be bombed. The Focke-Wulf, and other bombers employed against our shipping, must be attacked in the air and in their nests."

'Operations should, therefore, be directed against submarine and long-range aircraft activities when circumstances permit, until the menace has been dealt with. I am to say that this does not entirely exclude attacks on the primary objectives [i.e. oil targets] . . . against which you should continue to employ a proportion of your effort.

'Attached . . . is a list of suggested targets connected with submarines and long-range aircraft . . . Priority of selection should be given to those in Germany which lie in congested areas where the greatest moral effect is likely to result. You will appreciate that once a target has been selected it is particularly desirable that it should be subjected to a succession of heavy attacks.'

The list of suggested targets included the Germania shipyard, the Deutsche Werke and the Havaldtswerke Dockyard in Kiel, the Deschimag shipyard and the Focke-Wulf aircraft factory in Bremen, the Vulcan Werke in Vegesack, the Blohm und Voss shipyard and Havaldts in Hamburg, the MAN diesel engine factories in Augsburg and Mannheim, the Junkers factory at Dessau, submarine bases at Lorient, St Nazaire and Bordeaux, and the enemy airfields at Bordeaux-Merignac and Stavanger.

Some of these targets had been hit frequently by Bomber Command since the start of the air offensive against Germany, but it was only now that the RAF was given, as a primary objective, the task of mounting a concerted onslaught against Germany's sea power. The Battle of the Atlantic, which had begun during the very first hours of the war, had steadily been gathering momentum during 1940; by the spring of 1941, the struggle had reached heroic proportions. Hitler had not succeeded in defeating Britain in the air, but he might yet starve her into submission by means of a successful naval blockade.

Much of Bomber Command's effort during this new phase was directed against what the War Cabinet recognized as the greatest potential source of danger to the Atlantic convoys: the German Navy's capital ships *Scharnhorst*, *Gneisenau*, *Prinz Eugen* and *Bismarck*. In March 1941 the first two were assembled in Brest harbour, apparently in readiness for a breakout in strength into the Atlantic. Bomber Command's offensive against these warships and their harbours began with a raid on Brest on the night of 30-1 March; it was to last more than ten months.

Several attempts had been made to bomb the *Scharnhorst* during 1940, mainly in July when she was lying in dry dock at Kiel. It was against this warship that Bomber Command had first used a 2000-pound semi-armour-piercing bomb, dropped on the night of 1-2 July 1940 from a Hampden of 83 Squadron piloted by Flying Officer Guy Gibson. Gibson had made six attempts, diving across the target from 6000 feet, and five times the visibility was too poor to release the bomb. When it was finally released on the sixth attempt, it fell off too late and dropped in the middle of Kiel. The warship was hit by another 83 Squadron Hampden that night, but the damage was not serious.

The large number of night sorties flown against the warships in Brest during the spring of 1941 produced little result, and Sir Richard Peirse felt with justification that the tonnage of bombs wasted could have been put to good effect in attacks on the industrial complexes of western Germany. Area attacks on the big ports in north Germany, and on selected cities such as Cologne and Berlin, were far more profitable; night raids on these objectives continued to grow in strength, and for the first time Bomber Command began to inflict regular damage on a large scale. On the night of 12-13 March the RAF's new heavy bombers flew over German territory for the first time, when Halifaxes and Manchesters raided Hamburg, and on the last night of the month the town of Emden received an indication of the massive devastation to come when Wellingtons of Nos. 9 and 149 Squadrons dropped two of the new 4000-pound bombs, one falling in the old town and the other destroying the telephone exchange. The offensive reached a new level of intensity on the night of 8-9 May, when 360 aircraft were sent out to attack Hamburg and Bremen. It was the largest number of aircraft despatched by Bomber Command in a single night up to that date.

During this period, Bomber Command's policy was yet again altered by the turn of events, this time outside its immediate sphere of operations in western Europe. The first major factor that brought about the change was the German invasion of

Greece and Yugoslavia on 6 April; the second was the attack on the Soviet Union on 22 June. Both these events meant the withdrawal of several crack Luftwaffe fighter wings from the western front, which once again gave rise to hopes that Bomber Command might be in a position to renew daylight attacks on enemy targets without fear of crippling losses.

Air Vice-Marshal Baldwin, the AOC 3 Group, protested immediately against the idea of any of his Wellingtons being exposed again to the risk of suffering casualties on the scale of those sustained in December 1939. The Air Staff, although they believed that the degree of risk would be greatly reduced even on unescorted raids thanks to the strong defensive armament of the new heavy bombers, were well aware of the hazards attending this type of operation. At the same time, they thought that daylight raids over Germany would have more than a fighting chance of success if the enemy could be persuaded to concentrate their fighter defences in the Pas de Calais area. This could be achieved by launching strong and co-ordinated fighter and bomber attacks on objectives in the zone immediately across the Channel. It was hoped that such a step would not only induce the Germans to withdraw fighter squadrons from the air defence system of Germany itself – and possibly from other theatres of operations – but that it would also provide the Spitfires of 11 Group with an unrivalled opportunity of coming to grips with the Luftwaffe fighter formations sent up to intercept the bombers, paving the way for the RAF to establish a measure of air superiority over occupied France.

These 'Circus' operations – as daylight attacks by Bomber Command with strong fighter escort were known – had already been given a trial run on 10 January 1941, when six Blenheims of 114 Squadron, escorted by six squadrons of fighters, attacked ammunition and supply dumps in the Forêt de Guines. The result was encouraging: enemy fighters were sent up to intercept but the resulting dog-fights were inconclusive. One Hurricane was lost and two Spitfires crash-landed on their return to base, but all the others got back safely.

It was not until 14 June, however, that Circus operations

began in earnest. The majority were carried out by the Blenheims of 2 Group, although heavy bombers participated on several occasions. On 19 July, for example, three Stirlings of No. 7 Squadron, escorted by Spitfires, bombed targets in the Dunkirk area from 20,000 feet without loss.

The main drawback to the success of Circus operations was that the Spitfire was totally unsuitable for bomber escort duties. It was only when escorting bombers attacking targets near the coast that the Spitfire pilots enjoyed some freedom of action in seeking out the enemy fighters; when escorting raids that penetrated deeper inland they were forced to stay close to the bombers in order to conserve fuel, and there was very little margin left for actual combat. Messerschmitt 109 pilots had faced precisely the same problem during the Battle of Britain.

Nevertheless by the end of June it was decided that the Circus operations had achieved sufficient success in their primary object of keeping the enemy fighters occupied within certain areas to allow heavy bombers to carry out unescorted missions in daylight over Germany and occupied France, and on 30 June a force of Halifaxes of 35 Squadron made a daylight attack on Kiel without loss. This was followed by a dramatic daylight raid on Bremen on 4 July, this time carried out by fifteen Blenheims of 105 and 107 Squadrons. To reach the target the Blenheims had to fly at very low level across fifty miles of enemy territory and negotiate the formidable Bremen anti-aircraft defences on the final run-in. All the Blenheims were hit and four were shot down, but the target – a factory – was destroyed. The leader of the raid, Wing Commander Hughie Edwards, was awarded the Victoria Cross.

One of the biggest daylight attacks of this period took place on 24 July, when fifteen Halifaxes were sent out to attack the *Scharnhorst* at La Pallice. A smaller attack by Stirlings was made the day before. These raids were carried out in conjunction with diversionary attacks made by escorted Blenheims on the *Gneisenau* and *Prinz Eugen* at Brest. Originally it had been planned to make a large-scale daylight attack on all three warships in Brest under cover of several diversionary raids, a plan that was encouraged by the fact that the Luftwaffe's fighter defences in the area were relatively weak and that 11 Group's Spitfire squadrons were now being equipped with auxiliary fuel tanks which would enable them to escort the bombers all the way.

The raid was to begin with an attack by the most recent addition to Bomber Command's strength; the Boeing Fortress Is of No. 90 Squadron, twenty of which had been offered to the British Purchasing Commission by the United States Government. In view of the RAF's urgent need for four-engined heavy bombers they had been quickly pressed into service, and after several weeks of working-up they had carried out their first mission on 8 July. Three Fortresses, each carrying four 1100-pound bombs, were detailed to attack Wilhelmshaven at 27,000 feet, afterwards climbing to 32,000 feet to make their escape. Two aircraft bombed the target and the third, experiencing a severe oil loss, bombed Norderney instead. On 23 July three more Fortresses were detailed to bomb Berlin, but this mission had to be called off because of bad weather.

Returning to the projected raid on Brest, the attack by the Fortresses was to be followed by one made by eighteen Hampdens, escorted by Spitfires and bombing from medium level. It was hoped that this would bring the available German fighters in the area to combat, causing them to exhaust their supplies of fuel and ammunition before the main attack developed. The latter was to be carried out by about 120 Wellingtons and Halifaxes, without close escort but with two squadrons of Spitfires patrolling the area to engage any German fighters that tried to interfere. The main attack was to be completed within forty-five minutes, and while it was in progress a force of Blenheims was to make a diversionary raid in the Cherbourg area.

The carefully-laid plan, however, was thrown into confusion by the last-minute move of the *Scharnhorst* to La Pallice. As a result of this, the heavy bomber force earmarked for Brest was diverted to the attack on La Pallice instead. More trouble arose in the shape of the Avro Manchester units detailed for the raid; because of persistent engine trouble, these had to withdraw

from the operation completely while modifications to the Manchesters' Vultures were carried out. This meant that the total
number of aircraft available for the main Brest attack was reduced to seventy-eight.

Nevertheless the raid on Brest went ahead on schedule. Three
Fortresses dropped their loads from between 30,000 and 32,000
feet, the crews observing some of the 1100-pounders bursting on
the torpedo station along the west side of the quay and on one
corner of the dry dock. The Fortress crews reported seeing only
two or three enemy fighters, but the Hampdens which came
in a few minutes afterwards at a much lower altitude sighted
at least twenty-four. More fighters were up to meet the seventy-
eight bombers, mainly Wellingtons of the main force, but it was
the flak that caused the most trouble; the size of the raid did
not confuse the German anti-aircraft gunners, and the fire they
put up was both intense and accurate. Altogether the fighters
and the flak accounted for eleven of the ninety-nine bombers
which attacked Brest; two more crashed on the way back to
England. Proportionately, the attack by Halifaxes on La Pallice
suffered a far heavier loss. A warning that the heavy bombers
might encounter serious trouble over this target had come the
previous day, when the six Stirlings of 7 Squadron had attempted
to bomb the *Scharnhorst*; the aircraft had to fight their way
through strong fighter opposition and one of them had been shot
down.

Fifteen Halifaxes took part in the attack of 24 July. Fourteen
of them attacked the objective and were engaged by two squadrons (eighteen to twenty aircraft) of Messerschmitt 109s. Five of
the Halifaxes were shot down and all the rest were damaged
to some extent, but five direct hits were obtained on the
Scharnhorst, causing serious damage. That night, the great warship limped along the coast to join her sisters in Brest with three
thousand tons of water inside her.

The raid had succeeded in its object of putting the *Scharnhorst* out of action for some time, but the losses sustained by the
Halifaxes at the hands of a not greatly superior force of enemy
fighters – and during a raid on a target on the very fringe of

enemy territory – did nothing to encourage the Air Staff's view that heavy bombers could now carry out unescorted daylight raids over Germany with relative impunity. Of particular concern was the fact that the Halifax formation had been dislocated by the concerted fighter attacks; this had not only interfered with the bombing accuracy, but had also greatly reduced the effectiveness of the bombers' defensive firepower.

It was becoming increasingly obvious that daylight bombers could only hope to get away with attacks on strongly-defended enemy targets if one or more of the following conditions was fulfilled. Either the attacking force would have to be big enough to swamp the fighter defences, or escorted by long-range fighters – or else the attack would have to be made at very high altitude. The first two conditions were obviously out of the question; Bomber Command did not have the resources to mount a large-scale daylight offensive, and the only long-range fighter then in service, the Westland Whirlwind, was only available in small numbers. The third, however, was a possibility, for Bomber Command possessed one type of aircraft that was capable of high-altitude bombing: the Boeing Fortress.

During the raid on Wilhelmshaven of 8 July, one Fortress crew had reported that their aircraft had been able to outclimb enemy fighters sent up to intercept it at 32,000 feet, and that other fighters had been forced to abandon the attack after suffering an apparent loss of control. Consequently although the number of Fortresses in service was small, it was hoped that they might achieve a great deal in the way of precision daylight attacks.

The first Fortress mission after the Brest raid was flown on 26 July, when two aircraft took off from 90 Squadron's base at Polebrook to bomb Hamburg. Both aircraft failed to attack the primary because of heavy thunderstorms; one returned to base with its bombs still on board (a usual practice after an abortive mission, for the Fortresses' special 1100-pounders had to be obtained from America and were in short supply) and the other bombed Emden from 32,000 feet.

On 2 August a single Fortress made a successful attack on

Kiel, dropping four 1100-pound bombs, and a second aircraft bombed Borkum. The latter machine was engaged by enemy fighters at 32,000 feet and suffered some damage before getting away; the crew had been unable to return the fire because their machine-guns were frozen solid. On 6 August the target was once again the battle cruisers at Brest; one of the two Fortresses that set out claimed to have hit one of the ships, but the other bombs fell uselessly into the harbour as a result of a thick coat of ice on the bomb-sight. It was rapidly becoming apparent that high-altitude flying was attended by more than the usual share of problems; apart from icing and engine trouble, two of 90 Squadron's aircraft had been lost through structural failure following a loss of control during high-altitude training flights. Both these accidents were caused by turbulence, the extent and violence of which at altitudes of over 30,000 feet was still an unknown quantity.

Four Fortresses took part in the squadron's next mission, carried out on 12 August. One bombed the Dutch airfield of De Koogy, another bombed Cologne from 34,000 feet, and a third attacked Emden from 33,000 feet. The fourth aircraft had engine trouble and was forced to abandon the mission. These raids – and others made by heavy and medium bombers that day – were diversionary attacks in support of a daring low-level raid by fifty-four Blenheims of 2 Group on two power stations near Cologne, the Goldenberg plant at Knapsack and the Fortuna plant at Quadrath. This was the longest daylight penetration into enemy territory so far made by Bomber Command. The Blenheims were escorted by Whirlwind fighters of 263 Squadron, the only RAF fighter aircraft with sufficient range to carry out this task. If more Whirlwinds had been available, their use might have made a considerable difference to Bomber Command's daylight bombing plans. They were highly manoeuvrable, faster than a Spitfire at low altitude, and their armament of four closely-grouped 20-mm cannon made them a match for any Luftwaffe fighter of the day. As it was, the Whirlwind experienced a spate of troubles with its twin Rolls-Royce Peregrine engines, and only two squadrons were ever equipped with the type. Eventually, they were used in the fighter-bomber role and chalked up an impressive record on ground-attack operations over occupied Europe.

Four days after the attack on the power stations, on 16 August the Fortresses of 90 Squadron suffered their first loss due to enemy action. Four aircraft were sent out, two to bomb Düsseldorf and two to attack Brest, but bad weather compelled the first pair to return with their bombs still on board. The other two dropped their bombs on the warships in Brest from 35,000 and 32,000 feet respectively, and immediately afterwards the lower of the two Fortresses was attacked by seven enemy fighters. The aircraft was badly damaged, but thanks to the altitude at which it was flying the pilot managed to nurse it back to the English coast, which was crossed at 600 feet. While attempting to make a forced landing at Roborough near Plymouth, however, the bomber crashed and burst into flames, killing three of the crew. The enemy fighters had made twenty-six attacks on the Fortress, chasing it until it was only thirty miles from the British coast.

On 19 August an attempt to raid Düsseldorf by two Fortresses had to be abandoned when the guns of one aircraft froze up and the other began to spin a very distinctive contrail over the Dutch coast, giving away its position. The ever-present contrails at high altitude were a continual source of worry to the Fortress crews, but there was nothing they could do about them except descend to a lower level – where they would be easy victims for the flak and fighters. A second attempt to bomb Düsseldorf on 21 August was also called off when two of the three aircraft taking part experienced severe icing and the other was forced to return with engine trouble, jettisoning its bombs in the sea, and a third mission planned for 29 August was equally unlucky. This time, one of the two aircraft detailed went unserviceable just before the mission and the other aborted because of the tell-tale contrails.

A whole series of abortive operations followed. On 31 August one Fortress, bound for Hamburg, had to drop its load in the sea and return to base with oil trouble; a second aircraft was more fortunate and bombed Bremen, but because of heavy cloud the crew were unable to see the results. A third Fortress set off for Kiel, but returned with supercharger trouble. Bremen was attacked successfully by a lone Fortress on 2 September, but another aircraft bound for the same objective returned because of unfavourable cloud conditions and a third had to call off an attack on Duisburg when its intercom system failed. The same aircraft experienced intercom trouble again on 4 September, causing the crew to abandon an attack on Hamburg. That same day two Fortresses set out for Hanover; one returned with engine failure and the other, experiencing the usual dense contrail problem, bombed the docks at Rotterdam instead. This aircraft was attacked by a lone Messerschmitt 109 at 31,000 feet, but got away safely.

On 6 August, four Fortresses were detached to Kinloss for a mission against the battleship *Admiral Scheer*, which was lying in Oslo harbour. One aircraft returned to base with supercharger trouble; the other three reached Oslo but failed to locate the warship, aiming their bombs at the harbour installations instead. Four more Fortresses again set out for Oslo on 8 September. One of them, the last to take off, encountered ten-tenths cloud and returned to Kinloss. The other three, soon after entering Norwegian territory at 26,000 feet, were intercepted by a strong force of Messerschmitt 109s and two of the bombers were destroyed within a matter of minutes. The third Fortress climbed rapidly to 35,000 feet and turned for home, but some of the crew members began passing out through lack of oxygen and the pilot came down to 29,000 feet. The Messerschmitts immediately pounced, killing one gunner and wounding another. Bullets cut the wireless operator's oxygen lead and he collapsed. Another bullet hit the glycol tank, causing a long trail of white vapour which made the enemy fighter pilots think the Fortress was finished; they broke off the attack and disappeared. The Fortress staggered home with one engine out of action and its controls severely damaged. Another engine failed during the return flight and the bomber crash-landed at Kinloss, being completely written off.

Two more Fortress missions from Polebrook – with Cologne as the target – proved abortive. They were both carried out by the same aircraft on 15 and 16 September; on the first occasion the pilot turned back when he saw many enemy fighter contrails heading in his direction, and on the second the mission was abandoned following a major power loss on two engines. On 20 September a Fortress dropped four 1100-pound bombs on Emden, but a further mission to the same target on the twenty-fifth was abandoned when the aircraft began to produce contrails at 27,000 feet. It was the last bombing mission carried out by the RAF's Fortresses in Europe. A detachment of 90 Squadron went to the Middle East in October, where it was joined by a detachment of 220 Squadron, and the Fortresses flew several missions in North Africa; but these were at night. There was no escaping the fact that as a high-altitude day bomber, the Fortress I had fallen far short of expectations.

De Havilland's
'Wooden Wonder'.
Mosquitoes of No.
105 Squadron

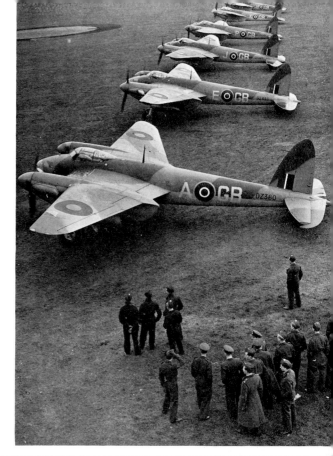

Mosquitoes of No.
105 Squadron in
flight above the
clouds

Below Brest harbour, showing the *Scharnhorst* and *Gneisenau* in dock under cover of a smoke-screen. Note bombs bursting in docks area. Photograph taken during a daylight attack by Halifaxes of No. 35 Squadron

Below centre The flash of a bomb-burst illuminates the surrounding countryside during an attack on Abbéville by Wellingtons of No. 115 Squadron on the night of 9/10 June 1940

Right and below far right Two remarkable shots of the attack on the Philips Factory at Eindhoven, 6 December 1942, by Bostons, Venturas and Mosquitoes of 2 Group. The aircraft shown in the top photograph is a Boston

Bombs burst
on Stavanger
as an attacking
Blenheim races
for home

Bombs burst on
a snow-covered
Norwegian
airfield during
a daylight raid
by 2 Group's
Blenheims. Note
Messerschmitt
109s taking off
in clouds of
snow

Fairey Battles of
the Advanced
Air Striking
Force attacking
a German
convoy in
Belgium on
12 May 1940

9

The Price of Failure,
March-November 1941

The Met forecast for the night of 7-8 November 1941, was far from optimistic. Clouds were building up over Germany, with the probability of thunderstorms, hail and severe icing. It was anticipated that the cloud tops would rise to 20,000 feet, and that westerly winds would increase in strength during the evening. Conditions were far from ideal for a long-range attack on targets in Germany; and yet, even after the forecast had been studied, the planners of Nos. 1, 3, 4 and 5 Groups thought that it would be perfectly feasible to go ahead with an operation that had been projected for some time: a maximum-effort raid on Berlin.

Agreement on launching the bombers on their 1200-mile round trip, however, was not unanimous. One dissenting voice was that of Air Vice-Marshal Slessor, AOC 5 Group, who said later:

'I had been away visiting Bomber Command HQ that afternoon, and on returning to my headquarters was met by our senior meteorological officer, Mr Mathews, who told me in no unmeasured terms that in his view we should be undertaking a quite unjustifiable risk in sending the Hampdens to Berlin in the icing conditions to be expected. I had the utmost faith in him; he knew the aircraft and the crews and what could be expected of them almost as well as I did, and I had no hesitation in diverting my group from Berlin to a closer alternative target, and so informed Command.'

AVM Slessor was perfectly within his rights to make this decision; it was a Group Commander's prerogative to alter a target if he considered it essential. Some station commanders, realizing that the bombers would probably have to fight their way home in the teeth of strong headwinds, ordered only the most experienced crews to take part in the mission.

Of the 400 aircraft that took off that evening on Bomber Command's biggest offensive against Germany to date, 169 machines of Nos. 1, 3 and 4 Groups had Berlin as their objective. Another fifty-five went to Mannheim, while the Hampdens of 5 Group set course for the Ruhr and 'fringe' targets at Oslo, Cologne, Ostend and Boulogne. The majority were Whitleys and Wellingtons, with only a comparative few of the newer Stirlings, Manchesters and Halifaxes taking part. All the aircraft carried maximum fuel and bombs, and the crews of many of them – operating from bases in Yorkshire and East Anglia – had been briefed to land at airfields in southern England after the mission as they would have only a marginal amount of fuel left.

The crews soon discovered that cloud conditions were much worse than they had been led to expect. The cloud tops were higher than the forecast had indicated, which left the bombers with two equally depressing alternatives if they were to get through to Berlin; either they could fly through the clouds and risk the inevitable icing, or they could re-route around them and consume additional quantities of their precious fuel. Many of the crews chose alternative targets such as Lübeck, Warnemünde, Rostock, Kiel, Schleswig and Sylt; they were the fortunate ones, for they had sufficient fuel reserves to regain their English bases in safety. Nevertheless most of them had to come down to 300 feet or lower to get below the clouds on the way home, running through thunderstorms and severe turbulence. Many crews were horribly airsick during the whole return flight.

For the crews who decided to try and reach Berlin, the journey was a nightmare. Most of them tried to fly through the cloud tops, but this led to severe icing and the heavily-laden aircraft soon had to descend right into the murk, with little chance of climbing out of it again and even less hope of locating the target. The rear-gunner of one 102 Squadron Whitley, which managed to bomb Berlin but was later blown badly

off course on the return flight, described what happened: 'Near
the Dutch coast we ran into dense cu-nim cloud, iced up and
both our engines cut out. The pilot took the Whitley down in
a rapid glide from 12,000 to 2000 feet. In the centre of the cloud
the wireless operator got a shock from his set; great chunks
of ice flew off the props and wings and hit the fuselage. My
turret was completely frosted over and I could see nothing. It
suddenly became very cold and very still.'

This Whitley, its engines having started again, got back to
base safely. Other crews were not so fortunate. One Wellington
crew, for example, dropped their high-explosive bombs on Berlin
through an unexpected gap in the clouds, but this closed again
before they could release their incendiaries. They therefore
decided to keep the latter in the hope that they would sight a
worthwhile target on the way home. However, some time later,
when the aircraft was still well inside German territory, its load
of incendiaries was set on fire by an anti-aircraft shell. This also
smashed the bomb release mechanism, which meant that there
was no way of jettisoning the burning load, so the pilot closed
the bomb doors to hide the glare from the anti-aircraft gunners.
With the fire still raging inside it the Wellington crossed the
coast, losing height steadily over the North Sea. It eventually
ran out of fuel and had to ditch; all the crew got out safely, but
they drifted for fifty-seven hours in their dinghy before being
finally washed ashore on the Isle of Wight.

At 06.00 on 8 November, the various bomber bases began to
pick up signals from their returning aircraft, most of which
were approaching the North Sea. 'We are running short of
fuel . . . we are ditching in five minutes.' Time and again, the
signal was the same. In all, thirty-seven aircraft failed to return
from the night's operations. Although it was Bomber Command's
heaviest loss so far in a single night, it was only some two per
cent higher than the average losses of this period. What was
both alarming and tragic was that twenty-five of those aircraft
had been forced to come down in the sea when they ran out of
fuel; still more had crash-landed on the English coast. Twenty-
one of the missing aircraft had been among those which reached

Berlin; seven out of the fifty-five machines in the Mannheim attack also failed to return.

All the crews reported that enemy opposition had been surprisingly light. Three aircraft had been destroyed by a heavy flak barrage over Oslo and three more had been seen going down in flames over Germany, but one of the latter was believed to be an enemy fighter. The crews who came back reported no attacks by night fighters, and only thirteen bombers had been damaged by anti-aircraft shells. Ten out of the fifty-four Whitleys despatched failed to return, as did nineteen out of 161 Wellingtons. The Hampdens of 5 Group lost five aircraft out of nineteen. Remaining losses were two Manchesters and a Stirling.

That terrible night would never be forgotten by the crews who survived the raid. They had flown in temperatures as low as minus 66 °F, with icicles forming on their faces and hands frost-bitten where they had inadvertently removed a glove to make some adjustment; some had fallen asleep in the cockpits, utterly exhausted, almost as soon as the wheels hit the tarmac.

The raid was followed by a pathetic confusion of accusation and counter-accusation. Sir Charles Portal criticized Sir Richard Peirse for authorizing the raid in the first place; Sir Richard Peirse blamed inadequate forecasting by the meteorologists and, to some extent, inexperience on the part of the crews. Sir Wilfrid Freeman, the Vice-Chief of the Air Staff, called Sir Richard Peirse's report 'objectionable' and his suggestion that the losses were due to inexperience a 'damning admission'. All that emerged in the end was a general feeling that a searching enquiry into the disaster should be quietly forgotten in case of a possible adverse effect on the morale of Sir Richard Peirse's subordinates. The Air Staff were even unwilling to lay a full report on the raid before the Prime Minister; it was not until 4 January that Churchill was appraised of all the facts, and then only at the insistence of Sir Archibald Sinclair.

The raid of 7-8 November formed the unhappy climax to a phase of Bomber Command's operations where increasing losses had been sustained in return for little in the way of appreciable damage inflicted on the enemy. The growing awareness that a very high proportion of the bombs dropped at night, even in moonlight, were failing to fall anywhere near their targets had been substantiated on the night of 12-13 March 1941, when fifty-four Wellingtons set out to attack the Focke-Wulf aircraft factory at Bremen while thirty-two Blenheims bombed the town itself. The crews of thirty-three Wellingtons claimed to have hit the target with a total of 132 HE bombs and 840 incendiaries but post-raid reconnaissance revealed that only twelve bombs had actually hit the factory and only a further twenty-eight had fallen within 600 yards of it. This represented less than one-third of the bombs dropped; also twenty-one Wellingtons had failed to locate the target at all, even though it was in a fairly well-placed position for identification.

This raid shattered, once and for all, the peacetime assumption that the average aiming error was 300 yards. It forced the Directorate of Bomber Operations to be honest with itself and double the aiming error; even so, the new basis that allowed for an error of 600 yards was still highly optimistic. The raid on the Focke-Wulf factory brought about a marked lack of confidence in the effectiveness of attacks on precision targets, and Portal himself now turned increasingly in favour of using Bomber Command as a weapon against the enemy's morale. In this he was strongly supported by Lord Trenchard, who in May 1941 submitted a lengthy and somewhat flowery memorandum to the Prime Minister urging the creation of a massive bomber force for such a purpose. Having studied the memorandum, Portal commented:

'I agree with Lord Trenchard's main thesis that the most vulnerable point in the German nation at war is the morale of her civilian population under air attack, and that until this morale has been broken it will not be possible to launch an army on the mainland of Europe with any prospect of success. I also agree that to exploit this weakness the main weight of our air attack should be directed against objectives in Germany, so situated that bombs which miss their target will directly affect the morale of the German civilian population.

I share Lord Trenchard's view that absolute priority should be given to the building up of a bomber force of decisive strength equipped with aircraft capable of reaching all parts of Germany. I would add, however, that this should be done after the minimum force of aircraft (eg. fighter, general reconnaissance, Fleet Air Arm etc.) essential for our security has been provided.'

Sir Dudley Pound, the Chief of Naval Staff, and Sir John Dill, Chief of the Imperial General Staff, both agreed that the enemy's morale would probably be the most profitable objective in the long term, but that at the present time priority should go to the Battle of the Atlantic. The comments of both the CNS and the CIGS indicated tacit agreement with the Air Staff's demand for the creation of a 4000-strong bomber force; however, as Sir Archibald Sinclair pointed out to Sir Charles Portal in June 1941, Cabinet Ministers – by whom such a scheme had to be approved in any case – were reluctant to commit themselves to so big a concentration of effort upon one means of winning the war. Churchill himself, in a minute to the Chiefs of Staff Committee dated 8 June, expressed doubts about the value of a long-term bombing policy and suggested that it might be better to have a programme on a month-to-month basis.

The Chiefs of Staff did not agree, and said so clearly in a minute to the Prime Minister on 11 June. 'The Chiefs of Staff,' the minute read, 'are of the opinion that, in order to obtain the maximum offensive value from our Bomber Force, it is of the highest importance that its operations should not be conducted in a hand-to-mouth manner, but in accordance with a definite strategic aim.' The minute quoted the RAF's offensive against the enemy ports and warships as proof of its ability to maintain a definite aim, and pointed out that the morale of the bomber crews would doubtless be greatly boosted if they were aware that they were acting in accordance with a comprehensive plan. It continued:

'The selection of a short-term policy aiming to disrupt the

transportation system of Western Germany and the lowering of the morale of the industrial workers of that area was based on the following main factors :

a. The dependence of the German economic and military effort on the Ruhr-Rhineland area and the communications, that traverse and radiate from it.

b. The extended character of German military operations has considerably added to the strain on communications, which are now the weakest link in the enemy's economic and military system. Moreover, any serious interference with communications would interfere with the enemy's military plan and, in particular, would delay a concentration in the West for invasion.

c. With the size of the bomber force at present available this primary aim combines best with the secondary aim of morale. The targets lie among workers' dwellings in congested industrial areas, and their attack will have a direct effect on a considerable section of the German people. The interruption of supplies will influence to some extent the morale of the whole of Germany.

The Chiefs of Staff submit therefore that the policy they recommend is not "restricted". The targets to be attacked cover a wide area of Germany and allow for all weather conditions. In addition, the necessary diversions imposed by the Battle of the Atlantic would, as far as possible, have as a secondary objective the German civilian morale.

In conclusion, the Chiefs of Staff emphasize that the kind of attack on railway centres which they now contemplate bears no relation to the series of harrassing attacks which were delivered against marshalling yards, such as Hamm, earlier in the war, when our Bomber Force was insignificant and our primary objective was German oil.'

As a result of these conclusions, Bomber Command was directed on 9 July 1941 to switch the main effort of the night-bomber force to attacks on the German transportation system, with the secondary aim of destroying civilian morale. These attacks appeared to assume even greater importance following Germany's attack on the Soviet Union on 22 June; the Chiefs of Staff believed that the dislocation of the German railways was the quickest and most direct way of aiding the Russians. However this view was not shared either by Sir Archibald Sinclair or Lord Hankey, the chairman of a special committee set up at the beginning of the war to co-ordinate the efforts of all departments engaged in preventing supplies of oil from reaching Germany, both of whom advocated a return to attacks on oil targets. In a memorandum to the Chiefs of Staff dated 15 July 1941 Lord Hankey stated:

'The argument in favour of striking at the morale of the population is impressive ... It is, however, just as important to strike at the morale of the High Command as at that of the people. We did not like it when in a single air raid at Pembroke we lost 70,000 tons of Admiralty oil. We should like it less if we lost, say, a month's imports or one-tenth of our tanker tonnage or of our storage plants. We should strike a heavy blow at the morale of the German High Command if, on top of the loss of Russian supplies and of some Romanian supplies, and of the closing of the Mediterranean route, were to come progressive attacks on synthetic supplies – at a time when they are already drawing on reserves of oil.

'It has been suggested that attacks on oil targets will not give immediate help to Russia. If the above remarks on morale are correct, however, this would not seem to be the right view. Leuna, which was attacked last week, is reported to be heavily defended. This is a measure of the importance the Germans attach to synthetic oil plants. It seems unlikely that they would allow them to be destroyed in detail without withdrawing fighter forces to protect them, as in the case of other decisive air targets. The Committee on Preventing Oil from reaching Enemy Powers does not ask for a relaxation of attacks on other decisive targets, but that synthetic oil should come into the programme of decisive targets.'

Sir Charles Portal's reply was that although a renewed oil

offensive was certainly strategically desirable, it was tactically not a sound proposition. The short-term offensive against the enemy's transport system appeared to hold far more promise. In the long term, assuming that the required increase in bomber strength was obtained, the thoughts of the Air Staff were channelled towards what now appeared to be the ultimate strategic aim of Bomber Command: a series of massive and devastating attacks on selected German cities.

It was not long, however, before this plan suffered a heavy blow. Early in August 1941, at the instigation of Lord Cherwell – scientific and technical adviser to the Prime Minister – a member of the War Cabinet Secretariat named Butt made a detailed analysis of over six hundred photographs taken by Bomber Command on night raids during June and July. His conclusions shocked even those who had harboured serious doubts about Bomber Command's claims to accuracy for some time, even though Butt admitted that his findings were subject to confirmation by an analysis of day photographs. His conclusions were as follows:

1 Of those aircraft recorded as attacking their target, only one in three got within five miles.

2 Over the French ports, the proportion was two in three; over Germany as a whole, the proportion was one in four; over the Ruhr, it was only one in ten.

3 In the full moon, the proportion was two in five; in the new moon it was only one in fifteen.

4 In the absence of haze the proportion was over one half, whereas over thick haze it was only one in fifteen.

5 An increase in the intensity of A.A. fire reduced the number of aircraft getting within five miles of their target in the ratio three to two.

6 All these figures related only to aircraft recorded as attacking the target; the proportion of the total sorties which reached within five miles was less by one-third. Thus, for example, of the total sorties only one in five got within five miles of the target. i.e. within the seventy-five square miles surrounding the target.

Sir Richard Peirse found it hard to reconcile these findings with the damage that Bomber Command was known to have inflicted on enemy targets, and his Group Commanders put forward various theories – such as bad weather – to explain why the results for June and July, assuming that Butt was correct in his analysis, should have been so poor. The Prime Minister, however, took a serious view of the report, and told the Chief of Air Staff that it seemed to require his most urgent attention. Nevertheless he was inclined to agree with Professor Lindemann that, no matter how inaccurate the report might be, it revealed an urgent need for the improvement of night bombing through the scientific study of navigation and the development of radio and radar techniques that would enable average bomber crews to pinpoint their objectives.

This was precisely what the Air Staff had been advocating for years. Far from damaging the prospects for the forging of Bomber Command into a mighty and accurate weapon of destruction, the Butt Report actually helped to hasten the achievement of this ultimate goal by bringing home the difficulties faced by the bomber crews to the highest ministerial level as no other document had succeeded in doing before. The Prime Minister believed that the report had pinned down the trouble that had dogged Bomber Command's operations up to that date, making it possible to decide on a firm course of action to improve matters; as a result, his confidence in the future ability of Bomber Command to deal severe punishment to the enemy, which had been on the wane during the first half of 1941, was now considerably restored.

By the beginning of September Churchill, having succeeeded in overcoming lingering opposition on the part of some Cabinet members, fully accepted the plan for a first-line bomber force of 4000 aircraft. His one aim now was to harness the available national resources to achieve this figure. On 7 September he wrote to Sir John Anderson, Lord President of the Council:

'I have been deeply concerned at the slow expansion of the production of heavy and medium bombers. In order to achieve a first-line strength of 4000 medium and heavy bombers, the Royal Air Force requires 22,000 to be made between July 1941 and July 1943, of which 5500 may be expected to reach us from American production. The latest forecasts show that of the remaining 16,500 only 11,000 will be got from our own factories. If we are to win the war we cannot accept this position, and, after discussion with the Minister of Aircraft Production and Sir Charles Craven, I have given directions for a plan to be prepared for the expansion of our effort to produce a total of 14,500 in the period instead of 11,000 . . .'

The Air Staff did not intend to allow Churchill's confidence to falter again. On 25 September Sir Charles Portal presented the Prime Minister with a plan detailing the massive area attacks which Bomber Command would carry out when its increased force became available. The plan called for repeated and devastating raids which, it was hoped, would result in the total destruction of forty-three selected German towns, the majority of which had a population of over 100,000. In his covering letter, the CAS suggested that with 4000 bombers employed at maximum effort on this task, Germany could be broken within six months.

It was a rash suggestion, and one that irritated the Prime Minister. In a minute of 27 September 1941, he told Portal:

'It is very disputable whether bombing by itself will be a decisive factor in the present war. On the contrary, all that we have learnt since the war began shows that its effects, both physical and moral, are greatly exaggerated. There is no doubt the British people have been stimulated and strengthened by the attack made upon them so far. Secondly, it seems very likely that the ground defences and night fighters will overtake the Air attack. Thirdly, in calculating the number of bombers necessary to achieve hypothetical and indefinite tasks, it should be noted that only a quarter of our bombs hit the targets. Consequently an increase in the accuracy of bombing to 100 per cent would in fact raise our bombing force to four times its strength. The most we can say is that it will be a heavy and I trust seriously increasing annoyance.'

The description of Bomber Command's effort as an 'annoyance' served to widen the rift that had developed in the ideals of Churchill and Portal, which until now had run closely parallel. It was little short of a humiliation and Portal, whose position had been won in the face of considerable opposition from some members of the War Cabinet – not least because the new CAS was a good deal younger that the other Chiefs of Staff – saw Churchill's reply as a personal challenge. He immediately countered by asking the Prime Minister to produce a new strategy. Churchill replied on 7 October in somewhat patronizing fashion, and the minute he wrote revealed a well-camouflaged retreat from his hard-hitting position of a few days earlier.

1 We all hope that the Air offensive against Germany will realize the expectations of the Air Staff. Everything is being done to create the bombing force desired on the largest possible scale, and there is no intention of changing this policy. I deprecate, however, placing unbounded confidence in this means of attack, and still more expressing that confidence in terms of arithmetic. It is the most potent method of impairing the enemy's morale we can use at the present time. If the United States enters the war, it would have to be supplemented in 1943 by simultaneous attacks by armoured forces in many of the conquered countries which were ripe for revolt. Only in this way could a decision certainly be achieved. Even if all the towns in Germany were rendered largely uninhabitable, it does not follow that the military control would be weakened or even that war industry would not be carried on.

2 The Air Staff would make a mistake to put their claim too high. Before the war we were greatly misled by the pictures they painted of the destruction that would be wrought by air raids . . . This picture of air destruction was so exaggerated that it depressed the Statesmen responsible for the pre-war policy, and played a definite part in the desertion of Czechoslovakia in August 1938. Again, the Air Staff, after the war

had begun, taught us sedulously to believe that if the enemy acquired the Low Countries, to say nothing of France, our position would be impossible owing to the air attacks. However, by not paying too much attention to such ideas, we have found quite a good means of keeping going.

3 It may well be that German morale will crack and that our bombing will play a very important part in bringing the result about. But all things are always on the move simultaneously, and it is quite possible that the Nazi war-making power in 1943 will be so widely spread throughout Europe as to be to a large extent independent of the actual buildings in the homeland.

4 A different picture would be presented if the enemy's Air Force were so far reduced as to enable heavy accurate daylight bombing of factories to take place. This however cannot be done outside the radius of fighter protection, according to what I am at present told. One has to do the best one can, but he is an unwise man who thinks there is any *certain* method of winning this war, or indeed any other war between equals in strength. The only plan is to persevere.'

The Prime Minister's words reassured Portal that there was to be no sudden and dramatic insistence on a complete change in the Air Staff's bombing policy. The CAS realized, however, that what was badly needed now was concrete evidence that the bombing inaccuracy revealed by the Butt Report, and which had not improved since, was being dealt with and overcome. Bomber Command had to justify the Air Staff's aspirations by bringing off a massive coup against the enemy, so providing ammunition for the heavy guns that Portal was ready to turn on the dubious minds of the Cabinet.

It was for this reason that the massive attack on Berlin was planned and launched on the night of 7-8 November 1941. Had it succeeded, it would have produced the reaction that the Air Staff so badly needed. But the conditions prevailing that night made success impossible, and the raid was a disaster.

More depressing news followed quickly. On 8 November, the Blenheims of 2 Group and aircraft of Fighter Command suffered unusually heavy losses during the day's Circus operations. Two main factors appear to have contributed to this: poor visibility, which made it difficult for the bombers to rendezvous with their escorting fighters as planned, and a general lack of co-ordination. The Intelligence Summary of No. 118 (Fighter) Squadron gives a typical account:

'It was decided in the afternoon to carry out a most ill-conceived scheme, designated Rodeo 5, in which the Middle Wallop Wing rendezvoused with the Whirlwinds of 263 over Warmwell and carried out a sweep of the Channel Islands area. The whole sortie seems to have been one long muddle. The Whirlwinds led the Spits much too far south and then returned right over the flak area. 501 were sent to deal with a few Huns that put in an appearance when we were on the way back. 118 went back to help, but 501 were not located. The net result was at least three planes damaged by flak and enemy aircraft, and one shot down, and all we could claim was one enemy aircraft damaged . . .'

That evening Sir Richard Peirse went to Chequers, where he found the Prime Minister in anxious mood. Churchill told the AOC-in-C that he believed the RAF could not afford casualties on the scale that had been suffered lately, particularly by Bomber Command, in view of the small amount of damage inflicted on the enemy. Attempts to reassure him appeared only to increase his anxiety. He told Sir Richard that Bomber Command should now make an effort to conserve its strength, attacking only 'fringe' targets while building up its forces for a renewed offensive in the spring.

After considerable discussion in the Cabinet, the Prime Minister wrote the following minute to Sir Archibald Sinclair and Sir Charles Portal on 11 November:

'The losses sustained both by the night bombers and day fighters have lately been very heavy. There is no need to press unduly the offensive by the fighters over France; about two sweeps a month instead of four should be sufficient, combined with a continuance of the attacks on shipping. While the degree of attack may be lightened, the impression of its continuance should be sustained.

'I have several times in Cabinet deprecated forcing the night bombing of Germany without due regard to weather conditions. There is no particular point at this time in bombing Berlin. The losses sustained last week were most grievous. We cannot afford losses on that scale in view of the short fall of the American bomber programme. Losses which are acceptable in a battle or for some decisive military objective ought not to be incurred merely as a matter of routine. There is no need to fight the weather and the enemy at the same time.

'It is now the duty of both Fighter and Bomber Command to re-gather their strength for the spring. Let me have a full report about the heavy losses of bombers on the night of the last heavy raid on Berlin.'

These decisions were passed on by the Air Staff to Sir Richard Peirse in the form of a directive on 13 November. As we have already seen, it was not until 4 January 1942 that all the facts concerning the disastrous raid of 7-8 November were laid before Churchill, Having studied them, the Prime Minister agreed with the Air Staff that the whole unfortunate business was best forgotten. Nevertheless it cast a dark cloud of gloom over Sir Richard Peirse, who had already been the subject of strong criticism during his year as Commander-in-Chief.

Sir Richard was the victim of circumstances. He had presided over the fortunes of Bomber Command when they were at their lowest ebb, when bomber crews paid with their lives for the short-sighted policies and reduced standards of training brought about by decisions taken in previous years. He had been blamed for policy decisions that were none of his doing, such as the drain of vital aircraft and crews from Bomber Command to reinforce squadrons in the Middle East. Mistakes and fundamental errors of judgement he had certainly made, but then so had others in higher authority. Yet in the final reckoning it was he who had to bear the burden of failure; early in the new year he was appoointed C-in-C of the allied air forces in the combined American, British, Dutch and Australian Command in the Far East.

The man who stepped into his place as AOC-in-C Bomber Command was Air Marshal Arthur Harris.

10

The Mounting Offensive, December 1941-June 1942

The outlook for Bomber Command when Air Marshal Harris took command as AOC-in-C was infinitely more favourable than it had been when his predecessor's term of office began in October 1940. Several promising new tools were being forged which, at long last, promised to supplement the only asset that had sustained Bomber Command through the dark months of 1941 : the courage and dedication of its crews.

On 16 September 1941, the first prototype Avro Lancaster had been delivered to the RAF for trials with No. 44 Squadron at Waddington. On 24 December it was followed by three production Lancaster Mk.1s, and the nucleus of the RAF's first Lancaster squadron was formed. In January 1942, the new bomber also began to replace the Manchesters of No. 97 Squadron at Coningsby. Four aircraft of No. 44 Squadron made the Lancaster's first operation on 3 March, when they laid mines in the Heligoland Bight, and the first night bombing mission was carried out on 10-11 March when two Lancasters of the same squadron took part in a raid on Essen. In all, fifty-nine squadrons of Bomber Command were destined to use Lancasters during the Second World War; this splendid aircraft was to be sharp edge of the RAF's sword in the air offensive against Germany.

The spring of 1942 also saw the introduction of the first of Bomber Command's long-awaited radar aids: the TR 1335, known more familiarly as 'Gee'. The basis of Gee was that pulses transmitted from three separate stations in Britain were displayed on a cathode-ray tube in the aircraft. By measuring the time interval between each pulse the navigator was able to fix the position of his aircraft from the place where the appropriate

Gee co-ordinates intersected on his chart, converting this information into latitude and longitude and transferring it to a plotting chart. The apparatus could also be used as a means of bombing 'blind' through cloud or of homing to base; to do this, the navigator could set up the co-ordinates of his objective on the cathode-ray tube and then, by careful tuning, instruct the pilot to fly a series of headings until the pulses transmitted by the ground stations were brought into line. At this point, if the operation had been carried out correctly, the aircraft would be over the required place.

Gee was first tested under operational conditions in August 1941, when two Wellingtons of No. 115 Squadron – experimentally equipped with the apparatus – successfully bombed München Gladbach. Two more missions were carried out during the weeks that followed, but because Gee was susceptible to enemy jamming – which, in fact, happened frequently at a later date – it was not used operationally again until sufficient aircraft were equipped with it to operate in strength. The aid was first used on a large scale on the night of 8-9 March 1942, when it equipped seventy-four bombers out of a force of 211 despatched on an attack against Essen.

Another aid tested during the latter part of 1941 was an early blind-bombing device known as 'Trinity', which was a rudimentary form of the later 'Oboe' – a bearing and distance radar device designed to enable an aircraft to fly along a radio beam until it reached a pre-determined point. Oboe, which was considerably more accurate than Gee, was not brought into operational use until the end of 1942, but Trinity was first used under operational conditions in December 1941 when Stirlings of Nos. 7 and 15 Squadrons, carrying the equipment and with crew members of 109 Squadron acting as operators, made several attempts to bomb the *Scharnhorst* and *Gneisenau* in Brest. The equipment was used again on several occasions early in 1942.

Oboe, which was still under development early in 1942, was first used operationally in December of that year by one of the most potent and versatile aircraft ever used by the Royal Air

Force: the de Havilland Mosquito. When Air Marshal Harris took over as AOC-in-C Bomber Command in February 1942, the Mosquito was one of two aircraft types with which it was planned to replace the ageing Blenheims of 2 Group; the other was the American-built Douglas Boston. The Boston was the first of the two to enter RAF service, with No. 88 Squadron at Swanton Morley in October 1941; a few weeks later this unit moved to Hartford Bridge, and its new aircraft – together with Bostons from 226 Squadron – carried out their first operational mission on 12 February when they were sent out to attack the *Scharnhorst* and *Gneisenau* in the English Channel.

The breakout of the German battle cruisers from Brest and their race for the safety of the north German Harbours – the 'Channel Dash', as the incident was to become known – was a crisis that had to be faced by Air Vice-Marshal J. E. A. Baldwin, the AOC 3 Group, who was acting AOC-in-C Bomber Command from the time when Sir Richard Peirse left the post on 9 January 1942 until Harris took over on 22 February. Early in January air reconnaissance over Brest revealed what appeared to be preparations for a breakout by the *Scharnhorst, Gneisenau* and *Prinz Eugen,* and the Admiralty reasoned that the warships would try to bludgeon their way through the Channel. What the Admiralty did not suspect, however, was that the passage through the Straits of Dover would be forced in daylight. This masterly plan, proposed by the German Admiral Ciliax, would enable the Luftwaffe to provide large-scale air cover over the warships at the most critical point of their breakthrough, as well as allowing more scope for beating off attacking surface forces and dodging torpedo attacks.

On 4 February almost every available aircraft of Bomber Command was bombed-up and placed on two hours' readiness in expectation of the breakout by the German naval force. All other operations came to a virtual standstill. It was an intolerable state of affairs, and on the tenth the state of readiness was downgraded to four hours for a force of 100 aircraft. The remainder were released for a return to other operations, on the understanding that they must be ready to switch their effort against the warships at short notice. Meanwhile Coastal Command was desperately trying to assemble every available torpedo-carrying aircraft – a far from easy task, for the three squadrons of Beauforts operational in the UK were scattered all over the country. No. 42 was at Leuchars, in Scotland, where it had been deployed in case of a possible excursion by the mighty pocket battleship *Tirpitz* from the Norwegian fjord where she was sheltering; half of No. 217 was at Thorney Island, near Portsmouth, with the other half – composed mainly of new and untried crews – at St Eval in Cornwall. Also at St Eval was the newly-formed No. 86 Squadron, also with inexperienced crews. Between them, the three squadrons (a fourth, No. 22, was on the point of embarking for the Far East) could muster only thirty-five aircraft. As for the Fleet Air Arm, with most of its squadrons at sea the best it could do was fly six Fairey Swordfish biplanes to Manston, where they would be in a position to attack the enemy ships as they passed through the Straits.

It was apparent that the main hope of inflicting damage on the warships by air attack lay with Bomber Command. On 12 February, however, when the battle was joined, 100 of the 250 or so bombers that stood ready for the assualt were loaded with semi-armour-piercing bombs which, for maximum effect, had to be dropped from at least 6000 feet – and, with the cloud base at a mere 600 feet over the Channel, these were completely useless. Some squadrons retained their SAP bombs in the hope that their crews might find a gap in the clouds, but for the majority the prevailing weather conditions meant a last-minute change of bomb load. The result was that the first wave of bombers did not get airborne until 14.20, some time after the warships had already been subjected to a gallant and suicidal attack by 825 Squadron's Swordfish and a torpedo strike by a handful of Coastal Command Beauforts.

The 242 aircraft of Bomber Command attacked in three waves, and although most of them reached the target area only one in six managed to bomb the warships. Many crews failed to sight the enemy vessels at all; others located them but were unable to attack, despite repeated attempts, because of the low cloud base. Thirty-nine crews claimed to have aimed their bombs at the warships, but no hits were registered. Fifteen bombers were shot down, in addition to the six Fleet Air Arm Swordfish and three Beauforts.

The Air Staff had been well aware of the difficulties involved in hitting a warship travelling at high speed, a task for which Bomber Command crews had received no training, and they had suggested that instead of wasting time and strength in trying to achieve the impossible Bomber Command should instead concentrate on dropping large numbers of mines along the warships' route, particularly on the approaches to the Elbe Estuary. After consultation with the Admiralty this plan was rejected and the whole strength of Bomber Command was committed to bombing attacks on the enemy vessels. Nevertheless it was mines laid previously by Bomber Command that ultimately caused serious damage to both the *Scharnhorst* and *Gneisenau* on the last stage of their run for the Elbe.

The escape of the warships through the Straits of Dover in broad daylight was a serious blow to British pride, especially that of the Admiralty. Churchill, however, while acknowledging this, took the view that it was no bad thing to have all the German warships penned up in one place in northern Germany; their escape from Brest meant that Bomber Command would now be free to devote the whole of its effort to the resumption of bombing attacks on Germany – provided such attacks did not result in heavy bomber losses through the combined effect of bad weather and enemy action. This indicated that the Prime Minister was prepared to relax the policy of conservation which had been brought into force at his insistence the previous November, and Sir Archibald Sinclair told the CAS that the bombing offensive should be resumed as soon as a fine spell was forecast. On 14 February a new bombing directive was issued which authorized Bomber Command to operate at maximum intensity whenever possible and without restriction. The reason was that great hopes were pinned on the use of Gee, which would give the RAF bombers an accuracy and power of concentration which had hitherto not been possible; it was, however, anticipated that the enemy would have found an effective method of jamming this device within six months, and the Air Staff consequently wished Bomber Command to achieve as much as possible with the help of the new equipment before this happened. There was a considerable element of uncertainty at play, for here, no one knew whether the Germans had succeeded in salvaging the Gee equipment from the 115 Squadron Wellington shot down during the trials a few months earlier, and it was consequently impossible to tell how far advanced enemy counter-measures were likely to be.

The targets that were to be hit during the new offensive were all selected because they lay within range of Gee. The primary targets, picked with the morale of industrial workers in mind, were Essen, Duisburg, Düsseldorf and Cologne; Bremen, Wilhelmshaven and Emden were selected as alternative area targets, while several others outside the range of Gee – including Berlin – were added to the list for attack when conditions were particularly favourable.

The bombing directive of 14 February 1942 which in effect called for an all-out attack on the enemy's morale, was to remain unchanged for a year. Its aims were received with mixed feelings in Parliament where some Members felt that the continued emphasis on building up a massive bomber force amounted to a waste of Britain's resources now that she was no longer alone in the struggle against Germany, and the Admiralty were concerned that the plans for large-scale area attacks would conflict with the Navy's demands for the assistance of Bomber Command in the Battle of the Atlantic. The Admiralty were already pressing for direct help in the form of the transfer of six and a half Wellington squadrons from Bomber to Coastal Command, where they would be used for the vital role of general reconnaissance, and were also asking for two bomber squadrons to be sent to Ceylon for long-range work over the Indian Ocean. With the situation in the Atlantic showing little signs of improvement in the spring of 1942, the Air Staff had little alternative but to part with some Bomber Command units to strengthen Coastal's offensive against the U-Boats, but in the event only two of them were equipped with Wellingtons. The remaining four were equipped with obsolete aircraft that were already being progressively withdrawn from operations over Germany; they were Nos. 51, 58 and 77 with Whitleys, and No. 144 with Hampdens.

The views of certain Members of Parliament on the Air Staff's latest policy were aired in a somewhat unfortunate speech by Sir Stafford Cripps, the Lord Privy Seal, in a speech to the House of Commons on 25 February. The gist of this speech was that the Government was fully aware of the other uses to which Bomber Command's effort could be put, and the implication was that discussions were under way at Cabinet level that might well result in a reversal of policy. Sir Stafford's comments were vague, but they produced unfavourable repercussions – particularly in the United States, where it appeared that even the British Government was now losing faith in strategic bombing. The RAF delegation in the USA at the time viewed the situation with gravity, for they were well aware that the US Government was under pressure to concentrate the weight of its war effort against Japan and they feared that any hint of disillusionment on the part of the British Government might have an adverse effect on the production of heavy bombers destined for the planned strategic air offensive in the European Theatre.

In an effort to dispel any doubts, the Air Staff quickly pointed out that the bombing directive had been approved by the Government and that to reverse the policy it contained would not only be difficult but damaging to the war effort. The directive was strongly supported by Sir Archibald Sinclair in a speech to the House of Commons on 4 March, in which he emphasized the fact that Bomber Command had already proved its value in co-operating with the Army and Navy in addition to its primary task of striking at the heart of Germany, and that in 1942 the RAF's bombers were still the only means at Britain's disposal of bringing home the war to the enemy nation.

Convincing though the Air Minister's words were, however, they were not convincing enough for some sectors of Parliament.

They were followed by a series of attacks from those MPs who were firmly opposed to the whole concept of strategic bombing and who laid continual emphasis on Bomber Command's lack of success so far in this field. Others put forward arguments that revealed a total lack of knowledge of either the aims or operational capability of Bomber Command; some were so ridiculous that they could be dismissed without difficulty. Nevertheless all this parliamentary opposition – coming as it did at a time when Bomber Command was under pressure from several quarters to have its effort split up and committed to tasks other than the primary one of strategic bombing – represented a serious threat to the Air Staff's plans. It was Lord Cherwell who stepped in at an opportune moment to sweep away much of the doubt and uncertainty that hung over the strategic bombing concept. He realized that what was lacking was an accurate means of estimating the material effect that a strategic bombing offensive was likely to have, and he attempted to set this right in a minute addressed to the Prime Minister on 30 March 1942 :

'The following seems a simple method of estimating what we could do by bombing Germany :

'Careful analysis of the effects of raids on Birmingham, Hull and elsewhere have shown that, on the average, one ton of bombs dropped on a built-up area demolishes 20-40 dwellings and turns 100-200 people out of house and home.

'We know from our experience that we can count on nearly fourteen operational sorties per bomber produced. The average lift of the bombers we are going to produce over the next fifteen months will be about three tons. It follows that each of these bombers will in its lifetime drop about forty tons of bombs. If these are dropped on built-up areas they will make 4000-8000 people homeless.

'In 1938 over 22 million Germans lived in 58 towns of over 100,000 inhabitants, which, with modern equipment, should be easy to find and hit. Our forecast output of heavy bombers (including Wellingtons) between now and the middle of 1943 is about 10,000. If even half the total load of 10,000 bombers were dropped on the built-up areas of these fifty-eight German towns the great majority of their inhabitants (about one-third of the German population) would be turned out of house and home.

'Investigation seems to show that having one's house demolished is most damaging to morale. People seem to mind it more that having their friends or even relatives killed. At Hull signs of strain were evident, though only one-tenth of the houses were demolished. On the above figures we should be able to do ten times as much harm to each of the 58 principal German towns. There seems little doubt that this would break the spirit of the people.

'Our calculation assumes, of course, that we really get one-half of our bombs into built-up areas. On the other hand, no account is taken of the large promised American production [6000 heavy bombers in the period in question]. Nor has regard been paid to the inevitable damage to factories, communications etc. in these towns and the damage by fire, probably accentuated by breakdown of public services.'

This minute, which was circulated by the Prime Minister, came under attack because the figures Lord Cherwell had quoted were optimum; for example, it was likely that Bomber Command would receive 7000 new aircraft over the stated period, and not 10,000. But Lord Cherwell had never intended his figures to be taken literally; he had sought merely to sweep away some of the haze that clouded the issue of strategic bombing and to show that decisive results could be achieved. His comments were welcomed by the Air Staff, who lost no time in pointing out to the Prime Minister that Lord Cherwell's calculations could only be transformed into reality if full priority were given to the production of new heavy bombers and to the navigational aids that would help them to find their targets, and if the main effort of Bomber Command were not frittered away on other tasks.

There was nothing new in all this; Lord Cherwell had simply summarized facts and estimates which had been known for a long time. Nevertheless his minute was important because Churchill held his opinions in high esteem; it averted what might easily have blown up into a major crisis over the employment of Bomber Command during 1942-3. As it was, the directive of 14 February stood unaltered; the mighty air offensive against Germany's cities would take place.

Air Marshal Harris realized that his first task as AOC-in-C would be to succeed where Sir Richard Peirse had failed by demonstrating conclusively that Bomber Command was capable of inflicting a shattering blow on the enemy. To this end, he set in motion a plan which at first seemed beyond the bounds of possibility. It envisaged an attack, in a single night, by one thousand bombers on one of the towns on the list of Bomber Command's area targets. The objective eventually selected was Cologne, and the venture was given the code-name of Operation Millennium.

It would be weeks, however, before Bomber Command would be ready to undertake a mission of this kind, even assuming that it was given Cabinet approval. Meanwhile the night offensive had got under way in March, and the first results were highly encouraging.

As yet, only a relatively small proportion of the RAF's bomber force was equipped with Gee, and in order to make the greatest use of these a technique known as 'Shaker' was devised. This involved the splitting of the bomber force into three sections: the illuminators, the target markers and the followers. The idea was that twenty or so Gee-equipped Wellingtons would arrive over the target in five flights at three-minute intervals, each aircraft dropping twelve bundles of flares at ten-second intervals upwind of the target and finally bombing the target with high explosive. The result, it was hoped, was that the position of the target would be indicated by long lanes of burning flares; these would guide a second wave of bombers, also fitted with Gee, which would hit the target with full loads of incendiaries. This would cause a concentrated area of fire into which the following bombers would drop their loads of high explosive.

This method was first tried out operationally on the night of

8-9 March, when 211 aircraft set out to bomb Essen. It was the first of eight big attacks launched against this target during the next seven weeks, all using the Shaker technique. Success however, was strictly limited, not least because the crews had trouble in operating their Gee equipment. There was also a great deal of opposition from searchlights and flak, and to add to the confusion the Germans fired dummy flares. A raid against Hamborn and Duisburg on the night of 9-10 March was more successful and considerable damage was inflicted on both these objectives. The only trouble was that they had been bombed by mistake. Once again, Essen had been the real target; the flares had gone down in the wrong places.

In fairness to the bomber crews, Essen – because of its massive anti-aircraft concentration and the fact that it was invariably shrouded by a dense layer of industrial haze – was one of the hardest targets in Germany. An attack on Cologne on the night of 13-14 March, carried out by 134 aircraft – of which fifty were equipped with Gee – produced a much better result. Despite poor conditions – cloud and haze – twenty aircraft dropped their flares on the target with the help of Gee, and nineteen out of twenty-six hit the target with incendiaries a few minutes later. Subsequent reconnaissance photographs showed considerable damage within the area marked by the incendiaries, and revealed that about half the attacking force had managed to place their bombs within five miles of this area – a far more encouraging result than had hitherto been achieved.

As a preliminary to these Gee-assisted raids, Bomber Command had carried out a full-scale operational trial to find out whether the use of flares would light up the target for long enough to enable the following crews to identify it visually and bomb it. The trial was carried out on the night of 3-4 March, and the objective was the Renault Factory at Billancourt, near Paris. The plan called for an advance force of Stirlings, Halifaxes and Manchesters, all flown by picked crews, to drop flares on the factory and then to bomb it visually with 1000-pound bombs. They would then drop more flares upwind of the target, indicating its position to the leading bombers in the main force.

These in turn were to drop flares after attacking with their 1000-pounders, lighting the way for the final wave which would consist of Manchesters, Halifaxes and Wellingtons, all carrying 4000-pound bombs. The main force was to concentrate its attack within the space of thirty minutes, and the final wave fifteen minutes.

Everything worked closely to plan. Of the 235 aircraft despatched, 223 claimed to have attacked the target. Only one aircraft, a Wellington, failed to return. The raid lasted one hour and fifty minutes, during which time there was an average concentration of 121 aircraft per hour over the target. Fifty-nine aircraft attacked the factory in one ten-minute period alone. As a result of the raid almost every building in the factory was more or less severely damaged, and some forty per cent of the Renault machine tools were destroyed.

The Renault Factory was, of course, a very different target to those in the Ruhr; there was nothing like the same concentration of flak and searchlights, and the inevitable industrial haze was absent. Nevertheless it was a good indication of what might be achieved with the use of the right techniques.

Another experiment was carried out in March, this time involving a saturation attack with incendiaries instead of high explosive. The target was Lübeck, selected because many of its buildings were old and inflammable and its streets narrow, affording good conditions for the development of firestorms. The centre of Lübeck – the Altstadt – was also densely populated, containing some thirty thousand people. Another ninety thousand lived in the suburbs.

On the night of 28-9 March 234 aircraft set out for this target, most of them carrying incendiaries. The final wave, which was to attack an hour after the main force, consisted of forty-seven Wellingtons and eighteen Manchesters carrying high explosives, including 4000-pound bombs. A total of 191 aircraft claimed to have attacked the target, and the raid was a complete success. Two hundred acres of the city centre were destroyed, mainly by fire, and there was additional heavy damage in the suburbs. The raid caused considerable panic, not only among the population of Lübeck and the surrounding area but also among the German administration in Berlin. It was thirty-two hours before the last fires were put out. One thousand dwellings were destroyed and 4000 damaged; 520 civilians were killed and 785 injured. Eight bombers were shot down, mostly by night-fighters on the way home.

A month later the experiment was repeated when Rostock was attacked with incendiaries on four consecutive nights, 24-7 April. Rostock was selected for much the same reasons as Lübeck, but this time there was a difference. On the southern suburbs of the city, at Marienehe, lay the important Heinkel aircraft factory, and this was allotted as a precision target for part of the attacking force. The attacks on the first two nights, carried out by 142 and ninety-one bombers respectively, were disappointing; the fires started in the town were scattered and the Heinkel factory appeared to be undamaged. In contrast, the third attack was highly successful. Out of the 128 aircraft despatched, 110 attacked the town and sixteen bombed the factory, causing heavy damage. Yet even this was surpassed by the fourth attack, in which forty-six bombers raided the town and a similar number attacked the factory out of a total force of 107. It was no mean achievement, since – as Rostock, like Lübeck, was outside Gee range – success depended on visual identification. At the end of the fourth night, sixty per cent of the old city of Rostock lay in smouldering ruins. For the first time, the phrase 'Terror Raid' became part of the German people's vocabulary.

These were the results Harris had been waiting for. The stage was now almost set for his master-stroke: the projected thousand-bomber raid. On 18 May he placed the scheme before Sir Charles Portal, stating that in order to carry it out he proposed to commit not only the whole of Bomber Command's first-line strength, but also a high proportion of the aircraft employed by the Operational Training and Conversion Units. By also using a large part of his bomber reserves he hoped that he could assemble a force of 700 machines; the remainder, he hoped, would be loaned by other Commands.

The Chief of Air Staff and the Prime Minister were enthusiastic about the plan; both were captured by its sheer audacity. So were the C-in-Cs Coastal and Flying Training Commands, Sir Philip Joubert and Sir William Welsh. The former promised Harris the use of 250 aircraft, including those that had been detached from Bomber Command to Coastal earlier in the year, and the latter thought that he could scrape together thirty or so Wellingtons.

In the event, Admiralty pressure compelled Joubert to withdraw his offer completely, and of the aircraft promised by Flying Training Command only four Wellingtons actually materialized. Nevertheless Bomber Command's own resources were greater than even Harris had envisaged; in all, the operational and training groups managed to scrape together 1042 aircraft for the operation. The biggest surprise was provided by the two Operational Training Groups, Nos. 91 and 92; the former provided 259 aircraft and the latter 108.

Harris had the required number of aircraft; what was necessary now was careful planning. The AOC-in-C was the first to admit that Operation Millennium was in the nature of a gigantic gamble that could reap an enormous reward or end in massive disaster that could destroy the entire structure of Bomber Command. Nothing must be allowed to go wrong.

Because of the size of the force and the inexperience of many crews, the target would have to be one which lay close to Germany's western frontier and which, above all, was easily identifiable. Also, the raid would have to be carried out in bright moonlight; the less time the bombers had to spend over enemy territory, the less chance there would be of interception by night-fighters. With these factors in mind, two alternatives were considered: Hamburg and Cologne. The final choice depended entirely on the weather.

The raid was tentatively scheduled to take place on the night of 27-8 May or on the first suitable night after that date. All the participating aircraft had to be at their allotted airfields by 26 May; this in itself presented a massive problem of administration, for many of the OTU aircraft had to be moved from their own bases to other stations. This caused an unavoidable dislocation of Bomber Command's training schedules. One of Harris's main worries was that the bombers from the OTUs would suffer heavy casualties. Many of them were flown by crews sent to the Training Units for a rest after completing tours of operations; they were among the RAF's most experienced aircrew and the loss of a high proportion would have incalculably damaging consequences.

A careful plan of attack was worked out for each of the two potential targets. The Cologne plan envisaged a ninety-minute assault, the first fifteen minutes of which would be allocated to all aircraft of Nos. 1 and 3 Groups equipped with Gee. The last fifteen minutes would be devoted to an attack by the heavy bombers of Nos. 4 and 5 Groups, and to photography of the result by eight selected crews. In between the two fifteen-minute periods would come the main body of the force. All aircraft taking part were to carry the maximum load of incendiaries. Nos. 1 and 3 Groups were given an aiming-point in the centre of the town; Nos. 4 and 92 (OTU) Groups were to aim at a point about a mile to the north of this, and Nos. 5 and 91 (OTU) Groups at a point a mile to the south. No flares or markers would be dropped, as these were considered unnecessary in the bright moonlight. Aircraft unable to find Cologne were to bomb Essen or any other built-up area in the Ruhr. The approach to and exit from the target were worked out in meticulous detail to minimize the risk of collision, and crews were left in no doubt of the vital importance of adhering strictly to the timetable.

Bad weather, with thunderstorms and a great deal of cloud on the bombers' route, caused the operation to be postponed on the night of 27-8 May. There was very little change the following night, although Bomber Command flew a small-scale mission over France and carried out some mine-laying. The weather was now causing serious concern; the massive armada could not be held poised indefinitely, and the moon would soon be on the wane. On the morning of 30 May the forecast still indicated thundery conditions over Germany, but promised good weather over the bombers' bases. After studying the weather reports, Harris decided that an attack on the Rhineland might offer some chance of success under the prevailing conditions; in his view, the fact that the bombers would have clear weather for their return to base more than outweighed the risk of a possible entanglement in cloud over the target. At noon, the order went out to the Groups; Operation Millennium would take place that night, and the target would be Cologne.

At dusk, the sky over eastern England vibrated to the roar of engines as the bombers took off from the runways of fifty-two airfields and set course for Germany. The bulk of the armada – 708 aircraft – was made up of the veterans of Bomber Command, Wellingtons, Whitleys and Hampdens. The remaining 338 consisted of the 'heavy brigade'; Stirlings, Halifaxes and Manchesters, with a sprinkling of the new Lancasters.

While the main bomber force headed across the North Sea, fifty aircraft of 2 Group, Army co-operation and Fighter Commands began a series of diversionary attacks on enemy airfields in France, Belgium, Holland and Western Germany. These intruder missions were scheduled to continue until the attack on Cologne was over. Meanwhile as they approached the enemy coast, the bombers began to encounter dense cloud and a great deal of icing was experienced. The cloud began to break up over Holland, and by the time the searchlights of Cologne were sighted the sky was clear except for a small amount of cirrus.

At 00.47, seven minutes ahead of schedule, the first bombs fell on the target. The last bombs were dropped at 02.25, exactly on time. Everything went according to plan; the first wave navigated by Gee until the crews were close enough to identify the target, and their bombs started fires that were easily recognized by the subsequent waves. Fighters and flak were active for the first forty-five minutes of the attack, but after that the defences, apparently saturated, 'became weak and confused'.

A total of 898 crews claimed to have attacked the target, dropping 1445 tons of bombs, two-thirds of which were incendiaries. The standard of accuracy was high and the AOC No. 3 Group, Air Vice-Marshal Baldwin – himself flying in one of the Stirlings in the first wave – reported that the first bombs had started fires within half a mile of the aiming-point. As the last bombers turned for home, the entire target area appeared to be in flames and the fires were visible from a distance of 150 miles.

Over 600 acres of Cologne's built-up area had been destroyed; the raid had caused almost as much devastation as all previous raids on German towns added together. About 250 factories, including metal works, rubber works, blast furnaces, chemical works, an oil storage plant and other establishments manufacturing many different types of component had been destroyed or badly damaged. The German report on the raid listed 486 people killed, 5027 injured and 59,100 made homeless. The toll of property included 18,432 houses, flats, workshops and public buildings destroyed and 40,586 damaged, 9516 of them severely. Fifty per cent of the city's power supply was put out of action, and the gas and water supplies were also disrupted. The railway repair shops, employing 2500 people, were totally destroyed, as were 484 of the city's businesses. About half the industrial plants in the city – 328 – had been damaged to a greater or lesser extent. 12,000 fires were started, some of which burned for days.

The aircraft losses were a good deal lighter than Harris had anticipated. Forty aircraft in the main force, as well as two of those engaged on the intruder missions, failed to return. 116 aircraft were damaged, twelve of them so badly that they were classed as unrepairable and a further thirty-three badly enough to keep them out of action for several weeks. The overall loss was 3.8 per cent of the attacking force, which was considerably lower than the average of 4.6 per cent experienced by Bomber Command in conditions of cloudless moonlight over Germany up to that time. Harris's fear that the Operational Training Groups might suffer heavily had not been justified; in fact, they sustained a lower loss rate than the operational groups.

To help clear away the damage and restore essential services, the German administration in Cologne drafted in 3500 soldiers 2000 prisoners of war and 10,000 labourers. They had only just started work when, at 05.00, the sirens wailed again. High above the pall of smoke that towered up to 15,000 feet over the shattered streets, four fast, twin-engined aircraft raced over the heart of the stricken city and dropped several 500-pound bombs into the inferno. They were the Mosquitoes of No. 105 Squadron, carrying out their first bombing mission of the war.

11

The Advent of the Pathfinders,
1942

For the first time, the thousand-bomber raid on Cologne brought brought home to the Nazi hierarchy in Berlin the full inadequacy of Germany's night-fighter defences. The night-fighters claimed to have destroyed thirty-six bombers during the raid on Cologne, but it was not enough. With remarkable short-sightedness, the whole of the German anti-aircraft system had been geared up to deal with small numbers of night bombers slipping through the ground-controlled interception zones of north-west Germany; now the bombers were pouring through on an unprecedented scale and the defences reeled under the impact.

Nevertheless the German night-fighter force of May 1942 had come a long way since 20 July 1940, the night when Lieutenant Werner Streib had shot down a Whitley over northern Germany and scored the Luftwaffe's first night victory over the Royal Air Force. After that the small band of night-fighter pilots had begun to register an increasing number of successes, but their effort still lacked any real co-ordination. By October 1940 the Luftwaffe had three night-fighter squadrons; these had no really permanent base, being shuttled around western Germany to areas believed to be in danger of attack by Bomber Command. At first, the rest of the Luftwaffe – geared as it was to offensive operations – regarded the night-fighter force with amusement and not a little disdain, but this began to give way to grudging admiration after the night of 1-2 October 1940, when Werner Streib shot down three Wellingtons inside forty minutes and other night-fighters accounted for two more.

Under the command of Major-General Josef Kammhuber, the night-fighter force at the end of 1940 found itself committed to two distinct types of activity: defensive operations in the searchlight belt stretching along the west German frontier, and offensive intruder operations over the British Isles. For the latter purpose Kammhuber assembled three squadrons of Junkers 88s and Dornier 17s to form a long-range fighter Group, which he stationed at Gilze-Rijen in Holland. These fighters usually operated in three waves: the first, alerted by the German radio-interception service that monitored the RAF bomber frequencies, attempted to attack the bombers as they took off on a raid from their bases in East Anglia; the second wave patrolled the bombers' route over the North Sea and the Low Countries, while the third followed the returning bombers and endeavoured to shoot them down as they joined the landing-pattern over their airfield at the close of their mission.

The success of these early intruder operations was limited. Nevertheless they came as a nasty surprise to Bomber Command, and their psychological effect on the bomber crews was considerable. The knowledge that they ran the risk of being shot down over their own territory, perhaps within a minute or two of safety, added greatly to the nervous tension and strain that afflicted every bomber crew by the summer of 1941.

The long-range night-fighters themselves suffered heavy losses during their early missions, but Kammhuber was convinced that intruder operations on a large scale was the Luftwaffe's only real answer to the ever-growing activity of Bomber Command. The main drawback was that, despite repeated requests, Kammhuber never succeeded in obtaining more than thirty or so aircraft for this kind of work. The final blow came when, after a particularly bad spell with heavy losses during the first week of October 1941, Hitler himself ordered intruder operations to cease forthwith. The force's aircraft were subsequently transferred to the Mediterranean theatre.

Deprived of what he considered to be the most effective weapon in his night-fighting arsenal, Kammhuber had no alternative but to set about re-organizing and expanding the night-fighter zones in western Germany. Working from his HQ at Zeist, near Utrecht, he created an air defence system that became known as the Kammhuber Line. This consisted of a masive searchlight belt some twenty-two miles deep; ahead of it, stretching in a giant arc over the Low Countries, was a series of fighter control zones known as 'Himmelbett' zones, each one overlapping its neighbours. Within each Himmelbett zone was a radar station consisting of a 'Freya' early warning set, with a range of up to 100 miles, and two 'Würzburg' sets, one for plotting the bomber and the other for directing the fighter on to it. The biggest snags with the whole system were that only one fighter could be controlled at a time within each zone, and that the fighter could not be handed over from one zone to another. The fighter controller could bring the intercepter to within a mile or so of its target, but it was in that last mile – with the fighter pilot depending on his eyesight alone – that the trouble began. All too often, in spite of the fact that they knew they were within a few hundred yards of the bomber, the night-fighters failed to intercept.

Unlike the RAF's night-fighters, the Germans carried no airborne radar to bridge the gap created by those last few hundred yards until the summer of 1941. The first example of airborne interception radar, known as 'Lichtenstein B/C', was first installed in the Messerschmitt 110s of Nacht-Jagdgeschwader 2, and was first used in action on the night of 9-10 August 1941. From this moment on, the successes of the Luftwaffe's night-fighter arm began to mount steadily.

Kammhuber's whole programme was hampered by continual delays and frustrations. It would be more than two years before the German night-fighter formations were in a position to inflict substantial damage on Bomber Command, and by that time the British had developed effective radar counter-measures that made the task of the night-fighter pilots immensely difficult.

Yet it was neither the vicissitudes of the German High Command, nor the delay in producing aircraft specifically designed as night-fighters, that defeated Kammhuber in the end. The factors that played a really decisive part in crippling his aspirations were the entry of the United States into the war and the subsequent daylight offensive by the USAAF over Europe, with the resulting emphasis on the mass production of day-fighters for the defence of Germany. Also, many night-fighters were subsequently destroyed when they were flung into the great daylight battles that began to develop over the Third Reich in 1943.

This, however, was still in the future. In 1942, although the first units of the mighty US 8th Air Force were beginning to assemble on British soil, the strategic offensive against Germany was sustained by Bomber Command alone, and in their fight against the British bombers the future of the Luftwaffe night-fighter force appeared increasingly promising. It would not be long before the night-fighter crews received a badly-needed boost to their morale when they went into action against the RAF's third thousand-bomber raid on Germany.

Air Marshal Harris lost no time in taking advantage of the prevailing moon conditions to launch a second massive attack on the enemy; he did not intend to allow the Germans time to recover from the hammer-blow his Command had inflicted on Cologne. On 1 June, with the weather still favourable, he authorized a thousand-bomber raid on Essen, the target that had eluded the bombers earlier in the year. The attacking force was to use the 'Shaker' technique, with Gee-equipped Wellingtons of 3 Group lighting the target with flares and the first wave of the main force carrying incendiaries.

A force of 956 bombers was despatched, and Harris was optimistic that similar results to those of the Cologne raid would be achieved. The result, however, was disappointing; 767 crews reported that they had dropped their bombs in the target area, but the latter had been obscured by up to ten-tenths cloud at 8000 feet and the usual layer of industrial haze. Subsequent reconnaissance photographs showed hardly any damage in Essen, and the precision target allocated to part of the attacking force – the Krupp factory – had not been hit at all. The photographs also showed severe damage to Oberhausen, Mulheim and Duisburg, which indicated that a high proportion of the bombs had fallen in the wrong places. Thirty-one aircraft, or 3.2 per cent of the attacking force, failed to return and another ninety-nine were damaged, five of these being destroyed when they crashed on landing. Most of the casualties had been suffered by the aircraft attacking in the first wave; there was evidence to show that here, as in the Cologne attack, the enemy's defences had decreased in intensity after the first thirty to forty-five minutes or so, which appeared to justify the policy of concentration in time and space.

After the attack on Essen the thousand-bomber force was temporarily disbanded, the various groups returning to their normal duties. It was reassembled during the third week of June for a third mission, this time with Bremen as the target. Harris hoped to persuade the Admiralty to release a force of Coastal Command aircraft to take part in this raid, and to this end he laid great emphasis on the fact that the destruction of Bremen would have a tremendous effect on the German naval effort. He also enlisted the support of the Prime Minister, who gave the Admiralty the necessary nudge by telling them to ensure that they did not interfere with Coastal Command's participation. The First Sea Lord, Sir Dudley Pound, agreed to release 100 Coastal Command Hudsons for the raid, and also offered the use of one of the Polish Wellington squadrons provided it was replaced at a later date. There was a good reason for this last offer; the Polish temperament had been found totally unsuited to the long, monotonous hours of patrol work that was the lot of Coastal Command, and morale in this particular unit was at a low ebb.

In the event Coastal Command provided a force of 102 aircraft, the great majority of which were Hudsons, bringing the total bomber force despatched to 1006 aircraft. The plan of attack, which was to be carried out on the night of 25-6 June, envisaged an assault by three waves of bombers. Fifty Halifaxes and fifty Stirlings were to go in first and attack the centre of Bremen, and they were to be followed by 124 Gee-equipped Wellingtons of 1 and 3 Groups. The main force had various targets allotted to it, including the Focke-Wulf factory, the docks and the Deschimag submarine yards. The attack was to be completed by another wave of Stirlings and Halifaxes, and the whole assault was timed to last sixty-five minutes.

The attack was hampered by dense cloud, both en route to Bremen and over the target itself. Most of the aircraft in the advance force had to bomb blindly with the aid of Gee, and the aircraft in the main force aimed their bombs at the glow of fires seen dimly through the cloud layer. Only one aircraft was able to bomb visually, and that was because its pilot disobeyed orders and dived down through the cloud layer to 3000 feet. Nevertheless the attack was accompanied by a certain degree of success. A lucky 4000-pound bomb had hit the Focke-Wulf factory, destroying a sizeable portion of it, and large areas of the town itself were gutted. The docks area, however, was undamaged.

In all, the attacking force had lost forty-nine aircraft, five of them Coastal Command machines. This represented a loss of 4.9 per cent. In addition, sixty-five aircraft received varying degrees of damage. The crews of ten of the damaged aircraft reported that they had been attacked by fighters, and the latter were believed to have accounted for at least twenty of the aircraft shot down. The Manchesters had suffered particularly heavily, and in fact this raid was their swansong; it was the last occasion when these machines were used operationally.

Air Marshal Harris was now forced to reconsider the whole question of future raids on this scale, which he had originally hoped could be mounted at the rate of up to five per month. The C-in-C's difficulty was that he now found himself astride a juggernaut; the three thousand-bomber raids carried out so far had received a huge amount of publicity, and both public and Parliament expected that they would continue. Even the Prime Minister took some convincing that it was necessary to call a halt to attacks on this scale, at least for the time being; Harris had to explain to him at length that the strength of Bomber Command was still not increasing in proportion to its losses, that nineteen squadrons had been transferred to other commands already in the course of 1942, and that he was left with only thirty operational squadrons, backed up by the OTUs, with which to carry on the air offensive. Quite apart from all this, he pointed out, Bomber Command was still expected to carry out a wide variety of tasks in addition to its primary function of bombing targets in Germany.

Churchill saw the point, and agreed that the thousand-bomber attacks should be halted until there had been a substantial increase in the strength of Bomber Command. The opportunity for launching another raid of this size was not to occur again until another two years had passed; meanwhile, the biggest attack launched by Bomber Command during the remainder of 1942 involved a raid by 630 aircraft against Düsseldorf on the night of 31 July-1 August, and this was not surpassed in strength until a raid on Dortmund carried out on 23-4 May 1943.

While it was true that the overall strength of Bomber Command was the subject of growing concern, the slow expansion was balanced to some extent by the fact that the new four-engined heavy bombers had the ability to carry a vastly bigger bomb-load than their predecessors. Nevertheless the situation in July 1942 was serious enough to provoke the following comments from the Prime Minister in his 'Review of the War Position' issued on the twenty-first of that month.

'It is at this point that we must observe with sorrow and alarm the woeful shrinkage of our plans for bomber expansion. The needs of the Navy and of the Middle East and India, the short-fall of our British production programmes, the natural wish of the Americans to fly their own bombers against the enemy, and the inevitable delay in these machines coming into action, all these falling exclusively upon Bomber Command have prevented so far the fruition of our hopes for this summer and autumn. We must regard the bomber offensive against Germany at least as a feature in breaking her war-will second only to the largest military operations which can be conducted on the Continent until that war-will is broken. Renewed, intense efforts should be made by the Allies to develop during the winter and onwards ever-growing, ever more accurate, and ever more far-ranging bomber attacks on Germany. In this way alone can we prepare the conditions which will be favourable to the major military operations on which we are resolved. Provision must be made to ensure that the bombing of Germany is not interrupted, except perhaps temporarily, by the need of supporting military operations...'

Three months earlier, Bomber Command had already demonstrated its ability to carry out the kind of 'far-ranging bomber attack' to which the Prime Minister referred when its new Lancasters carried out an audacious daylight attack on Augsburg – but the cost had been high. The target was the MAN diesel-engine factory, and the attack – which took place on 17 April 1942 – was carried out by eight Lancasters out of a total of twelve that set out. The raid is worth examining in some detail, not only because of its audacity, involving as it did a round trip of 1250 miles, most of it over enemy territory, but also because it was one of the most ambitious exercises in long-range navigation and precision bombing undertaken by Bomber Command. It was also the first occasion on which the new Lancasters were subjected to concentrated attacks by enemy fighters.

Twelve Lancaster crews, six from No. 44 Squadron at Waddington and six from No. 97 at Woodhall Spa, were selected for the mission and subjected to an intensive period of low-flying and navigational training. They had to hit just one building, the engine assembly shop which lay in the centre of the MAN factory complex. In this one building was produced a large proportion of the diesel power-plants for the German Navy's submarines. The outward flight was to be made in formation at the lowest possible altitude; the aircraft would attack with 1000-pound bombs, fitted with eleven-second delayed-action fuses, and afterwards return to base individually. Much of the flight back would be made in darkness, which meant that the bombers could select a higher altitude on this stage.

By flying at low level on the way out it was hoped that the Lancasters would escape detection by the enemy radar until the last possible moment. It was also thought that this technique would provide the best possible defence against fighter attack, enabling all the formation's guns to be brought to bear while at the same time preventing the fighters from attacking from below, the Lancaster's vulnerable spot. No fighter escort was planned, but the Bostons of 2 Group and aircraft of Fighter Command were scheduled to make a series of diversionary attacks on targets in northern France.

The aircraft crossed the French coast between Le Havre and Cherbourg. In two tight formations of six they flew on to Sens before turning eastwards. Visibility was about ten miles; there was an unbroken layer of cloud at 1000 feet, and the big bombers hedge-hopped across the French countryside at between twenty and fifty feet. As they approached Sens, they were attacked by between twenty and thirty enemy fighters and four of the Lancasters were shot down within fifteen minutes before the Messerschmitts unexpectedly broke off their attack and disappeared. (After the war, it was established that the enemy fighter squadron had already been on patrol for some time and was consequently short of fuel when it was vectored on to the Lancasters.

The eight surviving Lancasters flew on to Augsburg, bypassing Mulhouse and skirting the northern tip of Lake Constance. They were met by intense light flak over the target and three more aircraft were shot down, but the remainder pressed home their attack in the gathering dusk. Although all five remaining Lancasters were damaged, they all returned to base. Of the six aircraft from 44 Squadron, only one – piloted by Squadron Leader John Nettleton, the leader of the attack – got back. Nettleton was subsequently awarded a Victoria Cross. He was later killed in action on the night of 12-13 July 1943, during a raid on Turin.

Although reconnaissance later showed that the assembly shop had been damaged, the full result of the raid was not learned until after the war. It turned out that five of the delayed-action bombs which the Lancaster crews had braved such dangers to place on the factory had failed to explode. The others did severe damage to two buildings, one a forging shop and the other a machine-tool store. Out of 2700 machine-tools, eight were destroyed, sixteen badly damaged and eighteen slightly damaged. Five cranes were also destroyed and six badly damaged. The total effect on production was negligible, especially as the Maschinenfabrik Augsburg-Nürnberg had five other factories engaged in building U-boat engines at the time.

It was the last time that the RAF sent its four-engined heavy bombers on a daylight 'extreme danger' mission of this kind. The low-level tactics had not worked; although the task of the enemy fighters had been made more difficult by the low altitude at which the bombers flew, this had not prevented them from destroying one-third of the attacking force within a very short space of time. Had the fighters not run short of fuel, they might well have accounted for the whole formation before it was even halfway to the target.

The Augsburg raid consequently spelt the end of the RAF's attempts at daylight precision bombing and laid the emphasis on the development of this technique at night. The basis of this had already been laid with the use of Gee, which called for an advance force of bombers to locate and illuminate the target; even so results had been far from consistent and, as we have seen, the advance force did not always succeed in placing its flares on the right spot.

If better results were to be achieved, two things were required: radar apparatus that was considerably more accurate than Gee, and a nucleus of specially trained crews to operate it. The staunchest advocate of this idea was Group Captain S. O. Bufton, the Deputy Director of Bomber Operations at the Air Ministry, who put it forward to Air Marshal Harris in the form of a firm proposal in March 1942. His suggestion was for a force of six squadrons, which would be entirely responsible for target marking.

At this stage, the Bomber Group Commanders and the C-in-C were opposed to Bufton's scheme. They did not object in principle to the idea of target marking by carefully selected and trained crews, but they strongly opposed the creation of a separate force within Bomber Command to do the job. They believed, with considerable justification, that such a step would inevitably be accompanied by the draining of the best crews from the front-line squadrons, with a consequent lowering of both efficiency and morale. Besides, Air Marshal Harris thought that the results achieved in area attacks so far in 1942 had been fairly satisfactory, and expressed the view that the majority of bombs dropped had landed in built-up areas close to the intended target. Group Captain Bufton did not agree with Harris's optimistic viewpoint; he insisted that the inaccuracy accompanying area attacks had been greater than Harris was prepared to admit, and pointed out that area attack in itself was not the ultimate in Bomber Command's achievement but simply a step along the road to the real goal of devastating precision attack.

In spite of what he said to Bufton, the C-in-C was very much alert to the enormous wastage of effort experienced in Bomber Command's area attacks, and expressed his concern about this to his Group Commanders on 22 May. He pointed out that bomber crews had been too easily misled by decoy fires and that many had bombed conflagrations started in the wrong place apparently without ascertaining whether they were aiming their bombs at the target or not. All this meant that the overall result of area attacks against such targets as Mannheim and Rostock had been disproportionately small in comparison with the size of the bomber force despatched. The bomber force could only justify itself if it could repeatedly make effective attacks, and much could be done to remedy the hit-or-miss nature of many raids.

Intentionally or not, Air Marshal Harris was using precisely the same argument as Group Captain Bufton. By June 1942, the thoughts of the two men were running even more closely parallel; although Harris was still opposed to the creation of a special force for target marking, he thought it would be a good idea if each group used selected crews to fly in advance of the main force to illuminate the target with flares and incendiaries, and on 12 June he went a step further by informing the CAS that he was prepared to allow this task to be performed regularly by special crews within individual squadrons.

Group Captain Bufton's objection to this latest idea was that such individual crews would not have adequate facilities for the special training that would be required; this could only be achieved by the formation of a separate force whose sole task was target indication. Bufton was now receiving considerable support from the Air Staff, including Sir Charles Portal himself, and on 14 June the latter wrote to Air Marshal Harris indicating the Air Staff's belief that the creation of such a force would be the best method of improving Bomber Command's standard of accuracy. Portal's letter was in the nature of a suggestion – the inference was that the final decision must rest with the C-in-C Bomber Command – but it produced the desired effect. The machinery for the creation of the special force was set in motion; nevertheless there were a lot of administrative problems to be solved and it was not until 15 August 1942, that the Pathfinder Force officially came into being.

The order for the formation of the PFF, in fact, reached Air Marshal Harris on 11 August in the form of a direct request from the Air Ministry. With its headquarters at Wyton, in Huntingdonshire, the new Force consisted originally of five squadrons, one drawn from each operational Group. From No. 1 Group came 156 Squadron, with Wellingtons, and from No. 2 Group 109 Squadron with Wellingtons and Mosquitoes. No. 3 Group provided 7 Squadron (Stirlings), No. 4 Group transferred 35 Squadron (Halifaxes) and No. 5 Group contributed the Lancasters of 83 Squadron. All five squadrons were based on adjacent airfields within the area of No. 3 Group; No. 7 at Oakington, No. 35 at Graveley, Nos. 83 and 109 at Wyton and No. 156 at Warboys. The commander of the new force was an Australian, Group Captain D. C. T. Bennett, a former CO of Nos. 77 and 10 Squadrons. He was to remain with the PFF throughout its wartime career.

12

The Storm Breaks,
July-December 1942

The first operation by the newly-formed Pathfinder Force was carried out on the night of 18-19 August 1942. The success of the mission depended entirely on the skill of the crews, for the PFF aircraft carried no equipment that was not carried by the aircraft of the main force and even Gee was now of doubtful value, for the enemy had perfected a technique for jamming it.

The target on this first operation was Flensburg, and the plan of attack was simple and rather crude compared with the technique developed by the PFF during the months that followed. The first crews located the target visually and dropped lines of illuminating flares across it; then by the light of the flares more crews identified details of the objective – the port – and dropped target indicators to mark an aiming point. This simple visual technique was greatly developed during the ensuing months, but on this occasion only slight damage was inflicted on Flensburg.

The value of the Pathfinder Force soon became apparent. Before its creation, only thirty-five per cent of the night photographs taken by bomber crews claiming to be over the target were in fact taken within three miles of the aiming-point; by December 1942 the percentage had risen to fifty, which indicated a steady increase in concentration. Nevertheless there were a number of problems that still had to be solved during the PFF's early experimental operations, and not the least of these was that target indicators dropped in the wrong place – as happened all too frequently – proved far more misleading to the crews of the main bomber stream than did German decoy fires and flares.

It was clear that some means had to be found which would

enable the PFF crews to place their target indicators with a much higher degree of accuracy, but in the autumn of 1942 – with so much depending on the good eyesight and skill of individual crews – it was too much to hope for a dramatic breakthrough. It was only with the introduction of two new radar aids, Oboe and H2S, that the accuracy curve began to climb sharply.

The first of these, Oboe, opened up a whole new field of possibilities, and the device remained in use until the end of the war. Two fixed stations were used in its operation, known as the tracking or 'cat' station and the releasing or 'mouse' station. Each of these had pulse-transmitter, receiver and distance-measuring equipment, while the aircraft was fitted with a transmitter-receiver. Pulses from the fixed stations, received and re-transmited by the aircraft, were picked up by the ground stations and the total time of travel since transmission was measured. This meant that the distance of the aircraft from each station was known all the time, which enabled the stations – by correlating their reading – to transmit their information to the aircraft in the form of a fix.

In order to reach a pre-determined position for blind bombing or target marking, the pilot used ordinary navigational methods until he reached a point on the appropriate position line of the 'cat' station, when he switched on his Oboe. If he was correctly positioned on the Oboe beam, a continuous aural signal was picked up; any deviation caused this to break up into a series of morse Es and Ts. The beam itself was only fifty feet across, so very precise flying was required of the pilot.

As the aircraft continued along the beam, distance-from-target signals – in the form of four morse Bs, Cs and Ds – were picked up at eight, five and three minutes' time from the objective. At five seconds from the release point, the pilot heard five half-second pips followed by a two and a half second dash, at the end of which he released his load.

The main limitation of Oboe was that, because of the curvature of the earth, its range was limited when the device was used at normal operational heights – about 200 miles at 25,000 feet. Later, however, it was extended when used in conjunction with Mosquitoes operating at 30,000 feet or more. Another drawback was that during the run-up to the target, which might last as long as fifteen minutes, the pilot had to fly at a constant height and airspeed to hold the beam, which greatly increased the aircraft's vulnerability to flak – not to mention imposing an enormous amount of extra strain on the crew.

The second radar blind-bombing and navigational device, H2S, did not enter service until January 1943, but it was used on the majority of PFF operations after that date. Closely related to ASV (Air to Surface Vessel) – the first airborne radar apparatus, demonstrated as early as September 1938 during Fleet manoeuvres – H2S enabled bomber crews to 'see' through darkness and cloud for bombing, target marking or navigation. The H2S scanner was mounted in a blister below the mid-upper turret of a Lancaster and rotated at 50 rpm, driven by an electric motor. The echoes received, according to their intensity, showed up more or less brightly on a cathode-ray tube and produced a radar picture of the landscape features below the aircraft. The biggest advantage of H2S was that it was a completely self-contained unit and was therefore independent of such factors as range from base. It was, however, quite heavy – about 700 lb – and its operation and interpretation required a considerable amount of skill. Also, it was quickly discovered that the pulses of some of the earlier marks of H2S could be detected by the enemy, giving away the bomber's position.

Nevertheless H2S was by far the most effective aid devised for use by Bomber Command up to that time. Winston Churchill, who kept a close watch on its development during the summer and autumn of 1942, was firmly enamoured of it and expressed frequent concern at the slow progress that accompanied testing and production.

'I am glad [he wrote in a minute to Sir Archibald Sinclair on 7 June 1942] you have arranged with the Minister of Aircraft Production for Sir Robert Renwick to make a personal effort to accelerate production of the needed radio equipment. But I hope you will not let him disperse his efforts on too many bits of apparatus. The main thing is to hit the target, and this we can do with H2S. All the other items are of course useful, but nothing like so urgent.'

H2S was first used operationally on the night of 30-1 January 1943, when Stirlings and Halifaxes of Nos. 7 and 35 Squadrons PFF equipped with the device led the main bomber stream in an attack on Hamburg. Oboe came into use five weeks earlier, on the night of 20-1 December 1942, when Mosquitoes of No. 109 Squadron used it to bomb the Lutterade power station in Holland.

The development of both these aids was just one aspect of a new form of warfare that was becoming characteristic of the RAF's strategic bombing operations and the activities of the German night-fighters against them: a secret war fought in the darkness, its weapons electronic pulses and radio waves. The war had really begun in earnest on the night of 27-8 February 1942, when Whitleys of No. 51 Squadron dropped a force of British paratroops on the German radar station at Bruneval. The paratroops were subsequently evacuated by the Royal Navy, taking with them key parts of the station's Würzburg radar equipment, and an examination of these by British experts led the way to the development of effective countermeasures.

In the summer of 1942, however, the Luftwaffe's Lichtenstein airborne interception radar was still very much an unknown quantity. In July, the British radio monitoring service discovered that the enemy night-fighters over Holland were using a device code-named 'Emil Emil', but the exact nature of this device was not known. A radio search detected signals apparently coming from the enemy equipment, but further information about it could only be gained in one way: by sending out special aircraft, fitted with radio detection equipment, over enemy territory. The crews of such aircraft faced an extremely hazardous mission, for to collect as much information as possible on the German device they had to allow themselves to be attacked by night-fighters fitted with it.

In the autumn of 1942 Wellingtons of the RAF's special radio detection flight, No. 174, carried out seventeen missions over Holland without once being intercepted by an enemy fighter. Then, on the night of 3-4 December 1942, the radio operator of an eighteenth Wellington picked up weak signals at 04.30, probably from German AI radar, on 487 Megacycles. The signal strength increased rapidly, and the crew knew then that the enemy fighter was 'locked on' to them.

A few moments later the Wellington was heavily attacked by a Junkers 88. The captain of the British aircraft, Pilot Officer Paulton, took violent evasive action and his rear-gunner returned the fire. The radio operator, Pilot Officer Jordan, was badly wounded by the night-fighter's first burst of cannon-fire; nevertheless he went on transmitting information about the enemy radar signals back to his base for some minutes before he collapsed.

The Junkers 88 finally broke off the attack when Paulton took the Wellington down in a long dive from 14,000 to 500 feet. The bomber was severely damaged; both its throttles were jammed, its gun turrets were out of action and most of its instruments had been smashed by shell splinters. As the aircraft limped homewards the second wireless operator, Flight-Sergeant Bigoray – although himself wounded in both legs – continued to transmit vital information.

The Wellington eventually 'ditched' 200 yards off the British coast and the crew was rescued. For their part in the mission, Pilot Officer Jordan received the DSO, the pilot was awarded the DFC and Flight-Sergeant Bigoray the DFM. Thanks to the efforts of these men, the scientists developed jamming apparatus which, when brought into operation in 1943, threw the enemy airborne radar into confusion. They also devised a device known as Serrate, which enabled RAF night-fighters – mingling with the bomber stream – to home on to Lichtenstein-equipped enemy aircraft.

In 1942, however, counter-measures such as these were still in the future. In the meantime Bomber Command could counter the enemy radar in two ways; by launching raids of such size that the enemy defences were saturated, and by launching attacks on the German night-fighter airfields and radar stations as well as on factories that supplied components for them. Such attacks accounted for a large proportion of the RAF's medium-bomber activities, both by day and night, during the summer and autumn of 1942.

Although heavy losses had compelled them to cease temporarily in November 1941, daylight 'Circus' operations had enjoyed a fair amount of success. Although there was no denying that they had failed in their primary object of bringing the Luftwaffe to combat, they had nevertheless forced the Germans to concentrate some of their best fighter squadrons in the area across the Channel to the detriment of operations elsewhere, and although the enemy fighters could still choose combat on their own terms the RAF had taken an important first step towards establishing air superiority over an area where the Allies would ultimately set foot on the Continent once more.

After a break of nearly four months Circus operations were resumed in March 1942, with sweeps by medium bombers and fighters intensified in an effort to prevent the Luftwaffe from building up its forces after the losses it had sustained during the winter fighting on the Eastern Front. The mainstay of 2 Group's bomber force on these operations was still the elderly Blenheim, but by the spring of 1942 the Douglas Boston was beginning to enter service in increasing numbers. The first action against a land target by these aircraft was carried out on 8 March, when aircraft of Nos. 88 and 226 Squadrons bombed the Matford works at Poissy while other machines from the same squadrons carried out diversionary attacks elsewhere.

On the night of 17-18 August 1942 the Blenheims of 2 Group flew their last operational sorties when aircraft of No. 18 Squadron attacked enemy airfields in Holland and Germany. In September, the operational strength of 2 Group stood at four squadrons, three of them (Nos. 88, 107 and 226, equipped with Bostons and one (No. 105) with Mosquitoes. One more squadron was working up on Mosquitoes, while the remainder were in the process of converting to two new types of American-built aircraft: the Lockheed Ventura and the North American Mitchell.

The Ventura, a military version of the Lodestar transport, had been produced to meet a British contract placed in the summer of 1940. It bore a strong resemblance to its stablemate, the Lockheed Hudson, but its dorsal gun turret was positioned further forward to give an improved field of fire and the underside of the fuselage was re-designed to accommodate a ventral turret. The initial RAF contract had called for 675 of these aircraft, of which the first 188 were delivered from the summer of 1942 as the Ventura Mk. I. The first 2 Group squadron to re-equip with the new type was No. 12, in October 1942, and they were first used operationally on 3 November. The primary target was the diesel works at Hengelo, but instead the Venturas attacked railway communications in Holland.

A more spectactular effort was mounted on 6 December, when ninety-three aircraft of 2 Group – Bostons, Venturas and Mosquitoes – were despatched to attack the Philips radio and valve factory at Eindhoven, believed to produce about a third of Germany's supply of radio components. The target consisted of two clusters of buildings covering an area of about seventy acres, and it was particularly attractive because it was surrounded by open country – a fact that cut the risk of inflicting civilian casualties on the Dutch down to an absolute minimum.

The attack was to be made at low level, with the aircraft flying in three waves: the first consisting of thirty-six Bostons, the second of ten Mosquitoes and the third of forty-seven Venturas. However, all did not work according to plan. The bombers were harried by enemy fighters long before they reached the target; the leading formation became dislocated and arrived late over the objective, becoming tangled up with the Mosquitoes in the second wave. Afterwards, instead of re-forming into one compact defensive formation, the bombers straggled back to base in small groups.

The Philips factory had been badly damaged, but the cost to the attacking force had been high. Nine Venturas, five Bostons and a Mosquito failed to return, and another thirty-seven

Venturas, thirteen Bostons and three Mosquitoes were damaged. The enemy fighters had accounted for some of the missing aircraft, but the main body of the Messerschmitts and Focke-Wulfs had been drawn away from the area by a diversionary attack on Lille carried out by the USAAF. Many of the heavy losses sustained by the Ventura formation – which had attacked at considerably lower level than the others – had been caused by aircraft colliding with unseen obstacles in the smoke over the target, and some had been shot down by light flak. Of the damaged aircraft that returned to base, thirty-one had been the victims of bird strikes – a hazard that accompanied all low-level daylight operations. The result did not encourage future operations of this kind, and the unsuitability of the Ventura as a day bomber was further tragically underlined on 3 May 1943, when ten out of eleven Venturas of No. 487 Squadron, RNZAF, were shot down during an attack on a power station in Amsterdam.

Although deep-penetration attacks by the RAF's heavy bombers in daylight were halted after the heavy loss suffered by the Lancasters of 5 Group in the raid on Augsburg of 17 April 1942, two more major daylight raids were carried out by these aircraft in the course of that year, one of them on a target involving a round trip greater than that of the Augsburg attack. The target was the submarine yards at Danzig, against which forty-four Lancasters were despatched on 11 July. Most of the low-level flight to the target was made over the sea, which made accurate navigation very difficult; about thirty-three per cent of the total force failed to locate Danzig at all, and the remainder arrived late. Because of this, most of the attack, which had been timed to begin at dusk, in fact took place in darkness. No fighters were encountered, but the bombers ran into a very heavy anti-aircraft barrage over the target; two failed to return and a further eight were damaged. Because most of the aircraft bombed from heights of up to 15,000 feet, this attack in the event differed little from an ordinary night raid.

The third daylight raid by Lancasters in 1942 was attended by a considerably greater element of risk than the Danzig attack.

On 17 October ninety-four Lancasters drawn from Nos. 9, 44, 49, 50, 57, 61, 97, 106 and 207 Squadrons set out to make a dusk attack on two targets that lay 330 miles inside French territory: the Schneider Armaments Factory at Le Creusot and the nearby transformer station at Montchanin. On both the outward and homeward flights the bombers flew a long dog-leg into the Atlantic to avoid the stiff fighter and anti-aircraft defences in Brittany, crossing the French coast to the south of the Ile du'Yeu. This detour stretched the overall length of the round trip to 1700 miles.

The attack went ahead at dusk as planned. Eighty-six Lancasters made attacks on the Schneider Factory and seven more on the transformer. The crews reported that both attacks had been very successful, but this impression was not borne out by subsequent reconnaissance. The photographs showed that only a small area of the factory had been hit, most of the bombs having apparently fallen on houses to the east of the target. No fighters were encountered during the raid – which was fortunate, for the venture could easily have turned into a repetition of the Augsburg disaster on a far more massive scale – but one Lancaster was shot down by flak.

Neither these major raids nor the number of small-scale daylight raids on German targets – carried out during the first half of 1942 mainly by Hampdens and Wellingtons, operating under heavy cloud cover – indicated that anything worthwhile was to be gained by a return to precision heavy bomber attacks in daylight. If Fighter Command had been in a position to escort such attacking forces all the way to the target and back, it might have been a different story, but Fighter Command still possessed no long-range escort machines. Neither for that matter did the Americans, and for this reason the Air Staff were sceptical of the USAAF's intention to carry out daylight attacks with massed formations of heavy bombers, despite the formidable armament carried by the latter. As it turned out, the Air Staff's view was justified; the USSAF, encouraged by the results of strong attacks on 'fringe' targets in France, began to send its unescorted bombers over Germany in January 1943 – and it was then that the slaughter began. It was not until the close of that year, with the arrival of the first long-range P-51 Mustang fighter units in Britain, that the crucifixion of the 8th US Air Force over Germany ended.

For the Royal Air Force – although its heavy bombers were used for tactical operations in daylight on many occasions, particularly after the Allied invasion of Normandy – the concept of strategic daylight bombing died in 1942. The only missions of this nature carried out subsequently by Bomber Command, at least until the closing months of the war when the Allied Air Forces ruled the sky, were undertaken by Mosquitoes – which were fast enough and manoeuvrable enough to elude the majority of enemy fighters. Yet even the use of these promising aircraft during 1942 had been accompanied by an unexpected degree of disappointment; an attempt to raid Berlin in daylight by six Mosquitoes of No. 105 Squadron on 19 September, for example, proved totally abortive. Two of the bombers aborted, two more bombed Hamburg instead of the primary (one of them after being attacked and damaged by Focke-Wulf 190s), and only one reached the target area, bombing through ten-tenths cloud by dead reckoning. The sixth aircraft was shot down by enemy fighters.

The close of 1942 saw Bomber Command in a position of ever-growing strength. Squadrons were progressively re-equipping with Lancasters, Halifaxes and Mosquitoes, and a new operational Group – No. 6 (RCAF) – was ready to go into action. For the first time, in November, Lancasters had raided Italy, attacking Milan in daylight after flying over southern France in thick cloud and dropping 8000-pound bombs on Turin. With the aid of Oboe and H2S the old enemy of the bomber crews, bad weather, was on the verge of being beaten; the Pathfinder Force was seeking out its targets and leading the night bombers to them with growing accuracy.

Nevertheless, there were those in high places who felt that the true role of Bomber Command had still not crystallized and that its policies, particularly area bombing, were serving no useful purpose. It was time for more precise definitions, for reassurances that lives and costly equipment were not being wasted.

On 21 January 1943, that reassurance came in the form of the Casablanca Directive, issued by the Combined Chiefs of Staff. It was a document that was to lead to the massive, non-stop RAF night offensive that would be called the Battle of the Ruhr, and to round-the-clock bombing by the RAF and USAAF.

The main theme of the Casablanca Directive was simple. It read : 'Your primary object will be the progressive destruction and dislocation of the German military, industrial and economic system, and the undermining of the morale of the German people to a point where their capacity for armed resistance is fatally weakened.'

In the skies of the Thousand-Year Reich, the storm was breaking.

13

The Assessment

The moral implications of strategic bombing have been the subject of heated and prolonged discussion for half a century or more. Millions of words have been written and spoken about the total immorality of unleashing high explosives on civilian populations, or – depending on which side of the fence one happens to be standing – on the justification for taking such a step.

The net result, at the end of years of argument, is that precisely nothing has been resolved, and it is not hard to find the reason. The simple truth is that once the first shell has been fired and the first bomb dropped, once two nations are irrevocably committed to a course of total war, the words 'morality' and 'immorality' have little meaning. In total war, there is no dividing line between the two; there are only varying degrees of horror. When the two nations are more or less evenly matched, victory almost invariably hinges on the ability of one antagonist to punch harder and faster, with all the means at his disposal, than his opponent. And in such a conflict, there are no civilians.

In 1940-2, with the swastika flying over all Europe, RAF Bomber Command was Britain's only means of striking at the enemy's vulnerable heart. Weak and puny those early blows may have been, but in them was carried the fury and the frustration of the entire British people. The idea that the British are a peace-loving race is an old fallacy. They are quick to react when interfered with, and when their lives and homes are threatened they are capable of hatred and anger more terrible and more sustained than that of any other nation on earth. This is a fact which has been ignored by historians of Britain's wars so often in the past, yet it must be understood if, in turn, the underlying motives behind the conduct of war by the British people and their leaders are to be fully appreciated.

Much has been written since the war about the qualms experienced by British politicians and by senior officers of the Air Staff and Bomber Command when the decision was taken to launch unrestricted air warfare against Germany's cities, and still more about the horror and revulsion of the bomber crews whose task it was to carry out the act of destruction night after night. Yet there is hardly anything in the records and diaries of the period to support any claim to such feelings, and still less in the reminiscences of bomber crews who survived. Few, if any, doubted at the time that the decision to hit the German cities hard was the right one, and it is only with hindsight that it may be said that the decision was fundamentally wrong – but the considerations in reaching this conclusion are strategic, not moral.

In switching the emphasis to area attacks on selected German cities from precision attacks on oil plants and other vital targets, Bomber Command committed much the same kind of error that the Luftwaffe made during the Battle of Britain – although under vastly different circumstances and with less far-reaching consequences. In the Luftwaffe's case, the abrupt switch from the primary objectives – fighter airfields and Fighter Command's logistics organization – at a time when Britain's defences were virtually beaten to their knees resulted in the RAF maintaining complete air superiority over the British Isles, thwarting the Germans' invasion plans and so altering the course of the war. In the case of Bomber Command, the changeover to area attacks came at a time when the ability of average crews to find and hit precision targets was showing a marked improvement; had Bomber Command followed an unbroken programme of systematic precision attacks on German industry during 1942, there is little doubt that these would have had a serious effect on the enemy's war effort in the critical year of 1943, when he began to suffer his first real reverses. As it was, the full impact of bombing was not felt by the German industry until 1944, when daylight precision attacks by the USAAF began to cause serious breakdowns in some sectors of the enemy's war machine.

Nevertheless the RAF's attacks on German cities might have

produced more favourable results for the Allied cause than was actually the case. The trouble was that right from the start they lacked any real cohesion. Night attacks on cities were, up to the end of 1942, largely a matter of opportunity; they depended on a whole range of factors, not the least of which was Bomber Command's extensive commitment to other types of operation. There was also the problem of the Command's relatively slow rate of expansion; because of the shortage of aircraft during the first two to three years of the war, Bomber Command – having committed itself to a policy of area attack – was forced to step up its raids on German cities gradually, which made it possible for the enemy to strengthen his defences and gave the German population time in which to become hardened to air attack. The result of the German reaction to the gradual increase in the size of the RAF's raids was apparent during the Battle of the Ruhr, the year-long assault on the cities in Germany's industrial heartland that began in April 1943, when Bomber Command suffered staggering losses on several occasions and the German people's will to go on fighting stubbornly refused to be broken. By this time the population had developed a fatalistic attitude to Allied bombing, and although morale was low after particularly heavy air attacks a grim determination to carry on 'business as usual' was never absent for long.

The Germans themselves admitted after the war that the population came close to panic for the first time after the thousand-bomber raid on Cologne; in addition to being of unprecedented size and fury, the attack was totally unexpected and its repercussions were felt even in those areas of Germany at that time immune from air bombardment. Air Marshal Harris's 'Thousand Plan' policy was, therefore, basically correct; all that was lacking was the means to carry out similar raids at regular intervals. A far greater impact might have been achieved if, in 1942, Bomber Command had followed a policy of carrying out relatively small-scale precision attacks on industrial targets while husbanding the greater part of its resources to strike once a month – as Harris had originally planned – at selected German cities with a thousand aircraft. If such attacks had been directed at cities that were key points in, say, the German armaments industry, Bomber Command might well have succeeded in causing a major breakdown in the enemy's war production machine by the end of 1942. The fact that this was entirely possible was brought home to the German leaders by Albert Speer, the Reichsminister of Armaments and War Production, following the first massive attack on Hamburg in August 1943. Air Marshal Harris was fully aware of this possibility at the beginning of 1942, but his hands were tied. To pin down almost the whole of Bomber Command's effort in attacks on half a dozen or so enemy cities was a total impossibility at that time, and even if heavy bombers had been available in sufficient numbers it is doubtful whether the War Cabinet would have authorized such a policy; it was too much in the nature of a gamble, with the possibility of disastrous consequences to Bomber Command if it failed to pay off.

It has been suggested on more than one occasion that Bomber Command's strategic night offensive against Germany during the first three years of the war was a total failure. This, however, is only partly true. In the material sense, certainly, Bomber Command made hardly any impression at all on the German war effort before the end of 1942; on the other hand, the psychological effect of those early raids on the German people – including the Nazi leadership – was perhaps much greater than historians have so far dared to suppose.

It was as a direct result of Bomber Command's raids on Germany – particularly the thousand-bomber attacks in 1942 – that Hitler became obsessed with the idea of devoting the Luftwaffe's resources to carrying out revenge raids on the British Isles. Continual pleas by the Luftwaffe High Command for the development of advanced fighter aircraft – particularly night-fighters – for the air defence of Germany went unheeded until it was too late; instead, Hitler insisted on the adaptation of large numbers of superlative day-fighters such as the Focke-Wulf 190 as fighter-bombers, a role to which they were totally unsuited, and ordered that new types of fighter aircraft then on the drawing-board or flying in prototype form should be modified to carry bombs. A classic example of this was the case of the Messerschmitt 262 jet fighter, which first flew in July 1942; this aircraft might easily have been in full production as a day-fighter by the end of 1943, destroying all hope of the Allied Air Forces gaining a decisive victory in the Battle of Germany. Instead, months were wasted while – on Hitler's orders – various armament installations, particularly bomb-racks, were tried out on the prototypes. It was not until the spring of 1944 that a pre-production batch of 262s was built, and then production was set back still further by a series of heavy precision attacks on the Messerschmitt factory at Regensburg by the USAAF.

It is impossible to assess the full effect of Bomber Command's offensive on the morale of all sectors of the German people up to the end of 1942. What is certain, however, is that the RAF's attacks on cities had a more apparent effect on the German fighting troops than it had on the civilian population. This was particularly true of the men fighting on the Russian Front from the winter of 1941-2 onwards, when a progressive breakdown of communications often made it impossible for front-line troops to learn the fate of their families for days and sometimes weeks after they first learned that their home towns had been bombed. The uncertainty, the agony of waiting for news, combined with the intense suffering of the Wehrmacht's soldiers on the Eastern Front to produce a growing disillusionment with the Nazi leaders; the brash promises of earlier days that no enemy aircraft would ever fly over the Reich were remembered with increasing hatred for those who had made them.

In the final analysis, the outcome of any conflict – whatever the material damage inflicted on one side by the other – depends to a great extent on the will of the antagonists to go on fighting. To quote a more up-to-date example, the American bombing of North Vietnam – although it left a complete cross-section of the country's economy in ruins – failed uttterly to break the will of the North Vietnamese people; in fact, quite the reverse was true. It would, of course, be useless to try and draw any conclusions from a lengthy comparison between the American bombing of North Vietnam and the air offensive against Germany, as the matter involves not only two different types of war but also two alien ideologies and mentalities. There is, however, room for one definite comparison between the two offensives; a comparison that concerns the effect of sustained bombing on the morale, not of the civilian population subjected to the weight of the air attacks, but of the bomber crews themselves.

In the case of both the British offensive against Germany and the American air attacks on North Vietnam, crew morale was at its lowest at a time when the assault was still developing. The heavy losses that accompanied an increase in the scale of the offensive, although producing a sharp rise in stress and nervous tension, did not – curiously enough – bring about a further drop in morale. Instead, the routine of delivering nightly and daily loads of bombs brought with it a strange sense of inevitability; the crews became, for want of a better expression, punch-drunk. The same was true of the USAAF crews operating in the European theatre, but to a much lesser extent; the tour of operations flown by the average USAAF bomber crew over Europe was too short for any similar type of conditioning to take place.

At the end of 1942, RAF Bomber Command's crews had not yet reached this 'conditioned' stage. Morale, although far from rock bottom, was nevertheless still low enough to cause serious concern. It was only when Bomber Command began to strike telling blows at Germany's cities with the aid of its new heavy bombers in 1942 that the morale of the crews began to rise. The reasons for the disenchantment that prevailed before this time is, perhaps, best summed up in the words of two of the men who fought through those bitter years from 1939 to 1942, and who survived. The first was a wireless operator/air gunner who flew in Hampdens and later Manchesters, and the second a former Blenheim pilot.

'What I remember most about those early days [says the first] is the sheer boredom. True, there were moments of blind panic – on my first operation in July 1940, for example, we were bracketed by flak over Hamm and the aircraft turned completely over before the skipper regained control – but for the most part there wasn't a great deal to do. There was plenty of frustration, though; I lost count of the number of times during the first couple of years when we were briefed to go out on a job, only to be told at the last minute – when the aircraft was all fuelled and bombed-up – that it was scrubbed. This sort of thing had a far worse effect on us than actually flying on operations. Sometimes the reason was obvious – such as bad weather – but more often than not we just didn't know what was going on. Apart from air tests, there wasn't much we could do except go to the pictures or for a pint and curse everybody from the Station Commander upwards.

'When we did go off on operations, our own equipment gave us more trouble than the enemy did. When the flak came up there was usually a lot of it, but on many occasions we flew all the way to the target and back without even seeing so much as one searchlight. It was nothing like as dramatic as people imagine. In two years of operational flying I never saw an enemy fighter by day or night.

'The only time I started to get really frightened was when we converted on to Manchesters. During my very first trip in a Manchester the port engine burst into flames and we scraped in by the skin of our teeth. On another occasion we took a Manchester from Waddington to Boscombe Down to have some equipment fitted, and were marooned there for a week because the engines wouldn't start. Soon after that I went sick and was in hospital for three months. I'm convinced to this day that it saved my life; I lost a hell of a lot of good mates in Manchesters. They were bastards.'

The Blenheim pilot has a rather different story to tell. As a member of a squadron within No. 2 Group, his most vivid recollection is of the 'Circus' operations carried out in the spring of 1942.

'I can remember flying a lot of sorties without seeing anything, too, but when the Luftwaffe did come up all hell was let loose. Our Spitfire escort could usually cope with Messerschmitt 109s, but the Focke-Wulf 190s always got through, and they made mincemeat out of us. One thing sticks in my mind very vividly. We had had a very hectic week, with almost continual operations in the Pas de Calais area and heavy losses. We were so keyed up we practically didn't know what we were doing. Then, on the last mission, half our escort didn't show up on time and we lost three out of six aircraft. As we turned back towards the coast, I remember thinking that if I'd had an Air Marshal in front of my nose gun I'd have shot him without a moment's hesitation. It was totally irrational, looking back, but a lot of us felt like that at the time.

'Then, suddenly, as we flew along at low level, I saw some-one cycling along a road. Without thinking, I let him have it. He fell off his bike into a ditch. I've often wondered since who he was, and whether I hit him, but at the time I didn't give a damn. I fired out of sheer bloody-mindedness, and I know I wasn't the only one who did something of the sort.

'That was what the kind of war we fought did to a man.'

Appendices

ABBREVIATIONS

AASF Advanced Air Striking Force
A/C Aircraft
DFC Distinguished Flying Cross
E/A Enemy aircraft
F/Gunner Front Gunner
Fg Off (F/O) Flying Officer
FTR Failed to return
IAS Indicated air speed
IFF Identification friend or foe
Plt Off (P/O) Pilot Officer
R/Gunner Rear Gunner

SAP Semi-armour-piercing
S/B Starboard
S/E Single-engined
S/L Searchlight
Sqn Ldr (S/L) Squadron Leader
U/C Undercarriage
U/S Unserviceable
VC Victoria Cross
W/Op Wireless Operator
Wng Cdr Wing Commander
WW2 Second World War

APPENDIX I : CHRONOLOGY OF BOMBER COMMAND
OPERATIONS, 1939–42

September 1939

3 Blenheim IV N6215 of 139 Sqn photographs units of
the German Fleet in the Schillig Roads; first British aircraft
to cross the German frontier in WW2. Crew : Fg Off A.
McPherson, Cdr Thompson, RN, and Cpl V. Arrowsmith.

Armed reconnaissances flown over the North Sea as far as
the Heligoland Bight by 37 Sqn (6 Wellingtons), 44 (9
Hampdens), 49 (3 Hampdens), 83 (6 Hampdens) and 149
(3 Wellingtons).

3–4 First 'Nickel' or leaflet raid carried out on Germany by
Whitleys of 51 Sqn (3 a/c over Hamburg and N. Germany) and 58 Sqn (7 a/c over the Ruhr).

4 Ten Blenheims (five from 107 and five from 110 Sqn)
despatched to attack German warships in the Schillig
Roads, Four a/c of 107 Sqn and one of 110 FTR. Three
of 110 Sqn a/c bombed the *Admiral Scheer*, but with no
result. Raid leader Flt Lt K. C. Doran of 110 Sqn, subsequently awarded DFC. Failure of raid attributed to
' dud ' 500-pound bombs.

Six Wellingtons of 9 and eight of 149 Sqn despatched to
attack enemy surface forces at Brunsbüttel. Two of 9 Sqn
a/c FTR. One merchant vessel reported hit and set on
fire; no other result observed.

4–5 Three Whitleys of 102 Sqn drop leaflets on the Ruhr.

5–6 Two Whitleys of 77 Sqn drop leaflets on the Ruhr.

8–9 Two Wellingtons of 99 Sqn drop leaflets on Hanover.

9 Three Battles of 226 Sqn, AASF, reconnoitre the area
around Thionville.

10 Three Battles of 150 Sqn, ASF, reconnoitre the Franco-
German border.

September (cont)

15 HQ BEF Air Component created in France under Air Vice-Marshal C. H. B. Blount.

17 Three Battles of 103 Sqn and three of 218 reconnoitre Franco-German frontier in the Bouzonville-Lautenbourg area.

20 Three Battles of 88 Sqn despatched to patrol Franco-German border, operations having been curtailed for two days because of bad weather. Formation attacked by Bf 109s over Aachen and two Battles destroyed. R/Gunner of Battle K9243, Sgt F. Letchford, shot down one 109 – the first e/a claimed by the RAF in WW2.

22 Photo-reconnaissance over Homberg area of Franco-German frontier by five Battles of 142 Sqn.

26 144 Sqn carries out its first operational mission of the war : an armed reconnaissance over the North Sea to within twelve miles of enemy coast by twelve Hampdens. Two unidentified submarines sighted.

29 Photo-recce over enemy lines by six Battles of 105 Sqn, AASF.

Three Hampdens of 144 Sqn bomb two enemy destroyers in the Heligoland Bight. No results observed. Five more a/c of same squadron shot down by enemy fighters.

30 Five Battles of 150 Sqn despatched on a reconnaissance of the Saarbrücken area. Four a/c shot down by enemy fighters; Battles subsequently withdrawn from daylight operations until May 1940.

October 1939

1–2 Three Whitleys of 10 Sqn drop propaganda leaflets over Berlin – the first British a/c to fly over the German capital in WW2.

6 Six Wellingtons of 115 Sqn carry out an armed search for enemy warships reported to be off the Norwegian coast, but with no result.

13 One Blenheim of 57 Sqn, BEF Air Component, (pilot Wng Cdr H. M. A. Day) takes off from Metz at 11.40 hrs to carry out a recce of roads and railways in the Hamm-Hanover-Soest area and FTR. Two more Blenheims of 114

October (cont)

Sqn take off from Villeneuve to reconnoitre the Ruhr area; one completes the sortie, the other FTR.

16 Two Blenheims of 18 Sqn carry out a recce of the Siegfried Line and two more photograph areas of NW Germany. 18 Sqn's first operational mission of WW2.

27–8 Whitleys of 4 Group carry out their eighth leaflet raid of the month on Germany, 'Nickelling' the Düsseldorf-Frankfurt area in severe weather conditions.

November 1939

17 Four Blenheims of 21 Sqn, flying their first successful mission of the war, carry out a photo-recce of Wilhelmshaven and the Heligoland Bight.

Six Wellingtons of 39 Sqn carry out an armed recce over the North Sea : the Squadron's first war patrol.

December 1939

3 Enemy warships off Heligoland bombed by Wellingtons of 38, 115 and 149 Sqn. Two a/c of 38 Sqn attack the target and a third jettisons its bombs when intercepted by an enemy fighter; seven a/c of 115 and five of 149 Squadrons also attack the target. All twenty-four Wellingtons despatched return to base.

12 Following mine-laying operations by the enemy in British waters, Bomber Command is authorized to begin offensive patrols over German seaplane bases on Sylt, Borkum and Norderney.

12–13 Whitleys of 77 and 102 Sqns, operating in pairs, fly eight sorties against the enemy seaplane bases. No bombs fall on land.

13 Whitley of 51 Sqn attacks an unidenified submarine in the North Sea. Bombs miss the target and the submarine subsequently turns out to be British.

14 Armed reconnaissance over the North Sea carried out by Hampdens of 50 Sqn, this unit's first operational mission in WW2.

Twelve Wellingtons of 3 Group despatched from New-

December (cont)

market to carry out an armed patrol of the Schillig Roads. The bombers are subjected to concerted attacks by Bf 109s and 110s and five of them FTR.

18   Twenty-four Wellingtons of 9, 37 and 149 Sqn despatched to attack enemy warships in the Schillig Roads, Jade Estuary and Wilhelmshaven. Twelve Wellingtons FTR, destroyed by enemy fighters.

25   Eleven Hampdens of 61 Sqn, flying their first operational mission of the war, carry out an armed reconnaissance over the North Sea.

January 1940

12–13   Whitleys of 77 Sqn, operating out of Villeneuve, drop leaflets on Prague and Vienna.

February 1940

29   Eight Hampdens of 83 Sqn carry out an armed reconnaissance of the North Sea and one a/c attacks an unidentified submarine. No results observed.

Leaflet raids continue on a small scale, but all Bomber Command operations during this month and the previous one are severely hampered by bad weather.

March 1940

6   Wellingtons of 3 Group and Hampdens of 5 Group join 4 Group's Whitleys in making night reconnaissance flights over potential targets in Germany.

7–8   A Hampden of 61 Sqn, carrying out an offensive patrol of the Sylt-Borkum-Norderney triangle, bombs a German destroyer which opens fire on it. No results observed. A Whitley of 77 Sqn drops leaflets on Poznan, Poland.

11   Blenheim IV P4852 of 82 Sqn (Sqn Ldr M. V. Delap) hits the German submarine U-31 with two bombs in the Schillig Roads and sinks it. The RAF's first U-boat 'kill'.

19–20   First attack by the RAF on a land target, in reply to German bombing of Hoy in the Orkneys three days earlier. Twenty-six Whitleys of 10, 51, 77 and 102 Sqns (out of thirty despatched) and fifteen Hampdens of 44, 50, 61 and

March (cont)

> 144 Sqns (out of twenty despatched) claim to have success-
> fully attacked the seaplane base at Hörnum on the island
> of Sylt. Attack led by Whitley Mk V N1380 (Sqn Ldr
> J. C. Macdonald) of 102 Sqn. Negligible results; one
> Whitley FTR.

April 1940

4   First Commonwealth Squadron in Bomber Command, 75
    Sqn (New Zealand), formed at RAF Feltwell in Norfolk.

4–8   Formation of 10-17 Operational Training Units, the first
    in Bomber Command.

11   Following the German invasion of Denmark and Norway,
    Bomber Command is authorized to make its first raid on
    a mainland target. Three Wellingtons of 115 Squadron, out
    of six despatched, bomb Stavanger/Sola airfield. Fighter
    escort provided by two Blenheims of 254 Sqn, Coastal
    Command. One Wellington out of the three which did
    not bomb the target FTR.

    Hampdens and Wellingtons of 3 and 5 Groups, operating
    from bases in northern Scotland, begin offensive operations
    against enemy surface forces in Norwegian waters. Initial
    plans for daylight attacks frustrated through lack of cloud
    cover.

13-14   Bomber Command begins mine-laying operations in enemy
    waters. Fifteen Hampdens of 44, 49, 50, 61 and 144 Sqns
    lay mines off the Danish coast. One a/c FTR.

15   Six Blenheims of 107 Sqn, out of twelve despatched, attack
    Stavanger/Sola.

15–16   Twelve Whitleys of 10 and 102 Sqns despatched to attack
    Stavanger/Sola. Seven a/c claim to have bombed success-
    fully.

17–18   First successful bombing missions by 37, 75 and 99 Sqns.
    Total of fourteen Wellingtons despatched to bomb Stavan-
    ger/Sola. Five a/c aborted and one (99 Sqn) FTR.

18–19   Two Whitleys of 58 Sqn bomb Oslo/Fornebu airfield.

20–1   Two Hampdens of 83 Sqn bomb Aalborg airfield, Denmark.

May 1940

10 Germans invade Holland, Belgium and Luxembourg. First sorties against enemy columns flown by Battles of AASF; thirty-two a/c drawn from 12, 103, 105, 142, 150, 218 and 226 Sqns. Two attacks flown during the course of the afternoon; twenty Battles FTR and most of the survivors damaged.

Nine Blenheims of 15 Sqn bomb Waalhaven airport and nine Blenheims of 40 Sqn attack Ypenburg, also strafing enemy transports parked along the beaches between The Hague and Noordwijk. Four a/c FTR.

10–11 Raid on Waalhaven by thirty-six Wellingtons of 3 Group, causing some damage to airport buildings. Eight Whitleys of 77 and 102 Sqns carry out the first bombing raid on Germany, attacking lines of communication in the Geldern, Goch, Aldekerk, Rees and Wesel areas.

11 Eight Battles of 88 and 218 Sqns detailed to attack enemy columns advancing through Luxembourg. Seven a/c FTR; because of crippling losses, no further sorties flown by Battles on this day.

11–12 Eighteen Whitleys (51, 58, 77 and 102 Sqns) and eighteen Hampdens (44, 49, 50, 61 and 144 Sqns) detailed to attack road and rail communications around München-Gladbach. Five Hampdens aborted and three a/c (two Hampdens and one Whitley) FTR.

12 Bridges across the Albert Canal at Vroenhoven and Veldwezelt attacked by five Battles of 12 Sqn. Four aircraft FTR. Fg Off D. E. Garland and Sgt T. Gray posthumously awarded the RAF's first VCs of the war.

One Blenheim of 57 Sqn, Air Component, attacks Chaulnes during an armed reconnaissance mission (Sqn's first bombing attack of the war.)

Blenheims of 114 Sqn, AASF, suffer heavy losses on the ground when the squadron's base at Condé Vraux is bombed.

Nine Blenheims of 139 Sqn, AASF, attack enemy columns in the Maastricht-Tongeren axis. Formation attacked by enemy fighters and seven a/c FTR.

May (cont)

12–13   Bridges over the Albert Canal attacked by twelve Blenheims of 15 Sqn. Six a/c FTR; remainder all badly damaged.

Battles of the AASF fly fifteen more sorties against enemy columns in the Bouillon area; six a/c FTR. During the operations of 12 May, sixty-two per cent of all Battles despatched FTR.

13   Only one sortie flown by the AASF; small number of Battles from 226 Sqn bomb a factory in order to block the road near Breda and delay enemy advance.

14   One Blenheim of 114 Sqn attacks an enemy column near Bosseval. (First bombing attack made by the squadron in WW2.)

Ten Battles of 103 and 150 Sqns detailed to attack pontoon bridges near Sedan during the morning; mission completed without loss.

In the afternoon, all available Battles and Blenheims of the AASF are detailed to attack pontoon bridges and troop concentrations in the Sedan area. The seventy-one a/c taking part suffer crippling losses, as follows : 12 Sqn – four out of five; 142 – four out of eight; 226 – three out of six; 105 – six out of eleven; 150 all four; 114 – one out of two; 139 – four out of six; 88 – one out of ten; 103 – three out of eight and 218 – ten out of eleven. This represents a loss of fifty-six per cent of the entire force committed – the highest ever suffered by the RAF in an operation of this size.

15   War Cabinet authorizes Bomber Command to attack targets east of the Rhine.

15–16   Small force of Battles makes night attack on enemy bridgehead at Sedan; no losses.

The strategic air offensive against Germany begins. Ninety-nine Wellingtons, Whitleys and Hampdens of 3, 4 and 5 Groups despatched to bomb oil and steel plants and communications in the Ruhr. Results insignificant.

16   105 and 218 Sqns AASF disbanded; surviving crews and aircraft transferred to other units.

17   Twelve Blenheims of 82 Sqn despatched from the UK to

May (cont)

attack enemy concentrations in the Gembloux area. Eleven a/c FTR, one destroyed by flak and the remainder by enemy fighters. Surviving a/c badly damaged.

20 Battles of the AASF re-commence operations with small-scale night attacks against enemy communications.

20–1 Aircraft of 2, 3, 4 and 5 Groups step up night attacks on enemy bridgeheads, road and rail communications.

21/2 AASF Battles fly twelve sorties against enemy columns in the Arras area. More sorties flown the following morning against columns approaching Boulogne.

22 Blenheims of 2 Group make successful dusk attack on the HQ of a German mechanized division at Ribecourt.

27–8 Battles fly thirty-six sorties against enemy airfields, dumps and communications. This brings the total of sorties flown since 20 May to 200, for the loss of one a/c.

Bomber Command – particularly Wellingtons of 3 Group – begins intensive night bombing operations in Dunkirk area in support of 'Operation Dynamo'.

June 1940

3 Surviving Battles of AASF withdrawn to new bases in the Le Mans area.

Orders issued for the creation of British bombing force (Haddock Force) to attack targets in Italy from bases near Marseilles.

10 Italy declares war on Britain and France; initial attempt by Haddock Force to attack allotted targets frustrated by French non-co-operation.

11–12 Thirty-six Whitleys of 4 Group, drawn from 10, 51, 58, 77 and 102 Squadrons, despatched to bomb targets in Italy, refuelling in the Channel Islands. Twenty-three a/c abort because of severe weather; ten claim attacks on primary (Fiat works in Turin) or alternates. Two more bomb Genoa. One a/c FTR.

13 Ten Battles of AASF attack enemy columns along the Seine in the morning and thirty-eight more strafe troops on the Marne in the afternoon. Six a/c FTR.

June (cont)

14–15 Wellingtons of 214 Sqn drop incendiary bombs on the Black Forest east of Oberkirch-Geubach. 214's first operational mission of the war.

15 All serviceable Battles of the AASF ordered to be evacuated to England.

15–16 Eight Wellingtons of 99 and 149 Sqns despatched from Salon, near Marseilles, to bomb the Ansaldo factory in Genoa. One a/c of 149 Sqn claims a successful attack, the remainder bring their bombs back.

16–17 Aircraft of 99 and 149 Sqns claim successful attacks on industrial targets in Genoa and Milan. Last attack by a/c of Haddock Force; Wellingtons flown back to UK the following day.

18 Last RAF squadrons evacuated from France.

Beginning of phase two of Bomber Command's air offensive against Germany; attacks on aircraft factories, aluminium and oil plants and communications.

July 1940

1–2 Hampden L4070 of 83 Sqn (Fg Off G. P. Gibson) drops Bomber Command's first operational 2000-pound SAP bomb over Kiel. After six attempts to bomb warships in the harbour, the bomb finally falls in the town itself because of a defect in the release mechanism.

2–3 Sixteen Whitleys of 4 Group despatched to bomb the marshalling yards at Hamm. Ten a/c claim successful attack.

3–4 Ten Wellingtons of 3 Group claim successful attacks on the Focke-Wulf factory at Bremen and an airframe factory at Wenzendorf.

4 First operational mission by 101 Sqn in WW2; three Blenheims despatched to bomb oil targets at Ostermoor, Harburg and Oslenhausen. Two a/c abort and the third bombs Ostermoor.

4–5 Wellingtons of 3 Group claim successful attack on oil refineries at Emmerich.

7–8 Wellingtons of 3 Group claim attacks on marshalling yards at Osnabrück.

July (cont)

19–20 First operational mission by 78 Sqn; four Whitleys despatched to bomb Gelsenkirchen. One a/c bombs primary; the others bomb marshalling yards at Recklinghausen and a factory.

22–3 Nineteen Hampdens of 5 Group claim to have bombed the synthetic oil plant at Gelsenkirchen.

27–8 Wellingtons of 3 Group claim hits on oil refineries in Hamburg.

August 1940

2 First Short Stirling bomber enters service with 7 Sqn at RAF Leeming, Yorkshire.

8 Opening of initial phase of Battle of Britain with attacks tensifies its attacks on barges in enemy-held ports; these operations, which began on a small scale on 15 July, comprise Bomber Command's main effort until the end of on coastal towns and shipping. Bomber Command in-October.

12–13 Five Hampdens of 49 and 83 Sqns detailed to attack the Dortmund-Ems Canal. Mission successful; Flt Lt R. A. B. Learoyd of 49 Sqn awarded VC. Two a/c FTR.

17–18 Bomber Command's offensive against oil targets continues with the first of ten attacks on the plant at Leuna.

25–6 First raid by Bomber Command on Berlin. Industrial targets in the city attacked in reprisal for Luftwaffe bombing of London. Eighty-one Wellingtons, Whitleys and Hampdens of 3, 4 and 5 Groups despatched. Dense cloud down to 2000 feet over the target. Twenty-nine crews claim to have bombed Berlin; twenty-seven more believed they were over the city but could not locate targets : return to base with bombs on board or jettison bombs in the sea. Eighteen others claim bombing of alternate targets; seven a/c aborted and five FTR. Aircraft claiming successful attacks are from 44, 49, 50, 58, 61, 83 and 99 Sqn.

September 1940

9–10 First operational mission by 106 Sqn; mine-laying by three Hampdens off the French coast.

10–11 First operational mission by 311 (Czechoslovakia) Sqn.

September (cont)

Three Wellingtons despatched to bomb Antwerp-Deurne; one a/c bombed the primary, another a canal near Brussels and the third aborted.

14–15 First operational missions by 300 and 301 (Polish) Sqns; three a/c from each bomb barges in Boulogne harbour.

15–16 Hampdens of 83 Sqn bomb barges at Antwerp. Sgt John Hannah awarded VC for extinguishing severe blaze in his a/c over the target.

October 1940

7–8 Thirty Wellingtons of 3 Group and twelve Whitleys of 4 Group despatched to attack industrial targets in Berlin. Thirty-three a/c claim primaries attacked and seven more report attacks on alternates. One Wellington FTR and one crashes on return to UK.

15–16 Last operational sorties by Battles of Bomber Command; attacks on Boulogne by 301 Sqn and on Calais by 12 and 142 Sqns.

November 1940

6 Avro Manchester enters service with 207 Sqn at Boscombe Down. First a/c delivered is Mk I L7279.

7–8 Wellingtons, Hampdens and Blenheims despatched to attack the Krupp armament factory at Essen. Successful attacks claimed by twenty Wellingtons, six Blenheims and twenty-four Hampdens, but subsequent reconnaissance shows that few bombs fell in the target area.

13 Halifax enters service with 35 Sqn at Boscombe Down. First a/c delivered Mk I L9486.

13–14 Two Wellingtons of the RAF's Wireless Intelligence Unit, fitted with special equipment, deliver attacks on 'Knickebein' stations in the Low Countries after homing in on the enemy radio beams. One station badly damaged.

16–17 127 aircraft of Bomber Command despatched to raid Hamburg; largest RAF bombing operation in a single-night to date.

December 1940

16–17   134 a/c despatched to Mannheim on Bomber Command's first 'area' attack of the war. (Operation Abigail.) Forty-seven Wellingtons, thirty-three Whitleys, eighteen Hampdens and four Blenheims claim successful attacks.

January 1941

10   Six Blenheims of 114 Sqn, escorted by six squadrons of fighters of 11 Group, attack enemy supply dumps in France during the first RAF 'Circus' operation.

February 1941

10–11   First operation by Stirling bombers; attack on oil storage depot at Rotterdam by a/c of 7 Sqn.

Whitleys of 78 Sqn drop paratroops in Italian territory in a combined operation to destroy an aqueduct at Tragino (Operation Colossus).

24–5   First operation by Avro Manchesters; attack on warships in Brest harbour by a/c of 207 Sqn.

March 1941

1–2   First bombing attack by 106 Sqn; four Hampdens bomb Cologne.

10–11   First operational mission by Halifaxes of 35 Sqn. Six a/c despatched to attack Le Havre dockyard; four bomb primary, one bombs Dieppe and one aborts. One a/c shot down by British night-fighter over Surrey on return flight; two survivors.

12–13   First raid on Germany by new RAF heavy bombers; Halifaxes and Manchesters attack Hamburg.

Fifty-four Wellingtons of 3 Group despatched to bomb Focke-Wulf factory at Bremen and thirty-two Blenheims of 2 Group detailed to attack town centre. Thirty-three Wellingtons claim successful attack on the factory, but subesequent reconnaissance shows that only twelve bombs hit the target.

30–1   Beginning of Bomber Command's offensive against enemy battle-cruisers in French Atlantic ports.

April 1941

1 First operational use of 4000-pound bombs by Bomber Command. Two dropped on Emden in early hours of the morning by Wellingtons of 9 and 149 Sqns.

8–9 First operational mission in WW2 by 97 Sqn. Four Manchesters attack shipyards at Kiel.

14 Arrival of the first Boeing Fortress I destined for Bomber Command in Britain. Lands at Prestwick after the shortest Atlantic crossing yet recorded; 8 hrs 26 mins from Gander.

25–6 First operational missions by 304 and 305 (Polish) Sqns; one Wellington of 304 and three of 305 bomb oil storage tanks at Rotterdam.

27 First daylight mission by Stirlings; aircraft of 7 Sqn attack Emden.

May 1941

7 First Bomber Command Fortress Sqn formed: 90.

8–9 First operational mission by 104 Sqn in WW2. Six Wellingtons despatched to bomb Bremen. Four a/c bomb primary, one bombs Wilhelmshaven and one aborts.

360 aircraft despatched to bomb Bremen and Hamburg – the largest number so far sent out by Bomber Command in one night.

June 1941

12–13 First operational mission by 76 Sqn. Three Halifaxes despatched to bomb Hüls; one bombs Essen and the others abort.

First operational mission by 405 (Vancouver) Sqn, RCAF. Three Wellingtons bomb marshalling yards at Schwerte.

22 Inauguration of first three 'Gee' stations in the British Isles: at Ventnor, Daventry and Stenigot.

30 First daylight attack by Halifaxes of Bomber Command – on Kiel by six a/c of 35 Sqn.

July 1941

4 Daylight attack on Bremen by Blenheims of 105 and 107 Sqns. Fifteen a/c despatched; three abort and four FTR.

July (cont)

    Raid leader, Wng Cdr H. I. Edwards of 105 Sqn, awarded
    VC.

 8 First operational mission by Fortresses of 90 Sqn; daylight
    attack on Wilhelmshaven.

 23 Attack on the *Scharnhorst* at La Pallice by six Stirlings.
    One a/c FTR.

 24 Daylight attacks by seventy-eight Wellingtons, Hampdens
    and Fortresses on the *Gneisenau* and *Prinz Eugen* at Brest
    and on the *Scharnhorst* at La Pailice by fifteen Halifaxes
    under cover of diversionary 'Circus' carried out by Blen-
    heims in the Cherbourg area. Sixteen a/c (including five
    Halifaxes) FTR.

August 1941

11–12 First operational mission by 408 (Goose) Sqn, RCAF. Two
    Hampdens bomb Rotterdam docks and two more abort.

    Two Wellingtons of 115 Sqn make first use of Gee during
    a raid on München-Gladbach.

 12 Fifty-four Blenheims of 2 Group make large-scale daylight
    attack on two power stations near Cologne. Deepest day-
    light penetration so far. Bombers escorted to the target
    area by Whirlwinds of 263 Sqn. Attack made in con-
    junction with diversionary 'Circus' operations.

29–30 First operational mission by 455 Sqn, RAAF; attack on
    Frankfurt docks by one Hampden.

September 1941

 8 Two Fortresses of 90 Sqn destroyed by enemy fighters
    during a daylight mission over Norway; a third a/c, badly
    damaged, is written off in a crash-landing at Kinloss.

 25 Last operational mission by the Fortresses of 90 Sqn over
    Europe; an abortive sortie against Emden.

October 1941

12–13 First operational sortie by the famous Stirling N6086
    F-Freddie 'MacRobert's Reply' of 15 Sqn. A/c donated
    by Lady MacRobert in memory of her three sons, killed
    flying.

October (cont)

20–1 First operational mission by 458 Sqn, RAAF. Two Wellington Mk IVs despatched to Emden and eight to Antwerp.

November 1941

7–8 400 a/c of Bomber Command despatched to Berlin, Mannheim, the Ruhr, Ostend, Boulogne and Oslo. Thirty-seven
a/c FTR, about twenty-five running out of fuel when they
encounter strong headwinds during the return flight. Because of heavy losses in this and previous raids, Prime
Minister orders Bomber Command to conserve a/c and
carry out raids on a much reduced scale. Heavy losses in
daylight Circus operations bring about a temporary sus-
pension of the latter.

15 Mosquito light bomber enters service with 105 Sqn at
RAF Swanton Morley.

December 1941

24 Lancaster Mk I enters service with 44 Sqn at RAF Waddington.

During December, Stirlings of 7 and 15 Sqns make a series
of attacks on the *Scharnhorst* and *Gneisenau* using an early
type of blind-bombing device known as 'Trinity'.

January 1942

11 First operational mission by 419 (Moose) Sqn, RCAF. Two
Wellingtons despatched to Brest.

21–2 First operational mission by 420 (Snowy Owl) Sqn, RCAF.
Five Hampdens despatched to bomb Emden; two a/c
bomb primary, two bomb alternates and one FTR. One
other Hampden lays mines off the Frisian Islands.

28–9 Last operational mission by 458 Sqn, RAAF, in Bomber
Command; two Wellingtons bomb Boulogne harbour. Sqn
subsequently transferred to the Middle East.

February 1942

11–12 The 'Channel Dash'; *Scharnhorst, Gneisenau* and *Prinz
Eugen* leave Brest and make a daylight run through the

February (cont)

English Channel for north Germany. Bomber Command in action continuously against the enemy warships. First operational mission for the Douglas Bostons of 88 and 226 Sqns (12.2.42).

14–15   First operational mission by 158 Sqn. Seven Wellingtons detailed to bomb Mannheim; four bomb primary, one bombs Flushing aerodrome and two abort.

16–17   First operational mission by 156 Sqn; one Wellington despatched to drop leaflets in the Lille area. First bombing attack the following night; three Wellingtons bomb Essen.

27–8   Whitleys of 51 Sqn drop paratroops at Bruneval in a mission to capture parts of enemy Würzburg radar (Operation Biting).

March 1942

3–4   235 a/c of Bomber Command despatched to attack Renault Factory at Billancourt, near Paris. 223 crews claim to have bombed the target.

8   First attack on a land target by Bostons of 2 Group; day-light raid on Matford works at Poissy under cover of diversionary Circus operations (the latter newly resumed after a five-month break).

8–9   First large-scale use of Gee by Bomber Command. Seventy-four Wellingtons equipped with the device form the leading wave of a force of 211 a/c despatched to raid Essen.

10–11   First bombing attack by Lancasters; a/c of 44 Sqn raid Essen.

13–14   134 a/c (fifty carrying Gee) despatched to Cologne. Fifty per cent of crews claim successful attacks.

25–6   Last operational mission with Bomber Command by 58 Sqn; nine Whitleys despatched to bomb St Nazaire. Sqn transferred to Coastal Command.

28/9   191 aircraft of Bomber Command (out of 234 despatched) make a massive incendiary attack on Lübeck. 200 acres of the town devastated.

April 1942

10–11   First operational use of 8000-pound bomb; one dropped on Essen by a Halifax (R9457) of 76 Sqn.

April (cont)

15–16 Last operational mission by 455 Sqn, RAAF, with Bomber Command; three Hampdens bomb Dortmund, three more lay mines in St Nazaire area and one drops leaflets over Rennes. Squadron transferred to Coastal Command.

16–17 Last operational mission by 144 Sqn with Bomber Command in WW2; two Hampdens despatched to lay mines off Lorient. Squadron subsequently transferred to Coastal Command as a torpedo-bomber unit.

17 Daylight attack on the MAN diesel engine factory at Augsburg by eight Lancasters of 44 and 97 Sqns. Total of twelve a/c despatched and seven FTR, four shot down by fighters en route to Augsburg and three by flak over the target. Leader of the raid, Sqn Ldr J. D. Nettleton of 44 Sqn, awarded the VC.

23–4 Ninety-one a/c of Bomber Command despatched to make the first of four successive attacks on Rostock; eighty-three claim successful attacks. Heaviest damage caused on the nights of 26-7 and 28-9; Rostock attacked by 110 out of 128 a/c and ninety-two out of 107, dropping mixed incendiary and HE loads.

25–6 Last operation with Bomber Command by 311 (Czechoslovak) Sqn; four Wellingtons bomb the docks at Dunkirk. Squadron transferred to Coastal Command.

May 1942

30–1 First Thousand-Bomber Raid. 1046 a/c despatched to Cologne; 898 crews claim to have attacked primary. Forty a/c FTR.

31 First operational mission by Mosquitoes. Aircraft of 105 Sqn carry out a dawn bombing and photo-reconnaissance sortie over Cologne.

June 1942

1–2 Second Thousand-Bomber Raid. 956 bombers despatched to Essen; 767 crews claim to have bombed the target area, but reconnaissance shows little damage. Many crews bomb Oberhausen, Mulheim and Duisburg by mistake. Thirty-one a/c FTR.

June (cont)

Third Thousand-Bomber raid. 1006 a/c despatched to Bremen, including 102 Hudsons and Wellingtons of Coastal Command. Despite heavy cloud over the target the bombers caused considerable damage, particularly to the Focke-Wulf aircraft factory. Forty-four a/c of Bomber Command and five of Coastal FTR. Last operational use of the Avro Manchester (by 49, 50, 61 and 106 Sqns).

July 1942

11   Forty-four Lancasters of 5 Group despatched to make a dusk attack on the submarine yards at Danzig. Mission involves a flight of 1500 miles much of it over the sea. About one-third of the crews fail to find the target; two a/c FTR.

August 1942

15   Orders issued for the creation of the Pathfinder Force.
17–18   Last operational mission by Blenheim aircraft of Bomber Command; night attack on enemy airfields in Holland and north-west Germany by a/c of 18 Sqn.
18–19   First operational mission by the Pathfinder Force; target Flensburg.

September 1942

10–11   First operational use of 4000-pound incendiary bomb ('Pink Pansy'). Dropped by the Pathfinder Force during a raid on Düsseldorf.
14–15   Last operational mission by Hampden aircraft of Bomber Command. Four a/c of 408 Sqn, RCAF, carry out an attack on Wilhelmshaven.
19   First attempt to bomb Berlin in daylight by six Mosquitoes of 105 Sqn. Only one bombs the target area (through cloud). Two more bomb Hamburg, two abort and one FTR.
25   Low-level attack by four Mosquitoes of 105 Sqn on Gestapo HQ at Oslo. Target only slightly damaged; one a/c FTR.

October 1942

5–6   First operational mission by 425 (Alouette) Sqn, RCAF. Four Wellingtons bomb Aachen.

October (cont)

17 Ninety-four Lancasters of 9, 44, 49, 50, 57, 61, 97, 106 and 207 Sqns despatched to make a dusk attack on the Schneider Armament Factory at Le Creusot and the power station at Montchanin. Eighty-six a/c bomb the factory and seven the power station. One Lancaster FTR.

24 Seventy-four Lancasters of 5 Group (out of eighty-eight despatched) make a daylight attack on Milan after flying across France in cloud cover. Same target attacked by Halifaxes the following night. Total of 1336 sorties flown to Italy by 5 Group a/c before the end of November 1942.

November 1942

3 First operational use of Lockheed Venturas by Bomber Command. Aircraft of 21 Sqn despatched to bomb the diesel plant at Hengelo, in Holland; railways attacked instead.

28–9 Two Lancasters of 106 Sqn – R5551 (Wng Cdr G. P. Gibson) and R5573 (Flt Lt W. N. Whamond) – drop 8000-pound bombs on Turin. First use of this bomb against an Italian target.

December 1942

6 Ninety-three Bostons, Venturas and Mosquitoes of 2 Group despatched to make a daylight attack on the Philips Factory at Eindhoven. Thirteen a/c FTR and two more are lost on the way home; of the remainder, fifty-three a/c are damaged to some extent. First operational mission by 464 Sqn RAAF (fourteen Venturas despatched, three FTR) and 487 Sqn RNZAF (sixteen Venturas despatched, three FTR.)

6–7 First operational mission by 199 Sqn; five Wellingtons bomb Mannheim.

14 First operational mission by 427 (Lion) Sqn, RCAF; one Wellington lays mines of Frisian Islands.

20–1 First operational use of Oboe blind-bombing and navigation aid. Six Mosquitoes of 109 Sqn despatched to bomb power station at Lutterade; three a/c bomb primary, remainder develop faults in their Oboe equipment and bomb alternates.

156 Squadron
Wellington Mk III
A/C letter – 'F'
Night 16-17 September 1942
Primary – Essen
Time off – 20.02 hrs

Captain : Sgt Proudfoot
Navigator : Sgt Couchman
W/Op : P/O Tinkler
F/Gunner : Sgt Duke
R/Gunner : Sgt Belton
Time landed : 01.27 hrs

On the night of the 16-17 September 1942, Wellington Mk III A/C 'F' Captain Sgt Proudfoot was detailed as part of the Illuminator Force to light up Essen for the main force. Load : 173 flares and 13 marker flares.

A/C 'F' was airborne at 20.02 hrs and reached the target area without incident at approx 21.55 hrs at 18,000 feet. The defences did not open up immediately and we 'stooged' around for about five minutes, saw two cones of S/Ls and plenty of flak coming up on the S/B quarter. We decided that we had found the target; weather – 8/10 cloud at 10, 12,000 feet, moon up on the S/B quarter and some ground haze. Ground detail was not visible and it was decided not to drop the marker flares as the aiming point could not be definitely identified. At approx 22.00 hrs at 18,000 feet on a course of 160°, IAS 160, the bomb doors were open preparatory to releasing the flares.

The Captain was at the controls, Navigator on the bomb panel with front and rear gunners in their respective turrets and the W/Op was at the flare chute. At this moment the R/Gunner reported a S/E E/A (believed Fw 190) dead astern, slightly above; this approached to within approx 150 yards and opened fire, to which our R/Gunner replied. A cannon shell struck our A/C and the E/A broke off to port, but made a second attack from the port quarter whereupon our R/Gunner gave him a good burst. Strikes were observed on the E/A which burst into flames and dived down out of control with fire coming from the fuselage and both wings. It was last seen going down into cloud at about 8000 feet, and is claimed as destroyed, confirmed by Captain and W/Op. The W/Op was struck in both feet by cannon shell splinters; nevertheless he managed to push the photo flare down the chute, and staggered back to the astro-dome until our A/C was clear of the target area. Flames from the E/A lit up our A/C which was thought to be on fire, but it was found that the fabric from the astro-dome to the tailplane had been stripped off during the attack. When the R/Gunner saw the E/A approaching he had asked the Captain to fly straight and level to enable him to get in a good crack, but after the first attack the intercom unit must have been hit, and the Captain, hearing cannon shells bursting inside the A/C, made a steep banking turn to port.

It was then that he saw the E/A going down in flames. Captain then discovered that his S/B aileron was damaged for he found great difficulty in coming out of the turn. The A/C came down to approx 14,500 feet and elevator and rudder had to be used to get the A/C out of the turn. Captain then instructed the Navigator to jettison the flares, and pulled the jettison toggles. Flares were believed to have gone, but were not seen to ignite as the A/C was 4000 feet lower than it should have been for the flares to ignite (fused at 15,000 feet).

It was not known until the target was left that the W/Op had been hit; by this time he had flopped out on the bed, but it was decided to leave his injuries until the A/C reached base. Meanwhile the R/Gunner reported that his turret was U/S. Course was then set at 296° for Kampen, but the Captain had great difficulty in maintaining height as the fabric had been stripped from along the top of the fuselage from the astro-dome to the tail, and part of the trailing edge of the S/B wing and part of the aileron had been shot off during the combat.

Emmerich 22.45 hrs at 6000 feet: R/Gunner sighted a S/E unidentified E/A approaching from dead astern, which opened fire with one short burst. No strikes were observed on our A/C Captain side-slipped down into cloud tops at about 5000 feet but was unable to take evasive action owing to damaged aileron. Shortly after this the oil pressure on the port engine began to rise and fall and the engine began to cut.

The A/C lost height to approx 700 feet over the Zuider Zee and Captain had to open up S/B engine which got A/C up to 1200 feet. A/C was just crossing Dutch coast south of Ijmuiden when it was coned in S/Ls and some light flak was fired, but A/C was not hit. Mod IFF switched on approx forty miles from Dutch coast the crew saw what was thought to have been one of our bombers shot down into the sea.

The port motor cut 20/30 miles from the English coast and the Captain then tested all controls. It was found that the U/C was U/S, also the emergency system and the hand pump. Trip was continued on one motor. Rich mixture had been used from the target and when over Marham the nacelle tanks had to be pulled. When over base it was discovered that the TR.9 was U/S and a red Very cartridge was fired. It was then decided to crash-land and the crew braced themselves at crash stations. One side of the astro-dome could not be removed.

The Captain made a wheels-up landing, and the flares which were believed to have been jettisoned over the target came up through the floor and ignited. Captain got out through his escape hatch, saw several figures running from the A/C which was then well ablaze, and thought that the rest of the crew had escaped. He ran to the edge of the runway and could only see two members of the crew, but on looking back saw someone crawling and being half dragged along. He ran back and found the F/Gunner helping the W/Op, and lent a hand to get them out of range of the burning A/C, from which ammunition and marker flares were exploding.

The Navigator was last out of the A/C and did splendid work in helping to extricate the injured W/Op and other members of the crew. He was badly burned in the process, as was the W/Op. The R/Gunner ran from the blazing machine, crawled through the barbed wire on the perimeter track, and it was a considerable time before he could be found. Meanwhile tht A/C was completely burned out.

P/O Tinkler (W/Op) and Sgt Couchman (Navigator) were both taken to Ely hospital, P/O Tinkler with injuries to his feet and burns, and Sgt Couchman with burns on both hands and back. The rest of the crew, after being treated for shock, appear to be recovering.

APPENDIX 3 : BOMBER COMMAND ORDER OF BATTLE
ON 26 SEPTEMBER 1939

Unit	Base	Equipment
71 Wing AASF :		
15 Sqn	Bétheniville	Battle
40 Sqn	Bétheniville	Battle
72 Wing AASF :		
105 Sqn	Rheims-Champagne	Battle
226 Sqn	Rheims-Champagne	Battle
74 Wing AASF :		
103 Sqn	Challerange	Battle
150 Sqn	Challerange	Battle
75 Wing AASF :		
88 Sqn	Auberive-sur-Suippes	Battle
218 Sqn	Auberive-sur-Suippes	Battle
76 Wing AASF :		
12 Sqn	Berry-au-Bac	Battle
142 Sqn	Berry-au-Bac	Battle

No. 1 Group : Re-forming in the United Kingdom.

No. 2 Group		
82 Wing :		
114 Sqn	Wyton	Blenheim
139 Sqn	Wyton	Blenheim
83 Wing :		
107 Sqn	Wattisham	Blenheim
110 Sqn	Wattisham	Blenheim
79 Wing :		
21 Sqn	Watton	Blenheim

Unit	Base	Equipment
2 Group (cont)		
82 Sqn	Watton	Blenheim
101 Sqn (in reserve)	West Raynham	Blenheim
No. 3 Group		
9 Sqn	Honington	Wellington
37 Sqn	Feltwell	Wellington
38 Sqn	Marham	Wellington
99 Sqn	Mildenhall	Wellington
115 Sqn	Marham	Wellington
149 Sqn	Mildenhall	Wellington
214 Sqn (in reserve)	Feltwell	Wellington
215 Sqn (in reserve)	Bassingbourn	Wellington
No. 4 Group		
10 Sqn	Dishforth	Whitley
51 Sqn	Linton-on-Ouse	Whitley
58 Sqn	Linton-on-Ouse	Whitley
77 Sqn	Driffield	Whitley
78 Sqn (in reserve)	Dishforth	Whitley
102 Sqn	Driffield	Whitley
No. 5 Group		
44 Sqn	Waddington	Hampden
49 Sqn	Scampton	Hampden
50 Sqn	Waddington	Hampden
61 Sqn	Hemswell	Hampden
83 Sqn	Scampton	Hampden
106 Sqn (in reserve)	Cottesmore	Hampden
144 Sqn	Hemswell	Hampden
185 Sqn (in reserve)	Cottesmore	Hampden

No. 6 Group (Note: on 26 September 1939 No. 6 was a training group and the units within it were Group pool squadrons with the exception of No. 98 Sqn, which was a reserve unit.)

7 Sqn	Upper Heyford	Hampden
35 Sqn	Cranfield	Battle
52 Sqn	Benson	Battle

Unit	Base	Equipment
6 Group (cont)		
63 Sqn	Benson	Battle
75 Sqn	Harwell	Wellington
76 Sqn	Upper Heyford	Hampden
90 Sqn	Upwood	Blenheim
97 Sqn	Abingdon	Whitley
98 Sqn	Hucknall	Battle
104 Sqn	Bicester	Blenheim
108 Sqn	Bicester	Blenheim
148 Sqn	Harwell	Wellington
166 Sqn	Abingdon	Whitley
207 Sqn	Cranfield	Battle

The total number of operational squadrons in Bomber Command on 26 September 1939 was thirty-three, but of these ten – all equipped with Battles – were in France with the Advanced Air Striking Force. Six more squadrons were equipped with Blenheim medium bombers, leaving only seventeen squadrons with aircraft capable of mounting a strategic offensive against Germany from bases in the United Kingdom.

Since the established strength of an operational bomber squadron was sixteen aircraft, RAF Bomber Command in September 1939 had a first-line 'paper' strength of 528 machines. The actual figure of bombers of all types available for operations on 26 September was 280.

APPENDIX 4 : BOMBER COMMAND ORDER OF BATTLE ON 1 JANUARY 1943

Unit	Base	Equipment
No. 1 Group		
12 Sqn	Wickenby	Lancaster
101 Sqn	Holme-on-Spalding	Lancaster
103 Sqn	Elsham Wolds	Lancaster
460 Sqn RAAF	Breighton	Lancaster
166 Sqn	Kirmington (Re-forming with Wellington IIIs)	
199 Sqn	Blyton	Wellington
300 Sqn (Polish)	Ingham	Wellington
301 Sqn (Polish)	Hemswell	Wellington
305 Sqn (Polish)	Hemswell	Wellington
No. 2 Group		
88 Sqn	Oulton	Boston
107 Sqn	Gt Massingham	Boston
226 Sqn	Swanton Morley	Boston
105 Sqn	Marham	Mosquito
139 Sqn	Marham	Mosquito
21 Sqn	Methwold	Ventura
464 Sqn RAAF	Feltwell	Ventura
487 Sqn RNZAF	Feltwell	Ventura
98 Sqn	Foulsham	Mitchell
180 Sqn	Foulsham	Mitchell
No. 3 Group		
15 Sqn	Bourn	Stirling
75 Sqn	Newmarket	Stirling
90 Sqn	Ridgewell	Stirling
149 Sqn	Lakenheath	Stirling
214 Sqn	Chedburgh	Stirling

Unit	Base	Equipment
3 Group (cont)		
218 Sqn	Downham Market	Stirling
115 Sqn	East Wretham	Wellington
138 Sqn (Special Duties)	Tempsford	Halifax
161 Sqn (Special Duties)	Tempsford	Lysander
192 Sqn (Special Duties)	Gransden Lodge	Halifax

(Note: The primary task of these Special Duties squadrons was the dropping and collection of agents in Occupied Europe and the supply of arms etc. to Resistance Groups. Although on the strength of 3 Group, they were not therefore operational bomber squadrons.)

No. 4 Group		
10 Sqn	Melbourne, Yorks	Halifax
51 Sqn	Snaith	Halifax
76 Sqn	Linton-on-Ouse	Halifax
77 Sqn	Elvington	Halifax
78 Sqn	Linton-on-Ouse	Halifax
102 Sqn	Pocklington	Halifax
158 Sqn	Rufforth	Halifax
196 Sqn	Leconfield	Wellington
429 Sqn RCAF	East Moor	Wellington
466 Sqn RAAF	Leconfield	Wellington

No. 5 Group		
9 Sqn	Waddington	Lancaster
44 Sqn	Waddington	Lancaster
49 Sqn	Scampton	Lancaster
50 Sqn	Skellingthorpe	Lancaster
57 Sqn	Scampton	Lancaster
61 Sqn	Syerston	Lancaster
97 Sqn	Woodhall Spa	Lancaster
106 Sqn	Syerston	Lancaster
207 Sqn	Langar	Lancaster
467 Sqn RAAF	Bottesford	Lancaster

No. 6 Group, RCAF (forming on 1 January 1943)

405 Sqn RCAF	Beaulieu	Halifax
408 Sqn RCAF	Leeming	Halifax
419 Sqn RCAF	Middleton St George	Halifax
420 Sqn RCAF	Middleton St George	Halifax
424 Sqn RCAF	Topcliffe	Wellington
425 Sqn RCAF	Dishforth	Wellington
426 Sqn RCAF	Dishforth	Wellington
427 Sqn RCAF	Croft	Wellington
427 Sqn RCAF	Dalton	Wellington

Pathfinder Force (No. 8 PFF Group as from 8 January 1943)

7 Sqn	Oakington	Stirling
35 Sqn	Graveley	Halifax
83 Sqn	Wyton	Lancaster
109 Sqn	Wyton	Mosquito
156 Sqn	Warboys	Wellington/ Lancaster

APPENDIX 5: MONTHLY TONNAGES OF BOMBS
DROPPED BY BOMBER COMMAND 1932–42

(Note: These are approximate figures only. It is impossible to calculate the exact tonnage for a wide variety of reasons; for example, no one can say with certainty what happened to the bomb loads of aircraft which failed to return.)

Year and month	Tons dropped
1939	
September	6
October	–
November	–
December	25
1940	
January	1
February	1
March	31
April	112
May	1668
June	2300
July	1257
August	1365
September	2339
October	1651
November	1316
December	992
1941	
January	777
February	1431
March	1744
April	2396

Tons dropped	Year and month
1941 (cont)	
May	2846
June	4310
July	4384
August	4242
September	2889
October	2984
November	1907
December	1794
1942	
January	2292
February	1011
March	2675
April	4433
May	3234
June	6845
July	6368
August	4162
September	5595
October	3809
November	2423
December	2714

APPENDIX 6 : BOMBER COMMAND MONTHLY A/C
LOSSES, SEPTEMBER 1939–DECEMBER 1942

Year and month	Totals despatched Day/Night	FTR Day/Night
1939		
September	40/83	12/2
October	–/32	–/2
November	4/15	–/–
December	119/40	17/–
1940		
January	6/38	–/–
February	4/54	–/1
March	53/239	1/5
April	167/489	15/18
May	802/1617	49/21
June	812/2484	31/26
July	616/1722	32/40
August	417/2188	18/52
September	98/3141	1/65
October	172/2242	1/27
November	113/1894	2/50
December	56/1385	2/37
1941		
January	96/1030	3/12
February	124/1617	2/16
March	162/1728	4/35
April	676/2249	23/56
May	273/2416	20/39
June	531/3228	22/76
July	582/3243	66/91
August	468/3344	35/121

Year and month	Totals despatched Day/Night		FTR Day/Night
September	263/2621		14/76
October	138/2501		17/68
November	43/1713		-/83
December	151/1411		7/28
1942			
January	24/2216		-/56
February	252/1162		15/18
March	131/2224		2/78
April		246/3572	13/130
May	105/2702		1/114
June	196/4801		2/199
July	313/3914		19/171
August	186/2454		10/142
September	127/3489		6/169
October	406/2198		14/89
November	113/2067		11/53
December	200/1758		16/72

(Note : Totals do not include a/c destroyed accidentally or crashing on return to UK.)

Select Bibliography

Wing Cdr W. Anderson, *Pathfinders*, Jarrolds, London, 1946

C. Bekker, *Angriffshöhe 4000*, Gerhard Stalling Verlag, Hamburg, 1964

W. S. Churchill, *The Second World War*, Cassell, London, 1950, Vols I-IV

Major L. F. Ellis, *France and Flanders, 1939-1940*, HMSO, London, 1954

N. Frankland, *The Bombing Offensive Against Germany – Outlines and Perspectives*, Faber and Faber, London, 1965

Wing Cdr G. P. Gibson, *Enemy Coast Ahead*, Michael Joseph, London, 1946

MRAF Sir Arthur Harris, *Bomber Offensive*, Collins, London, 1947

W. J. Lawrence, *No. 5 Bomber Group, RAF (1939-45)*, Faber and Faber, London, 1951

E. Middleton, *The Great War in the Air*, Waverley, London, 1920, Vol IV

Ministry of Information, *Bomber Command*, HMSO, London, 1941

P. Moyes, *Bomber Squadrons of the RAF and Their Aircraft*, Macdonald, London, 1964

D. Richards and H. St G. Saunders, *Royal Air Force, 1939-1945*, HMSO, London, 1953, Vols I and II

H. St G. Saunders, *Per Ardua: the Rise of British Air Power, 1911-1939*, Oxford University Press, London, 1944

Sir C. Webster and N. Frankland, *The Strategic Air Offensive Against Germany, 1939-1945*, HMSO, London, 1961, Vols I, II and IV

Index